THE ECONOMIC DEVELOPMENT OF THE USSR

THE ECONOMIC DEVELOPMENT OF THE USSR

ROGER MUNTING

ST. MARTIN'S PRESS   NEW YORK

Library of Congress Card Catalog Number: 82-42545

ISBN 0-312-22885-6

CONTENTS

To my Father and Mother

A NOTE ON WEIGHTS AND MEASURES AND EXCHANGE RATES

Weights and Measures

Centner   = 10 kg
Desyatina = 1.1 hectares or 2.7 acres
Pud   = 16.4 kg or 36.1 lb
          (the pud was divided into 40 Russian pounds)
Milliard is used for one thousand million
Tonnes are metric (= 1,000 kg)

Exchange Rates

When the new ruble was introduced in 1961 it was fixed at a rate of 1 ruble = US $1.11 (US $1 = 0.90 rubles). Since then the ruble has appreciated, officially. In February 1980 the rate was 1 ruble = US $1.53 (US $1 = 0.65 rubles). These rates of exchange do not, however, represent market rates as the ruble is not freely exchangeable.

TABLES

The Republics of the USSR

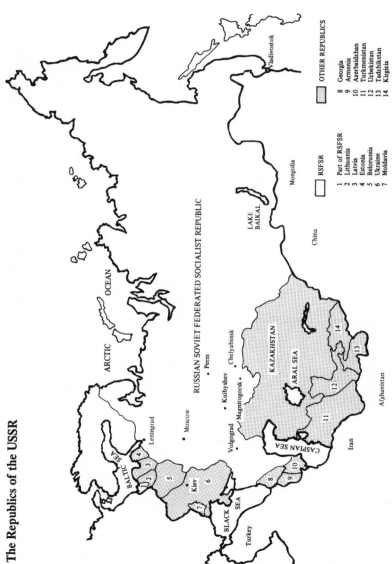

ARCTIC OCEAN

Leningrad
Moscow
Perm
Kuibyshev
Chelyabinsk
Volgograd
Magnitogorsk

RUSSIAN SOVIET FEDERATED SOCIALIST REPUBLIC

BALTIC SEA

Kiev

BLACK SEA

Turkey

CASPIAN SEA

Iran

KAZAKHSTAN

ARAL SEA

Afghanistan

LAKE BAIKAL

China

Mongolia

Vladivostok

	RSFSR		Part of RSFSR

	OTHER REPUBLICS	

1 Lithuania
2 Latvia
3 Estonia
4 Belorussia
5 Ukraine
6 Moldavia

8 Georgia
9 Armenia
10 Azerbaidzhan
11 Turkmenistan
12 Uzbekistan
13 Tadzhikstan
14 Kirgizia

PREFACE

This book was written, in response to invitation, as one of a series on European economic history. I say this not to justify its appearance but rather to explain its purpose. It is intended as an introductory text for students of modern European economic history. It may be that this is the first book on the USSR that the student might read; I hope it is not the last. More complete economic histories of the USSR are provided by the excellent works of Alec Nove, *An Economic History of the USSR* (1969) and Maurice Dobb, *Soviet Economic Development since 1917* (1966). In addition to these two books, I would make particular acknowledgement to the various works of R.W. Davies, former Director of the Centre for Russian and East European Studies, University of Birmingham, and Misha Lewin, also sometime of that institution, which have, in contrasting ways, greatly influenced my understanding of Soviet development. The selected bibliography also indicates the works on which I place most emphasis.

This is intended to be an economic history in particular, though Soviet experience clearly demonstrates the interdependence of the political and economic currents. It traces the main aspects of macro-economic change, though micro-economic problems are referred to, particularly in the case of agriculture. I have tried to bring the chronological coverage as up-to-date as possible, though, in historical treatment, that is always full of danger as the contemporary so very quickly becomes surpassed by events. And then there is the question of statistics. Dealing with Soviet statistics can be a very tricky exercise and the difficulties involved have been well explored elsewhere. It is possible to dispute the bases of many statistics but we must take as a reasonably reliable guide some body of statistical evidence. It is an essential tool in economic history, but by no means the only one. As far as possible, I present the most up-to-date figures available.

I owe acknowledgement for help to a number of people. First, I thank Professor Derek Aldcroft, University of Leicester, editor of the series; in no particular subsequent order, the Inter-library loan desk of UEA, Ms Jenny Brine of the Baykov Library, University of Birmingham, and Mr Stuart Rees of the University of Essex Library for his extraordinary assistance in making available the excellent resources of that library. The British Academy funded a short visit to Moscow, under the Cultural Exchange Agreement, which enabled use of materials in the Lenin Library, the Public Historical Library and, most valuably, the Library of the Social Science Institute (INION) of the Academy of Sciences. While attached to the Institute of History of the Academy of Sciences I was able to have fruitful discussions with V.P. Danilov and others. Steve Wheatcroft, University of Birmingham, Jim Holderness and Michael Miller, UEA, read drafts and made useful comments. I am very grateful to them, though I did not always follow their advice to the letter. I owe particular thanks to Steve Wheatcroft, Julian Cooper and Steve Tupper who have allowed me to use unpublished research papers. The debt owed to other works may be occasionally clear in the text, though as a rule I have endeavoured to keep footnote references to a minimum. Particular thanks are due to Miss Judith Sparks for assistance with typing. Above all I want to thank Elaine, Jo and Rebecca.

EDITOR'S INTRODUCTION

By comparison with the nineteenth century the twentieth has been very much more turbulent, both economically and politically. Two world wars and a great depression are sufficient to substantiate this claim without invoking the problems of more recent times. Yet despite these setbacks Europe's economic performance in the present century has been very much better than anything recorded in the historical past, thanks largely to the superboom conditions following the post-Second World War reconstruction period. Thus in the period 1946-75, or 1950-73, the annual increase in total European GNP per capita was 4.8 and 4.5 per cent respectively, as against a compound rate of just under 1 per cent in the nineteenth century (1800-1913) and the same during the troubled years between 1913 and 1950. As Bairoch points out, within a generation or so European per capita income rose slightly more than in the previous 150 years (1945-75 by 250 per cent, 1800-1948 by 225 per cent) and, on rough estimates for the half-century before 1800, by about as much as in the preceding two centuries.[1]

The dynamic growth and relative stability of the 1950s and 1960s may, however, belie the natural order of things, as the events of the later 1970s and early 1980s demonstrate. Certainly it would seem unlikely that the European economy, or the world economy for that matter, will see a lasting return to the relatively stable conditions of the nineteenth century. No doubt the experience of the present century can easily lead to an exaggerated idea about the stability of the previous one. Nevertheless, one may justifiably claim that for much of the nineteenth century there was a degree of harmony in the economic development of the major powers and between the metropolitan economies and the periphery which has been noticeably absent since 1914. Indeed, one of the reasons for the apparent success of the gold standard post-1870, despite the aura of stability it allegedly shed, was the absence of serious external disturbances and imbalance in development among the major participating powers. As Triffin writes: 'The residual harmonization of national monetary and credit policies depended far less on *ex post* corrective action, requiring an extreme flexibility, downward as well as upward, of national price and wage levels, than on an *ex ante* avoidance of substantial disparities in cost competitiveness and the monetary policies that would allow them to develop.'[2]

Whatever the reasons for the absence of serious economic and political conflict, the fact remains that through to 1914 international development and political relations, though subject to strains of a minor nature from time to time, were never exposed to internal and external shocks of the magnitude experienced in the twentieth century. Not surprisingly therefore, the First World War rudely shattered the liberal tranquillity of the later nineteenth and early twentieth centuries. At the time, few people realised that it was going to be a lengthy war and, even more important, fewer still had any conception of the enormous impact it would have on economic and social relationships. Moreover, there was a general feeling, readily accepted in establishment circles, that following the period of hostilities it would be possible to resume where one had left off – in short, to recreate the conditions of the pre-war era.

For obvious reasons this was clearly an impossible task, though for nearly a decade statesmen strove to get back to what they regarded as 'normalcy', or the natural order of things. In itself this was one of the profound mistakes of the first post-war decade since it should have been clear, even at that time, that the war and post-war clearing-up operations had undermined Europe's former equipoise and sapped her strength to a point where the economic system had become very sensitive to external shocks. The map of Europe had been rewritten under the political settlements following the war and this further weakened the economic viability of the continent and left a dangerous political vacuum in its wake. Moreover, it was not only in the economic sphere that Europe's strength had been reduced; in political and social terms the European continent was seriously weakened and many countries in the early post-war years were in a state of social ferment and upheaval.[3]

Generally speaking, Europe's economic and political fragility was ignored in the 1920s, probably more out of ignorance than intent. In their efforts to resurrect the pre-war system statesmen believed they were providing a viable solution to the problems of the day, and the fact that Europe shared in the prosperity of the later 1920s seemed to vindicate their judgement. But the post-war problems – war debts, external imbalances, currency issues, structural distortions and the like – defied solutions along traditional lines. The most notable of these was the attempt to restore a semblance of the gold standard in the belief that it had been responsible for the former stability. The result was a set of haphazard and inconsistent currency-stabilisation policies which took no account of the changes in relative costs and prices among countries since 1914. Consequently, despite the apparent prosperity of the latter half of the decade, Europe remained in a state of unstable equilibrium, and therefore vulnerable to any external shocks. The collapse of US foreign lending from the middle of 1928 and the subsequent downturn of the American economy a year later exposed the weaknesses of the European economy. The structural supports were too weak to withstand violent shocks and so the edifice disintegrated.

That the years 1929-32/3 experienced one of the worst depressions and financial crises in history is not altogether surprising given the convergence of many unfavourable forces at that point in time. Moreover, the fact that a cyclical downturn occurred against the backdrop of structural disequilibrium only served to exacerbate the problem, while the inherent weakness of certain financial institutions in Europe and the USA led to extreme instability. The intensity of the crisis varied a great deal, but few countries, apart from the USSR, were unaffected. The action of governments tended to aggravate rather than ease the situation. Such policies included expenditure cuts, monetary contraction, the abandonment of the gold standard and protective measures designed to insulate domestic economies from external events. In effect, these policies, while sometimes affording temporary relief to hard-pressed countries, in the end led to income-destruction rather than income-creation. When recovery finally set in in the winter of 1932/3 it owed little to policy contributions, though subsequently some Western governments did attempt more ambitious programmes of stimulation, while many of the poorer Eastern European countries adopted autarkic policies in an effort to push forward industrialisation. Apart from some notable exceptions, Germany and Sweden in particular, recovery from the slump, especially in terms of employment generation, was slow and patchy and even at the peak of the upswing in 1937 many countries were still operating below their resource capacity. A combination of weak real growth forces and structural imbalances in development would no doubt have ensured a continuation of under-resource utilisation had not rearmament and the outbreak of war served to close the gap.

Thus, by the eve of the Second World War Europe as a whole was in a much weaker state economically than it had been in 1914, with her shares of world income and trade notably reduced. Worse still, she emerged from the war in 1945 in a more prostrate condition than in 1918, with output levels well down on those of the pre-war years. In terms of the loss of life, physical destruction and decline in living standards Europe's position was much worse than after the First World War. On the other hand, recovery from wartime destruction was stronger and more secure than in the previous case. In part this can be attributed to the fact that in the reconstruction phase of the later 1940s some of the mistakes and blunders of the earlier experience were avoided. Inflation, for example, was contained more readily between 1939 and 1945 and the violent inflations of the early 1920s were not for the most part perpetuated after the Second World War. With the exception of Berlin, the map of Europe was divided much more cleanly and neatly than after 1918. Though it resulted in two ideological power blocs, the East and the West, it did nevertheless dispose of the power vacuum in central and eastern Europe which had been a source of friction and contention in the interwar years. Moreover, the fact that each bloc was dominated or backed by a wealthy and rival super-power meant that support was forthcoming for the satellite countries. The vanquished powers were not, with the exception of East Germany, burdened by unreasonable exactions which had been the cause of so much bitterness and squabbling during the 1920s. Finally, governments no longer hankered after the 'halcyon' pre-war days; not surprisingly, given the rugged conditions of the 1930s. This time it was to be planning for the future which occupied their attention, and which found expression in the commitment to maintain full employment and all that entailed in terms of growth and stability, together with a conscious desire to build upon the earlier social welfare foundations. In a wider perspective, the new initiatives found positive expression in terms of a readiness to co-operate internationally, particularly in trade and monetary matters. The liberal American aid programme for the West in the later 1940s was a concrete manifestation of this new approach.

Thus despite the enormity of the reconstruction task facing Europe at the end of the war, the recovery effort, after some initial difficulties, was both strong and sustained, and by the early 1950s Europe had reached a point where she could look to the future with some confidence. During the next two decades or so virtually every European country, in keeping with the buoyant conditions in the world economy as a whole, expanded very much more rapidly than in the past. This was the supergrowth phase, during which Europe regained a large part of the relative losses incurred between 1914 and 1945. The Eastern bloc countries forged ahead the most rapidly under their planned regimes, while the Western democracies achieved their success under mixed enterprise systems with varying degrees of market freedom. In both cases the state played a far more important role than hitherto, and neither system could be said to be without its problems. The planning mechanism in Eastern Europe never functioned as smoothly as originally anticipated by its proponents, and in due course most of the socialist countries were forced to make modifications to their systems of control. Similarly, the semi-market systems of the West did not always produce the right results, so that governments were obliged to intervene to an increasing extent. One of the major problems encountered by the demand-managed economies of the West was that of trying to achieve a series of basically incompatible objectives simultaneously — full employment, price-stability, growth and stability and external equilibrium. Given the limited policy weapons available to governments, this proved an impossible task to accomplish in most cases, though West Germany managed to achieve the seemingly impossible for much of the period.

Although these incompatible objectives proved elusive *in toto* there was, throughout most of the period to the early 1970s, little cause for serious alarm. It is true that there were minor lapses from full employment; fluctuations still occurred, but they were very moderate and took the form of growth cycles; some countries experienced periodic balance of payments problems; while prices generally rose continuously, though at fairly modest annual rates. But such lapses could readily be accommodated, even with the limited policy choices, within an economic system that was growing rapidly. And there was some consolation from the fact that the planned socialist economies were not immune from some of these problems, especially later on in the period. By the later 1960s, despite some warning signs that conditions might be deteriorating, it seemed that Europe had entered a phase of perpetual prosperity not dissimilar to the one the Americans had conceived in the 1920s. Unfortunately, as in the earlier case, this illusion was to be rudely shattered in the first half of the 1970s. The supergrowth phase of the post-war period culminated in the somewhat feverish and speculative boom of 1972-3. By the following year the growth trend had been reversed, the old business cycle had reappeared and most countries were experiencing inflation at higher rates than at any time in the past half-century. From that time onwards, according to Samuel Brittan, 'everything seems to have gone sour and we have had slower growth, rising unemployment, faster inflation, creeping trade restrictions and all the symptoms of stagflation'.[4] In fact, compared with the relatively placid and successful decades of the 1950s and 1960s, the later 1970s and early 1980s have been extremely turbulent, reminiscent in some respects of the inter-war years.

It should, of course, be stressed that by comparison with the inter-war years or even with the nineteenth century, economic growth has been quite respectable since the sharp boom and contraction in the first half of the 1970s. It only appears poor in relation to the rapid growth between 1950 and 1973, and the question arises as to whether this period should be regarded as somewhat abnormal, with the shift to a lower growth profile in the 1970s being the inevitable consequence of long-term forces involving some reversal of the special growth-promoting factors of the previous decades. In effect, this would imply some weakening of real growth forces in the 1970s which was aggravated by specific factors — for example, energy crises and policy variables.

The most disturbing feature of this later period was not simply that growth slowed down but that it became more erratic, with longer recessionary periods involving absolute contractions in output, and that it was accompanied by mounting unemployment and high inflation. Traditional Keynesian demand-management policies were unable to cope with these problems and, in an effort to deal with them, particularly inflation, governments resorted to ultra-defensive policies and monetary control. These were not very successful either, since the need for social and political compromise in policy-making meant that they were not applied rigorously enough to eradicate inflation, yet at the same time their influence was sufficiently strong to dampen the rate of growth, thereby exacerbating unemployment. In other words, economic management is faced with an awkward policy dilemma in the prevailing situation of high unemployment and rapid inflation. Policy action to deal with either one tends to make the other worse, while the constraint of the political consensus produces an uneasy compromise in an effort to 'minimise macroeconomic misery'.[5] Rostow has neatly summarised the constraints involved in this context: 'Taxes, public expenditure, interest rates, and the supply of money are not determined antiseptically by men free to move economies along a Phillips curve to an optimum trade-off between the rate of unemployment and the rate of inflation. Fiscal and monetary policy are, inevitably, living parts of the democratic political process.'[6]

Whether the current problems of contemporary Western capitalism or the difficulties associated with the planning mechanisms of the socialist countries of Eastern Europe are amenable to solutions remains to be seen. It is not, for the most part, the purpose of the volumes in this series to speculate about the future. The series is designed to provide clear and balanced surveys of the economic development and problems of individual European countries from the end of the First World War through to the present, against the background of the general economic and political trends of the time. Though most European countries have shared a common experience for much of the period, it is nonetheless true that there has been considerable variation among countries in the rate of development and the manner in which they have sought to regulate and control their economies. The problems encountered have also varied widely, in part reflecting disparities in levels of development. While most European countries had, by the end of the First World War, achieved some industrialisation and made the initial breakthrough into modern economic growth, nevertheless there existed a wide gulf between the richer and poorer nations. At the beginning of the period the most advanced region was north-west Europe including Scandinavia, and as one moved east and south so the level of per capita income relative to the European average declined. In some cases, notably Bulgaria, Yugoslavia and Portugal, income levels were barely half the European average. The gap has narrowed over time but the general pattern remains basically the same. Between 1913 and 1973 most of the poorer countries in the east and south (apart from Spain) raised their real per capita income levels relative to the European average, with most of the improvement taking place after 1950. Even so, by 1973 most of them, with the exception of Czechoslovakia, still fell below the European average, ranging from 9 per cent to 15 per cent in the case of the USSR, Hungary, Greece, Bulgaria and Poland, to as much as 35-45 per cent for Spain, Portugal, Romania and Yugoslavia. Italy and Ireland also recorded per capita income levels some way below the European average.[7]

It is perhaps apposite that this series should begin with a volume on the largest and most influential of the European countries, though not the richest in per capita terms, and the first major country to adopt full-scale socialist planning. The USSR has made enormous strides since Tsarist days and the holocaust that followed the Bolshevik revolution and its aftermath. In 1913 Russia's income per head was only about 61 per cent of the European average, whereas by the 1970s it was fast approaching the European level. As Dr Munting shows, such rapid progress was made only at great cost to a nation of people prepared to forego current consumption and to turn a blind eye to the atrocities committed by the ruling regime. Clearly, as the examples of Nazi Germany and Eastern Europe post-1945 also demonstrate, remarkable quantitative progress can be achieved but at a price which the freer Western capitalist societies would not be prepared to tolerate. Moreover, though the planning and control mechanism of the USSR produced striking results, it was by no means perfect as an allocative system, and in the case of agriculture it often failed to produce satisfactory results.

That the planning mechanism frequently came under strain is not altogether surprising given its inherently cumbersome and bureaucratic procedures and the fact that the planning authorities themselves sometimes deliberately overloaded it in order to try to achieve the impossible. Inevitably, therefore, such pressures gave rise to reforms and modifications in the system designed ostensibly to improve its efficiency.

From our own Western ideological commitment, with a predilection for 'free enterprise' or mixed systems of enterprise, it is tempting to be hypercritical of the apparent defects and inconsistencies of socialist planning. Yet one should bear in mind that the experience of the 1970s demonstrates that Western countries have not been particularly successful in terms of economic management. Nevertheless, it would be pointless to ignore the fact that socialist planning, both in the USSR and elsewhere, has encountered serious problems of a type which have not yielded readily to attempted solutions. Much has been written by Western observers about the limitations of planning, especially in the Soviet context. The value of Dr Munting's new work is not simply that it presents an up-to-date survey of the economic achievements of the USSR since the revolution but also that it analyses objectively the problems encountered in forcing the pace of modernisation while at the same time providing an impartial assessment of the merits and defects of the planning system of that country which subsequently served as a prototype for several other European countries.

Derek H. Aldcroft
University of Leicester

Notes

1. P. Bairoch, 'Europe's Gross National Product: 1800-1975', *The Journal of European Economic History*, 5 (Fall 1976), pp. 298-9.

2. R. Triffin, *Our International Monetary System: Yesterday, Today and To-morrow* (1968), p. 14; see also D.H. Aldcroft, *From Versailles to Wall Street, 1919-1929* (1977), pp. 162-4. Some of the costs of the gold standard system may, however, have been borne by the countries of the periphery, for example Latin America.

3. See P.N. Stearns, *European Society in Upheaval* (1967).
4. *Financial Times*, 14 February 1980.
5. J.O.N. Perkins, *The Macroeconomic Mix to Stop Stagflation* (1980).
6. W.W. Rostow, *Getting From Here To There* (1979).
7. See Bairoch, 'Europe's Gross National Product', pp. 297,307.

INTRODUCTION

The USSR is of interest if only because of its immense power. In achieving its position of economic power the Soviet Union developed a system of economic management and control through central planning. The creation of a planned economy was an untried and pioneering experiment and, until the extension of Soviet influence into eastern Europe after the Second World War, unique. For much of its history the Russian state was dogged by a sense of weakness, of economic backwardness. Thus the political push for industrial growth in the USSR was generated by the need to overcome this weakness, just as earlier 'phases' of industrial policy, early in the eighteenth or late in the nineteenth centuries, had tried to do. Planning under Stalin's direction, therefore, achieved in large measure what the predecessors of the Tsar's Empire had failed to do; create a great industrial power. The political dimension and the prime interest of the state was always paramount; planning became a sophisticated elaboration of state direction. In making such an observation, however, it is important to keep in mind the radical changes effected by the revolution — in social structure, the distribution of internal power and position in the world. The Soviet revolution brought a totally new ideology and economic system. In the first decades of its history the USSR stood alone, without allies, and with little by way of economic assistance from the industrialised world. The 'Great Patriotic War', 1941-5, marked a change, for, in withstanding the onslaught of German invasion and occupation, the Soviet Union emerged as a great power, extended its territory and secured 'socialist allies'. The system of political and economic organisation became a model for these allies, and much of the early practice of the Soviet economy established as a basis for 'socialist economics'.

Much of the strength of the Soviet economy has been, and remains, its great riches in natural resources, though many are in remote and extremely inhospitable locations. The extremes of climate and space present great demands on government and people. In the far north and east rivers remain frozen for up to two-thirds of the year; permafrost renders conventional building impossible. At the other extreme there are regions of desert. Thus, despite having the largest land area (at 22.4 million square km), population is relatively concentrated in European Russia (that part of the country west of the Ural mountains).

The population exceeds 260 millions and is made up of over 90 different nationalities (the official statistical handbook also lists a 'miscellaneous' category) and there are over 100 languages in use. The largest population group is Russian (or 'Great Russian'), and Russian is the major language. But the Soviet Union is very much more than Russia, though the terms are sometimes used indiscriminately. 'Russia' may be used to refer to the Russian Empire before 1917, or to the largest of the 15 republics, the Russian Soviet Federal Socialist Republic (RSFSR). (European Russia is also used in a geographical sense to refer to the country west of the Urals. It has no constitutional meaning.)

The USSR is a union of fifteen republics each with nominal constitutional sovereignty, though real limitations on their independence. More than half the population live in the RSFSR, which stretches from Europe to the Pacific Ocean. The smallest republic is Estonia, with fewer than 1½ million people. Government and administration may thus be on a national or 'all-union' basis, applying to the whole country, or operating at a republican level. For example *Gosplan*, the state planning body, is national or 'all-union' but each republic also has its *Gosplan*. Most of the material in this book deals with the whole country and central policy rather than its constituent regions.

From its earliest beginnings the USSR was regarded by many in the West as a model for future society. Few take such a concept seriously today; even among Marxists or other revolutionary socialists there has grown a sense of disillusion with the revolutionary policy of the Soviet state. In part this is attributable to the extent of state power and control in all aspects of life, not simply in economic affairs. The thread of continuity of state absolutism from the Tsarist Empire is at least as strong as the dynamic of the pursuit of socialism. Nonetheless the history of the Soviet economy is a peculiar story because it has been based on the first known non-market system. It has also been one of remarkable, if imperfect, economic success, substantial rates of growth and the creation of an industrial economy. The establishment of this great industrial power has been a consistent theme of Soviet economic history; ways and means have varied significantly over the years.

1 RUSSIA BEFORE 1917

Russia's was the most rigid of European autocracies. That it failed to yield adequately to forces of change was one explanation for its destruction in the revolution of 1917. In the words of the gifted commentator, Sir John Maynard, the Tsar 'had been the patriarchal housefather' to the nation (1962, p. 7). The nineteenth-century nation was a vast, but highly centralised, empire of peoples, with a myriad of languages and religions. The totalitarian state was always the dominant institution: all society was subordinate to the state; foreign contacts were restricted; even rank and status depended on service to the state. The major cultural and constitutional forces that had moulded Western Europe — the Renaissance, the Reformation, concepts of constitutional monarchy and parliament democracy — had failed to penetrate Russia. The Tsar ruled by divine right. Although there were significant liberalising reforms, from the emancipation of the serfs in 1861 to the constitutional gesture of the Dumas after 1905, they were too late and too little to secure the continuance of the monarchy and its government.

And yet, curiously, Russia had frequently been responsive to Western influence, with much of the initiative in opening doors to the West coming from the top. The determination to emulate Western technical and industrial expertise was most strongly expressed by Peter the Great early in the eighteenth century. Even Western styles of dress and the French language were slavishly adopted at court later in that century. In the nineteenth century Western technology in modern industry, as well as the capital to fund industrial projects, was welcomed. And, ultimately of most significance, it was a Western creed, Marxism, that was the fuel of revolutionary socialism which triumphed in October 1917.

The Empire, which was destroyed in 1917, was potentially rich yet with a poor population. Average income was low. In 1913 national income per capita was 107.3 rubles in European Russia (114.3 rubles for the whole Empire or 109.3 rubles in USSR territory) (Falkus, 1968). This was about one-third that of Germany, a quarter that of Britain and less than one-sixth of the USA. Differentials in income were probably greater than in Western industrial countries, though this is uncertain. Nominally society was rigidly stratified by rank and status into legal 'estates'. Although they accorded in part with occupational groups they were not equivalent to social classes. The gentry made up only about 1 per cent of the population, with the clergy, merchants (*kuptsy*) and tradesmen (*meshchane*) comprising minorities. The mass of the population were peasants, whose life-expectancy and per capita income were amongst the lowest in Europe. Yet social and occupational groups of industrial and other wage workers, businessmen and industrial entrepreneurs cut across these boundaries. In real terms society was more fluid than the legal structure suggested.

Agriculture and the Peasantry

Agriculture was both the strength and weakness of the Russian economy. One reason for the sluggish growth in per capita income, apart from the fast growth of population, was the predominance of agricultural employment. Agriculture has always tended to be a low-productivity sector compared with industry and hence a large agricultural sector weighted down average incomes. In Russia the problem was greater because the productivity of land, on average, was low. In the contemporary world the food-producing and exporting nations, particularly the USA, had high levels of labour productivity yet low yields. Within Europe (Britain, France, Germany and the Low Countries especially) farming was more intensive with higher yields but lower labour productivity than the USA. On average Russia had the worst of both worlds: lower yields than the USA and lower labour productivity than western Europe (Table 1.1).

Table 1.1: Crop Yields in Various Countries: 1911-1915 (in puds per desyatina)

Country	Wheat	Rye	Oats	Potatoes
Russia	45	54	52	489
USA	69	68	77	440
France	86	68	83	570
England	146	–	119	1,012
Germany[a]	146	120	127	904

Note: a. Germany for 1911-14.
Source: P.I. Khromov, *Ekonomicheskoe razvitie* (M. 1950), p. 413.

According to Goldsmith's estimates (1961, p. 441) overall crop production in the Russian Empire increased at an average rate of 2.3

per cent per annum from 1883 to 1915; industrial crops and potatoes increased at a faster than average rate but these represented a relatively small share of total production. The increase in production resulted both from an extension of area under cultivation and by improved yields. There was also an important improvement in distribution with the building of railways. Thus sales in one area could be increased, as could purchases elsewhere, with a general improvement in income with no necessary change in production. Yet, despite increased production and improved distribution, supply increases were moderated by factors other than the distribution of income. First, the growth of exports offset, to a large extent, the increase in domestic production. Priority to exports was maintained, even at times of famine, including the disastrous year of 1891. (A generation later, under Stalin, the same was to happen.) Second, the Russian harvest was invariably subject to fluctuation, so that years of great shortage were not uncommon. Third, there were great and growing regional variations of yields and production.

This point is often rather neglected, but it was profoundly important. At a simple level, European Russia was virtually divided between the northern part — the so-called 'consuming provinces' — and the southern 'producing provinces', the dividing line roughly coinciding with the northern edge of the rich black-soil belt. In other words, the south produced a net surplus of foodstuffs, and incidentally the greater part of exports, and the north were net 'importers' of food. However, in the Baltic provinces there was significant production of dairy produce and other animal products, much of which was exported to Germany; Tsarist Poland was a centre of sugar manufacture as was a number of provinces in the Ukraine. In Siberia a co-operative dairy industry had developed with notable success — producing butter for export.

The most serious problems were to emerge in central Russia, the heart of old Muscovy. In this area population density was at its greatest with consequent land hunger. Most of the peasant households were dependent to some extent on earnings from outside the farm, from crafts and trades (*promysly*) either casual or short-term factory labour, from work as agricultural labourers or from the production of some marketable commodity at home. Only a fraction of agricultural produce found its way to the market and many peasants indeed were net purchasers of foodstuffs on the market. For them, therefore, low grain prices meant lower food costs; the revival in prices after 1896 meant growing food costs. For all the peasant population, however, and indeed in some respects for the whole of Russian society, the size of crop was always more important than its price. There was a fine margin between sufficiency and hunger.

The emancipation of the peasants from serfdom in the 1860s granted plots of land in perpetuity, but the practical value of these allotments was severely reduced by the growth of population. Russia's population grew at a rate faster than any other major European country, from 74 million in 1860 to 126.4 million in 1897 and 174 million in 1913. The pressure of population imposed a great strain on the economy and a massive one on agriculture. The average per capita (male only) provision of allotment land at the end of the nineteenth century was almost half that provided upon emancipation, with the result of growing peasant land hunger.[1] Together with resentment at the need to make redemption payments for the allotment land, this land hunger fuelled peasant discontent. Various measures were taken by government to try to alleviate the 'peasant problem'. A peasant land bank was established in 1884 to help land purchase and local government (*zemstvo*) bodies began offering aid from the 1890s, while redemption demands were steadily reduced and finally written off in 1904. But the only way to solve such a problem from the peasants' point of view was to give them more land. No provision was made for further grants of land but peasants were able to buy land from the gentry. Collectively these purchases were vast.

The peasant commune (*obshchina*) was a long-established cultural influence and it was usual for most Russian peasants to undertake some contractual obligations on a collective basis. Even labourers offered themselves for work in gangs (*arteli*). The commune was a primitive form of welfare guaranteeing a minimum of subsistence to members, through periodic redistribution of land, and equity, through the division of farmland into strips. In this way all members received a share of the good and the bad. Such measures were eminently rational, but they did not make for optimum production. The persistence of intermingling of land and disincentives resulting from periodic redistribution were one reason for the low levels of productivity in Russian agriculture. However, under the emancipation measures, features of the commune were employed by the government both for tax collecting and to maintain social stability in the countryside. The rural community (*sel'skoe obshchestvo*) was instituted as being collectively responsible for the tax and redemption payment of its members. Often, but not always, this community was effectively the same in households involved as the traditional commune. However, in regions such as the western Ukraine, the Baltic and west Belorussia features of the commune were effectively imposed, through the institution of the rural community, where there had been no such tradition. Thus the collective responsibility for tax payment fostered and encouraged redistribution of land. Land was both an asset and a liability because it had to be paid for. Often, therefore, land was redistributed on a more rational basis, according to the number of mouths to be fed in the family or according to the hands to work the land. In some areas redistribution never took place. There was no rule; communes were effectively organs of self-government and the peasants were left to their own devices.

The Stolypin reforms of 1906-11 marked a substantial change in policy and official attitudes to the commune. The commune was no longer regarded as a bastion of stability in the countryside but as a threat to the regime. The revolts of 1905 in the countryside were attributed to the commune. Now individualism was to be encouraged. At the same time this would have the advantage of enabling individual enterprise through landownership and investment. Joint responsibility was abolished; peasants were encouraged to claim land as private property (previously allotment land had been the property of the commune) and establish independent farms.

The reforms met with limited success. The rate of leaving the commune was most spectacular in the north and west, where the commune had little traditional strength anyway, and in the south-east, where there was some evidence of a form of proto-capitalist farming developing. Here land was rich, productive and more plentiful than in central Russia. It is clear from the events of 1917 that the reforms did not achieve the desired political effects. There is also real doubt as to how far the traditional commune structure was weakened. The administrative functions of the rural community, dating from emancipation, were done away with but many of the traditional functions – joint control over land use (irrespective of who owned the land), even redistribution – persisted. This was particularly evident in the central provinces, where the problems associated with commune land holding were most severe. This meant that the great majority of peasant households, on average 85 per cent of the total for European Russia, continued to farm in a traditional three-course rotation, with all the disadvantages of strip-farming, isolation and dislocation of land. There is no doubt that such an institutional structure restricted total agricultural production. The major problem was one of production, though the peasants themselves and those sympathetic to the peasantry from whatever quarter saw the major problem as one of landownership. However, a contemporary estimate in 1906 calculated that a total redistribution of non-peasant land to the peasants would have made only a marginal difference to their average holdings.

Indeed, land sales accelerated after 1906 so that the peasantry were overwhelmingly dominant in Russian agriculture by 1917. In 1914 78 per cent of grain marketings came from peasant farms, and according to the 1916 agricultural census peasants owned over 90 per cent of live-stock and over 80 per cent of the sown area in European Russia. During the agrarian revolution of 1917 they acquired nearly all the remainder. This transfer did not solve the agrarian problem.

Despite the great rundown in gentry landownership before and during the First World War there remained some areas of widespread gentry landownership, particuarly in the commercially more successful regions of the Baltic and the southern provinces. It was in such estates that examples of productive enterprise, easily comparable with the best of Western Europe, could be found. The decimation of such estates, or their loss through boundary changes, was a serious if quantitatively limited loss to the Russian economy after the revolution.

Agriculture provided the major exports, up to two-thirds in 1913 or 75 per cent if timber is included (Table 1.2). This proportion had remained fairly steady from 1900 at a time when the total value of exports more than doubled. By 1913 Russia had become the world's largest exporter of wheat. Agriculture was far from a static or stagnant sector, for it was agricultural production and, in particular, exports which funded the rapid development of industry in the half-century before the First World War.

Table 1.2: Russian Exports (percentage share by value)

Year	All grains	Agricultural total	Timber	Metals and metal products	Oil
1861	39.1	78.4	3.3	1.1	0
1881	48.9	78.6	5.9	0.3	0.5
1900	42.8	64.6	8.1	0.2	6.5
1913	39.1	64.0	10.9	0.2	3.3

Source: Khromov, *Ekonomicheskoe razvitie* (M. 1950), appendix.

Industry

The dominant theme in much of the historiography of pre-revolutionary Russia is the emphasis on industrial backwardness, but the extent of this backwardness has been exaggerated. Industrially Russia was, in 1914, significantly less developed than Britain, Germany or the USA but nonetheless she had become one of the major industrial producers in the world. In the last quarter of the nineteenth century Russian industry grew at a rate of over 5 per cent per year – in excess of western Europe, though it must be said from a lower level. The 1890s saw the most spectacular levels of growth, at 8 per cent, associated with the rapid development of machine building, coal mining, iron and steel manufacture and the extension of the railway network (Table 1.3).

Table 1.3: Economic Indicators, 1890-1914

	1890	1895	1900	1905	1910	1913
Pig iron production (million puds)	56.6	88.7	179.1	166.8	185.8	283
Coal extraction (million puds)	367.2	555.5	986.3	1,139.7	1,526.3	2,200
Raw cotton consumption (million puds)	8.3	12.3	16.0	18.2	22.1	25
Railway construction (thousand km)	30.6	37.0	53.2	61.1	66.6	70
Imports (thousand rubles[a])	406.650	526.147	626.375	635.087	1,084.442	1,374.0
Exports (thousand rubles[a])	692.240	689.082	716.217	1,077.325	1,449.084	1,520.1

Note: a. Visibles.
Source: Khromov, *Ekonomicheskoe razvitie* (M. 1950), pp. 452-5.

A serious recession hit Russian industry after 1899. Some industrial disturbances followed – a precursor to the great revolt of 1905. Growth was renewed after 1907 at an average rate of 6.25 per cent to 1913. Between 1900 and 1913 total industrial production grew by 74.1 per cent (from 862 million rubles to 1665 million) and per capita production by 46.2 per cent. By 1913 Russia stood as the fifth industrial producer in the world, though in per capita terms her position was much lower. Significantly, however, Russia produced more steel and machinery than either France or Austria (Table 1.4).

Russia was also the second-largest petroleum producer, after the USA, and the biggest importer of machinery in the world, principally textile and agricultural machinery.

Table 1.4: Comparative Production Figures in Major Countries

Production in 1913	USA	Germany	UK	Russia	France	Austria
Pig iron						
(thousand tonnes)	31,462	19.312	10,425	4,635	5,311	2,435
Steel						
(thousand tonnes)	31,803	18,329	7,787	4,841	4,687	2,685
Machines (percentage						
world total)	50	20.7	11.8	3.5	1.9	3.4
Cotton spindles in use						
(thousands)	32,149	11,186	55,653	8,990	7,400	4,090

Source: K.C. Thalheim, 'Russia's Economic Development' in G. Katkov *et al.*
(eds.), *Russia Enters the Twentieth Century* (1971), pp. 92-5.

Russia also had the great asset of rich natural resources. As well as extensive forests she had large deposits of coal, iron ore, gold, platinum and oil. Before the revolution the major realised resources were in European Russia but these in themselves were vast. However, their location was remote from population centres. Thus it was only with the advent of railways that problems of distance could be overcome.

Railway building was costly in capital and expertise so, in common with most European countries, much of the programme was undertaken by the state. Before 1880, however, most railway lines had been built by private companies. Thereafter the state took a more direct role in railway construction and by 1913 owned two-thirds of the network. Apart from railway building and armaments factories, the state took little direct part in industry. The largest single industry (in terms of employment and capital stock) was textiles, particularly cotton, and this was developed totally by private enterprise. Of far greater importance was the indirect role of the state. The state was (sometimes excessively) regulatory and protective. State demand, particularly in railway buiding, provided an important market for iron and steel products. However, the state played a major and active role in encouraging the development of industry in private hands and in encouraging foreign businesses to invest in Russia. This policy is most closely associated with Sergei Witte, Minister of Finance from 1892 to 1904.

What Witte sought to do was create the atmosphere wherein a modern industrial economy could grow. Achieving this involved overcoming one problem that had plagued his predecessors, the instability of the ruble. The exchange value of the ruble was stabilised in 1894 and joined to the gold standard in 1896. This helped to make the ruble an attractive currency, and Russia an attractive country for foreign investment. Foreign capital imports to finance investment were by no means unusual, but in Russia they were more extensive than elsewhere. It was foreign investment that largely financed the development of new industries and new areas. By 1914 90 per cent of mining, almost 100 per cent of oil extraction, 40 per cent of the metallurgical industry, 50 per cent of the chemical industry and even 28 per cent of the textile industry were foreign-owned.

As well as direct, joint-stock, investment there was considerable foreign borrowing by the Russian government. The government sold interest-bearing bonds in foreign capital markets, most successfully in Paris. Witte extended this practice, which had developed earlier in the nineteenth century, and borrowed heavily, principally for railway building. But his financial policy was only partially successful. In some years government foreign borrowing was used to maintain a budget surplus. The state was never able to reduce its level of foreign borrowing; rather it increased. The proportion of government debt held overseas increased from 30 per cent in 1895 to 46 per cent in 1904, when Witte left office as Minister of Finance, to 48 per cent in 1913. The growth of the economy was never sufficiently self-sustained to enable a reduction in foreign capital dependence. Nonetheless it is unlikely that the heavy industrial investment, particularly on railways, could have been achieved without government action.

The Russian economy was highly protected by tariffs – the highest in Europe. These had the effect of protecting 'infant' industries and raising revenue. The high duties on foodstuffs and some raw materials, for instance, were more evidently for revenue than protection. By 1902 import duties accounted for 40 per cent of the value of all imports, ranging from 28 per cent for manufactured goods, through 31 per cent for raw materials to 96 per cent for foodstuffs. In 1898 duties on complex agricultural machinery, which did not compete with Russian manufacturers, were removed altogether as an aid to commercial agriculture. Overall the average tariff burden moved more heavily to goods and raw materials in the 1890s. This, therefore, tended to increase domestic prices and restrict consumption. There has thus been a common view that a restraint on consumption was a deliberate, if incidental, aspect of policy; that the high tax burden necessitated by fiscal policy significantly restricted home market demand. Indeed, Witte virtually admitted as much in his secret memorandum on industrial policy to the Tsar in 1899.

By the end of Witte's period of office one-third of government ordinary revenue came from tariffs and one-third from the state vodka monopoly. Only 17 per cent of revenue came from direct taxes (12 per cent in 1910). The remainder came from taxes on sugar, tea, matches, kerosene and other products, and profits from government enterprises and postal services. Increases in revenue, from taxes on everyday items of consumption, led to a view that the government 'exploited' the masses for the sake of economic policy. This is particularly stressed in connection with revenue from spirit sales. However, it has been convincingly argued (Crips, 1976, p. 28) that increases in revenue resulted from increases in consumption rather than a restriction of living standards.

In particular, the idea that the peasantry suffered unduly from government fiscal policy does not seem to bear scrutiny. First, tariffs had little effect on mass consumption, being more heavily borne by purchasers of luxury goods and capital goods. Second, the relative burden of direct taxes was shifted from the rural to the urban sector. The poll tax was abolished in 1881, while redemption payments (not strictly a tax but with the same effect on the peasant) were removed in 1904. In 1913 land tax accounted for only 2.5 per cent of ordinary revenue. Third, the effective 'burden' of indirect tax was far higher in urban than rural communities. Consumption of taxed items such as kerosene, sugar and tea was far higher in urban than rural areas. The same was true for spirit consumption, which in any event was far lower in Russia, per capita, than in other European countries. The image of a rapacious government growing rich from an oppressed peasant mass drowning its sorrows in government-produced vodka is hardly tenable! Olga Crisp concludes that, at worst, government fiscal policies had a neutral effect on consumption. This is not to say that the mass of the population were not poor; indeed they were.

Nonetheless, there was a well-developed home market and widespread movement of goods and people across the vast country long before the advent of railways. Local and national fairs provided a network of market outlets and the most famous, that at Nizhni-Novgorod (Gorky), reputedly had goods from all parts of the world. Trade turnover of the Nizhni-Novgorod fair (which was held once a year) reached a peak in 1881, after which date permanent urban retail outlets became more important, and mass-produced consumer goods, particularly cotton textiles, took a larger share of consumpton. Each large town had its own market quarter (*gostinnyi dvor*) and there was a well-developed mercantile system. The home market was also served by peasant domestic handicrafts (*kustar*) and artisans.

Industrial recession after 1900 contributed to the widespread discontent which boiled over into attempted revolution in 1905, following the abortive war with Japan. The government responded with a variety of constitutional reforms and the establishment of the Duma, a first attempt at representative government. This 'constitutional experiment' was shortlived and of limited impact. The economic gains were more tangible. Renewed growth was linked to an expansion of real incomes, though at a rate slower than in the West.

Labour

The October revolution was made in the name of the proletariat, yet the proletariat was very small, and indeed declined in size during the months of 1917 as workers and soldiers returned to the village. The strong links maintained with the village when a peasant left to work in the factory were a peculiarity of the Russian labour market. In part this was because he or she still had legal rights and obligations in the village, at least until 1906, and in part because of family ties. There was a strong seasonal element in factory work, with workers often returning to the village for the harvest. In the northern and central provinces of European Russia a majority of peasant households received some income earned outside the farm, in agricultural labour, building and mining services as well as factory work. A permanent proletariat was very small; indeed it had been part of state policy to avoid this phenomenon. Internal passports were required to move about the country and these were issued — in great numbers — by the communes. There was thus no real shortage of labour, despite the expected restrictions on mobility after emancipation, though there were shortages of skilled labour and some local labour shortages. The Stolypin legislation after 1906 enabled easier permanent migration, both to new lands in the east and to the urban centres, so that migrant workers became a permanent hereditary urban proletariat (Antonova, 1951, p. 81). There was a substantial growth in the total number of wage labourers between emancipation and the outbreak of war (Table 1.5).

The total wage labour force grew four and a half times. However, agricultural labour and casual work were far more significant than factory work. Also small-scale domestic and artisan workshop industry was as important as factory employment. There was thus a dual structure to the labour market. Russian factories, since the days of Peter the Great, had been large, employing hundreds or even thousands of workers. In 1913 the famous Putilov engineering works in St Peters-

Table 1.5: Wage Labour in European Russia

Category	1860	1913
Total	3,960	17,815
of which:		
Industry		
Factories and mines	800	3,100
In own homes	800	3,000
Construction	350	1,500
	1,950	7,600
Railways	11	815
Shipping	500	500
Agricultural labour	700	4,500
Other (services,		
general unskilled work, etc.)	800	4,865

Source: A.G. Rashin, *Formirovanie rabochego klassa Rossii* (M. 1958), p. 172.

burg had 10,000 workers. Size was often a substitute for high technology. The ratio of workers to capital was higher than in Britain or Germany because of relative costs, and also because round-the-clock shifts were more common in Russia. Further, and more significant, was the fact that the general industrial infrastructure was less well developed in Russia, so that new plants were often forced to be more integrated than Western counterparts. This tended to encourage large size. If the large enterprise did not dominate the labour market entirely it had a disproportionate influence, for it was in the large enterprises that strikes and other disturbances were the more frequent. The Putilov factory, for instance, was the centre of the St Petersburg soviet in 1905.

Revolutionary Background

When Marx's ideas were published in Russia they fell on peculiarly fertile ground. Curiously, Marx's works were widely read as classical political economy. But more significantly his ideas of revolution and concept of future society were taken up with enthusiasm by revolutionaries. Russia had a revolutionary movement (or rather a number of revolutionary movements) long before the name of Marx was voiced.

The revolutionary and the clandestine developed because there were no channels for legitimate political dissent within Russian society; and this political intolerance became more vigorous from the 1880s. There was a further peculiarity of Russian society; the phenomenon and social role of the intelligentsia. A body of well-educated, often well-to-do, intellectuals with a highly developed critical attitude to society and the political structure had emerged through the nineteenth century. The intelligentsia was by no means a revolutionary body but it did throw up a number of revolutionaries. What is significant is that nineteenth-century 'liberalism' had an intellectual nature, very different from the bourgeois commercial character of Liberal England. From amongst the intellectual elite came forth a revolutionary leadership often remote from the masses they sought to lead.

In the last quarter of the nineteenth century reformist and some-times revolutionary ideas took many forms, but a strong thread was evident in what later came to be called 'populism' (*narodnichestvo*). A very few populists became revolutionary terrorists. The basis of all populist thought was a desire to see an improvement in the life of the masses, the peasantry. Their radical thinking was attracted to Marxist ideas[2] because of the emphasis on mass revolution. Later Marxist revolutionaries put more faith on the industrial proletariat as a revolutionary body and a concept of future industrial socialism. Best known of these, of course, was Lenin. Lenin became a Marxist but he was first of all a revolutionary, and he adapted (some would say distorted) Marxian ideas to Russian conditions. In so doing he introduced ideas and strategy that had developed in the peculiar circumstances of Russia. The notion of revolutionary leadership by a tight-knit, cell-like, clan-destine organisation had nothing to do with Marx but everything to do with revolutionary populism; the use of agitation and terror in pursu-ing revolutionary ends had again grown out of Russian experience; the feasibility of a revolutionary seizure of power by a well-organised party and motivated, yet small, proletariat was also alien to Marx. Lenin's Theory of the Party, as the vanguard of revolution, on behalf of the workers, developed from this. It was essential to Marx's doctrine that the proletarian revolution would be a mass movement. However, in Russia the proletariat were not the mass but a minority, so this was a further reason for the importance of the party role. A revolutionary movement was favoured in Russia by the absence of developed trade unions. Lenin's attitude to trade unions vacillated, but initially he was hostile to their 'economistic' aims of improving wages and working conditions which diverted workers from the political aims of taking power. Although trade unions did develop, legally, after 1906, the political revolutionary movement in Russia had deeper roots. Where Lenin and other Marxists (and it must be said that Plekhanov is legiti-mately regarded as a founder of Russian Marxism with great influence on Lenin) differed from earlier revolutionaries was in their attitude to the peasantry.

Put simply, it may be said that they regarded the peasantry not as revolutionary but as petit bourgeois, whose rising against the landlord or regime had merely been to secure more land rather than change the political structure. However, they also supposed that class relations, determined by property relations, and class antagonism, detected by Marx in industrial England, were evident in rural Russia. Hence they supported the poor (*bednyak*) against the exploiting rich (*kulak*). Such a concept of differentiation was to be of crucial significance after 1917.

In becoming a committed Marxist Lenin opposed populist thinkers and their support for the peasantry. The so-called 'doctrinaire' populists of the late nineteenth century (particularly Nikolai Danielson and Vasily Vorontsov) were hostile to capitalism in general and industry in particular. Their notion of a utopian future was one where peasant-type agriculture was the basis of the economy. In other words, they believed that Russia could and should avoid Western industrial capitalism, 'jump over' a stage in Marxian historical progression, so to speak, to an agrarian-socialist future. Lenin countered the view by asserting that, far from avoiding capitalism, Russia was, in the 1890s, already a capitalist economy. He wrote his celebrated *Development of Capitalism in Russia* (first published in 1899 under a pseudonym) to prove his point. But the idea of 'accelerating history', driving forward to socialism before capitalism had fully matured, was not totally forgotten, and echoes of this debate on Russia's destiny were to be heard in the 1920s, after Lenin's death.

The intellectual differences between 'populist' and 'Marxist' crystallised into political parties. Populist ideas were carried forward into the Socialist Revolutionary (SR) party, which had much peasant support, and the Social Democrats (SD) became a revolutionary Marxist party, with support amongst urban workers. A division over policy split the SD's in 1903, the majority faction on this occasion, the *bolsheviks*, being more radical than the *mensheviks* or minority. Thus the Bolshevik Party was born.

War and Revolution

The First World War threw the Russian economy into disarray and destroyed the old regime before the Bolshevik revolution was brought about. Foreign trade dwindled to a trickle because of the closure of the western frontier through which 90 per cent of Russia's trade had passed before 1914. Imports of machinery fell from 317,000 tonnes in 1913 to 47,000 in 1915. Against that, exports of grain declined accordingly thus releasing more than sufficient margin to feed the army. The position was alleviated a little with allied supplies through the White Sea, but the rail link with Murmansk was completed only in 1917.

The major economic problem during the war was with distribution rather than production. Despite army recruitment, agricultural production was maintained, with wartime harvests exceeding 1913 levels. Yet, in spite of this, food shortages in urban centres had become acute by 1917. The major causes were transportation bottlenecks and, more seriously, a breakdown in the market. Rapid inflation and shortages of consumer goods encouraged peasants and speculators to hold on to grain stocks. In 1916 it was estimated that 40 per cent of grain reserves were held by banks as a hedge against inflation. There was no absolute shortage; increased army demand was less than the savings on exports. Food shortages aggravated urban discontent where workers had already seen their wages rendered valueless by inflation. Strikes and riots multiplied through 1917.

The army numbered more than 15 million men of which the greater part (10 to 11 million) were peasants. Conscription also affected the industrial labour force with as many as 40 per cent of workers being under arms, according to an estimate by Olga Narkiewicz (1970, p. 35). The effects of this were crucial. Many of the peasants under arms deserted to claim land during the tempestuous months of 1917. The remaining industrial labour force was packed with women and young men as well as peasants avoiding conscription in the village. The proletariat, on whose support the Bolsheviks sought to rely, was very different in 1917 from what it had been in 1913. Desertions from the front contributed to the loss from the army but the greatest losses were because of capture (over 3½ million). Varying estimates put the numbers killed at 600,000 to 650,000. Total 'losses' (including dead, wounded, prisoners) reached over 7 million (or higher by some estimates), close to half the army.

A nation at war could not withstand decimation at the front and dislocation in the economy, and the old regime was quickly removed in the February revolution in which the Bolsheviks played no part. A government, based on the Duma and to be provisional for the duration of the war, was set up and plans made for the election of a Constituent Assembly by universal suffrage. The provisional government clearly failed because there was no change to the social ills which had brought it into being, all of which stemmed from the war. Further, it lacked a popular power base, being effectively rivalled for influence by the workers councils or soviets which had been formed.

After returning to Russia in the famous sealed train in April, and an abortive attempt to seize power in July, Lenin led the Bolsheviks to revolution in October 1917 (6 November by the new calendar). His opportunism led him to oppose the war and thus win a measure of popular (if by no means majority) support. It was Trotsky who saw the political capital to be made from claiming the support of the soviets, though the slogans 'all power to the soviets' had little ultimate truth. The Bolsheviks thus came to power on a tide of popular discontent rather than clear support. From the beginning they were necessarily a minority regime. It is interesting to note that, in common with many observers, the then British ambassador thought their power would be shortlived. It was some time before the significance of the October Revolution became apparent.

Notes

1. Rural population density was much lower in Russia, on average, than in western Europe but much of the land was infertile or unsuitable for farming. The rate of change was greater than elsewhere in Europe. The average allotment in 1861 was 4.8 desyatinas (5.2 hectares); by 1900 it was 2.6 desyatinas (2.8 hectares).

2. It was a populist, Nikolai Danielson, who first translated Marx's *Capital* into Russian.

2 NEW ECONOMIC POLICIES

After the October Revolution the Bolsheviks held the reins of power but had few specific plans about which direction to take the economy. Early economic measures amounted to little more than a recognition of *de facto* developments. Nationalisation of the land, the first measure, in effect recognised real peasant possession. The land was granted rent-free to those who worked on it. The decree on workers' control similarly accepted that many factories had been taken over by workers. Nationalisation, the only clear policy, proceeded piecemeal. The state bank was nationalised on 27 November when it refused to grant loans to the new government. All other banks were nationalised a month later. In December 1917 the Supreme Economic Council (*VSNKh*) was created, and thus marked a significant step in establishing central control over the economy. VSNKh had power to take over factories, control finance and subordinate the Council of Workers control. Real exercise of these powers came with the outbreak of civil war in April 1918.

Agriculture and the Land

The land decree became law in January 1918. Under its provisions land was to be in possession of those who used it — not a socialist measure but one recognising the customary peasant concept of ownership and effectively implementing the agrarian programme of the SRs. Nominally land was to be distributed to local peasants — the landless getting priority — on equal terms. Some priority was also given to collectives over individual claimants. In fact, land redistribution was undertaken at a local level by peasant organisations — and that meant the commune for the most part. How much land peasants gained, of course, depended on the general availability — and in the central provinces that was relatively little. According to Pershin, the largest land funds from private estates were in the south-east (Samara, Saratov, Penza, Simbirsk) (Pershin, 1966, vol. 2, p. 202). The average gains were small, between 0.09 and 0.39 desyatinas per head — though with substantial regional variations. According to the 1916 census, in European Russia, excluding Stavropol, there were 1,110,157 private farms (non-peasant), with an average sown area of 69.8 desyatinas, and 15.5 million peasant farms. A rapid redistribution at that stage would have increased peasant farm-holdings by half a desyatina each. In addition there was some state land, principally forest, and a small amount of church land. By 1917, of course, the peasant population had increased somewhat. Yet in some localities there were pickings to be had and the process of distribution was over quickly.

Quite apart from the takeover of private estates there was a wide-spread redistribution of peasant land in which most of the 'Stolypin' individual farmers were reabsorbed into the commune. (There were enormous regional contrasts here; in Belorussia, for instance, this trend was not evident.) This, and the general growth in the rural population, led to more family divisions and thus more poor peasant households. Regional disparities remained, but there was a levelling down in the locality of the village. The net gains, on average, to the peasants were few. The effects on the economy were negative.

War Communism

The period of the civil war ushered in a new form of economic organ-isation which became a totally centralised dictatorship. The war with Germany was formally closed with the treaty of Brest-Litovsk signed in March 1918. This brought forth reaction from left and right and an attempt at counter-revolution. There was also intervention from erst-while Allies (including Britain, France and USA) to try to secure Russia's place in the war and maintain a second front against Germany. There was also, of course, the wish to secure foreign-owned assets. The future of foreign property was uncertain and much was nationalised later. More significantly, all debts on loans secured by the Tsarist regime before and during the war — which were considerable — had been abrogated by the new government.

The Bolsheviks thus found themselves literally fighting for survival yet with reduced resources. The German Peace treaty had involved sub-stantial territorial losses which had disproportionate economic signifi-cance. The Baltic provinces and Tsarist Poland were lost, Finland became totally independent and, under the treaty, much of the Ukraine remained under German occupation.

The demands of war gradually called forth more and more central control. Nationalisation was extended to all industrial enterprises, trade became outlawed and money virtually ceased to have value, though this was a function of inflation rather than decree. Workers' control was abolished. But the main problem was to secure food supply to the towns and to the army. A state grain monopoly had been introduced in February 1918 (and was now matched by monopolies in other commodities). This proved insufficient, for the money paid to peasants in return for their produce was virtually useless.

In May 1918 the decree on grain control was published with some urgency(by telegraph). This made for the compulsory delivery of *all* surpluses, over and above subsistence and seed, to the state; any concealment could lead to seizure without payment (payment was little enough anyway). Specific provision was made in the decree for the use of armed force if need be. The government was clearly attacking the peasantry, though the attack was nominally only against *kulaks* and black marketeers. Responsibility for collection was vested in local organs of *Narkomprod* (the supply commissariat) which also employed gangs of workers and members of the *cheka*, the political police, to seize food by force where needed. In June 1918 an attempt to ally the poor peasants with the town was made with the formation of the so-called committees of the poor (*Kombedy*) to take grain from the 'class enemy' the kulak. The use of *Kombedy* amounted to little, in fact, and the practice was discontinued in November of that year. The whole basis of war communism was therefore the compulsory seizure of foodstuffs (*prodrazverstka*) and its distribution without the market mechanism. In so doing the policy perhaps helped to win the war by keeping the army fed at least minimally, but it had other, negative, consequences. Distribution by ration did not work. No-one who did not work productively received a ration card. This simple fact explains why so many anti-Bolsheviks worked for them often in highly responsible posts. But the ration card was insufficient, and workers resorted to the black market, which was never destroyed. During 1918-19 it was found that less than half of the urban population's food supply came from the state mechanism (Conjuncture, 1928, p. 7). Workers went into country areas to barter for food, and made consumables such as cans and cigarette lighters in their workplaces to trade for food. This diversion and the time spent in looking for food aggravated the overall decline in production. Surrogate media of exchange developed — salt being a favourite and universally accepted one. The dependence on barter affected all strata. An artist in the Bolshoi at the time told the author how she exchanged most of her family's clothes for food (it is a tribute to the government that the Bolshoi remained open). Another result was that the urban population continued to decline. The population of Moscow and Leningrad fell by 58 per cent between 1917 and 1920. The course of the war and territorial changes caused serious supply problems. The centre of Bolshevik control was central European Russia, and often this was cut off from the 'producing region' of the south. This applied not only to foodstuffs but coal supplies as well. Coal mines in the Moscow region could not meet demand adequately.

Through a combination of tactical brilliance by the Red Army under Trotsky, a patriotic desire to drive out foreign interventionists and the fact that nobody wanted a return to the old regime, the counter-revolution was resisted, but it left its toll. In order to maintain power the Bolsheviks had resorted to arbitrary and sometimes cruel measures. A reign of terror at the hands of the *cheka* emerged. This political police force (curiously referred to as 'secret') shot 50,000 people during the war.

Above all, there was a disastrous fall in production, and a vast gulf between the interests of the government and the peasantry. This had always been evident throughout Russian history but for the Bolsheviks it had grown worse. It was not to be healed in the 1920s. Agricultural production fell by about 40 per cent. Sown area was reduced in passive response to grain seizure, on average by 34 per cent from 1916 to 1920; the decline was less for staples such as rye (20 per cent) and more for technical crops such as cotton (81 per cent). Compared with the pre-war figures (1913), yields of the major grains fell by more than 25 per cent in 1920. Industrial production fell by 70 per cent (1913 to 1921), that of heavy industry by nearly 80 per cent; coal extraction fell by 77 per cent (1913 to 1920).

The result was serious famine and other supply shortages. Revolt was threatened in the countryside, workers rioted in the streets of Petrograd and sailors at Kronstadt mutinied in March 1921. There was urgent need for reform, and in the same month as the Kronstadt rebellion the tenth party congress approved the ending of war Communism. This period had been an experimental one and was even welcomed by some as a blueprint for full Communism. Money had ceased to have a function; supply was by centralised rationing. Earlier notions of workers' control had disappeared and been replaced by central command. Much was to change in the next few years but some essentials remained. The economy was never wholly decentralised again. The Council of Labour and Defence (STO), established in 1918 (under a slightly different name) and which introduced centralised control of industry, remained. In February 1921 it spawned an offshoot, the state planning commission, or Gosplan. In March 1920 the first organ of planning – the state commission for the electrification of Russia (GOELRO) – had been established.

However, the economy had ground virtually to a halt and a radical change of direction was required; it came with the introduction of the New Economic Policy (NEP) in March 1921. This policy was designed to effect a recovery in production from the trammels of world war, internal turmoil and revolution and civil war aggravated by administrative incompetence. At the opening of the decade of the 1920s the Soviet economy was at its lowest possible ebb.

To effect recovery from wartime and post-war dislocation was the priority of all European governments, but in Soviet Russia the problems were somewhat greater than in most other countries of Europe. Inflation was rife, and famine struck the country in 1921. Despite victory in the civil war, the regime's support was fragile. NEP was conceived as a compromise between state control and private enterprise. Lenin was the architect of the new policy and it proved to be his legacy to the new state, for he died in 1924. The basis of the policy was a return to legal market exchange and thus a concession to commercial capitalism, but it was in Lenin's words:

> a capitalism we must and can accept, and to which we can and must assign certain limits, for it is necessary to the great mass of the peasantry and to the trade that enables the peasants' needs to be satisfied. We must arrange things in such a way that the regular operation of the economy and patterns of exchange characteristic of capitalism become possible. It must be so for the sake of the people. Otherwise we should not be able to live. (*Collected Works*, XLV, 1970, pp. 85-6)

The policy was therefore pragmatic. Before the end of 1920 the rigid control of labour, introduced in the civil war, had been removed, but the policy is generally acknowledged to have begun with the introduction of a tax in kind for the peasantry on 15 March 1921. This replaced the system of arbitrary compulsory procurement (*prodrazverstka*) of foodstuffs. The tax was fixed at a level below the previous level of procurement, and it was to be progressive (*Resheniya*, vol. 1, 1967, p. 200). There was thus no disincentive to produce; indeed the opposite, for anything produced over and above the tax level could be sold freely and legally. The freedom to exchange on the market in turn meant the re-emergence of private traders – *Nepmen* as they came to be called – now acting quite legally (as opposed to the illegal 'bagmen' in war Communism). There were also state and co-operative trading organisations. Trade also required the return to a money economy, and a stable currency became a renewed objective, though stabilisation took some years to achieve.

The Structure of NEP

At the heart of the policy lay the abstract notion of a link or alliance, a unity of thinking, between town and country, industry and agriculture, proletariat and peasantry. This was known as the *smychka*. If it was to have any real form it was to be in the market-place. Concessions to private traders and economic freedom to the peasants were matched by the denationalisation of small-scale production in May 1921. A number of factories, although remaining state-owned, were leased out to private entrepreneurs (often their former owners), who operated them effectively on capitalist lines. By 1922, 10,000 had been leased out, though nearly all of these were very small enterprises; only 76 sizeable establishments were returned to former owners. From June 1921 artisans and craft workshops were able to operate freely.

The government retained control of what Lenin called the 'commanding heights of the economy'; the central bank (reopened in November 1921), the budget, large-scale industry and foreign trade. The supreme economic council (*VSNKh*), which had had authority over the whole economy during war Communism, retained a large measure of managerial control over industry during NEP, though the real extent of this control varied from time to time and from industry to industry. Nominally, VSNKh could influence industry through control of the budget (until 1922), by appointing or dismissing managers and setting general output targets. This control was limited, in effect, to large-scale heavy industry. Consumer-goods industries were more fully governed by the market. Regional economic councils (*SNKh* or *sovnarkhozy*) exercised control over industries in their respective regions or republics (the Ukraine or Belorussia, for example). VSNKh was more concerned with industry of nationwide or 'all-union' significance.

From 1920 responsibility for overall regulation of the economy as a whole and for some limited degree of planning was vested in the Council for Labour and Defence — STO. Economic planning has become synonymous with the Soviet economy, but in their early years of power the Bolshevik leaders were vague and uncertain about how to introduce it. To some the command economy of war Communism had been a pattern for the future but, as we have seen, it was practically and polit-ically essential to abandon that policy. However, some concept of planning, albeit modest, was retained. Lenin himself had been much influenced by the planning and control of the German war economy under Walter Rathenau, though early Soviet concepts of planning had been ones of an engineering rather than economic nature. Krzhizhan-ovsky, who first developed theoretical approaches to planning with Gosplan, was an engineer.

STO was chaired by Lenin and included representatives of the major commissariats (war, agriculture, transport and supply) and the trades unions. It was here that the real economic power of the state lay, for STO had the power to issue binding decrees. Day-to-day industrial business was in the hands of VSNKh and the Peoples' Commissariat of Production (*Narkomprod*), which in these early years often acted independently of one another.

The first attempt at any co-ordinated planning was the establish-ment, in March 1920, of the state commission for the electrification of Russia (GOELRO) which was approved in December 1920 by the Eighth Congress of Soviets. As its title suggests, its aim was to increase electrical production capacity to enable widespread electrification. This involved building 30 new power stations, over 10 to 15 years, which in turn required an expansion of heavy industry to double the 1913 level, light industry to one and a half times the 1913 level and a general extension in the agricultural area and rail network. Such a plan illus-trates how early the thinking developed that future production could be determined by government. A year later, in February 1921, STO established a state planning commission (Gosplan) with the brief of working-out a single co-ordinated, general plan for the economy and the means of putting such a plan into effect. This also demanded prep-aration of a budget and an examination of banking and credit and the location of industry. Gosplan had no power to command, merely to advise, but it was bound to collect data on the economy. It examined all proposals from VSNKh, to co-ordinate various demands and direc-tives. Ironically, many of the first and most able economists working there were not even Bolsheviks. Two of the leading economists, S.G. Strumilin and V.G. Groman, had both been Mensheviks. Groman joined Gosplan in 1922 and his arrival signalled a change from seeing planning as a job for engineers to one for economists. One of the early tasks of Gosplan was to draw up a balance sheet of the national economy; a huge macro-economic cross-tabulation similar in concept to, though infinitely more complex than, Quesnay's *Tableau écon-*

omique. The Central Statistical Office collected the data on which this 'balance', for 1923-4, was based. This was the first such exercise, for a national economy, undertaken, and it was to be the foundation for the 'control figures' drawn up by Gosplan in later years. These control figures, the first being for 1925-6, formed the basis for economic forecasts.

The process of economic planning which emerged after 1928 followed a path different from the early work of Gosplan, being commands rather than forecasts. Yet the conceptual and statistical basis of the five-year plans had its roots in the pioneering work undertaken early in the 1920s.

Despite the beginnings of centralised planning forecasts, state control over the economy was limited. Large-scale industries quickly began to organise temselves into trusts, bringing together productive enterprises in the same industiy. These trusts had a large degree of independence; they had legal responsibility, and they were also required to cover their costs on a commercial basis (from 1922 when they were removed from the budget). Indeed *Yugostal*, a trust of south Russian ferrous metallurgy concerns formed in 1921, had the right to deal on the world market. By mid-1923 there were 478 such trusts, including 56 in textiles and 45 in food products. Of these 133 were nominally subordinate to VSNKh, being 'all-union', and 345 to regional *sovnarkhozy*. Later in 1923 the number of trusts was reduced through amalgamation. These trusts were not productive units but combinations which could exercise control over the internal budget and level of output of any member-factory or enterprise.

Internal trade was conducted by state trading organs, which were relatively few, private traders (*Nepmen*) and co-operatives. Co-operative trading bodies were actively encouraged by the government and became relatively successful in the sale of consumer goods in rural areas. State-controlled trade was virtually confined to wholesale trade in urban areas. In Moscow in 1922 83 per cent of retail trade was in private hands, and only 7 per cent in state hands, whereas 77 per cent of wholesale trade was handled by the state and 14 per cent privately (Malafeev, 1964, p. 50). In some remote rural areas only the *Nepman* could provide a trading outlet or source of supply. There were thus likely to be local and regional variations in price level, as well as differences between state, co-operative and private prices. As the decade progressed state and co-operative organs increased their share of total trade (see p. 77).

The private sector was extensive, including innumerable small-scale industries, artisans, workshops and craftsmen in town and country and above all almost all of agriculture.

Agricultural Structure

The revolution did little to improve the productive capacity of agriculture as a whole, though it improved the lot of many poor, and previously landless, peasants. The *average* landholding of peasant households increased over the country as a whole, and there was a general levelling tendency (Table 2.1). Already by 1922 there was some reversal of the levelling effected in the revolution.

Table 2.1: Peasant Households in RSFSR

	1917[a]	1920	1922
Poor and middle peasants (less than 4 desyatinas)	69.3	91.8	87.5
Well-to-do (4 to 8 desyatinas)	21.7	6.5	9.0
Kulaks (over 8 desyatinas)	9.0	1.7	3.5

Note: a. There appears to be a small error in the original; the column adds up to 99.0.
Source: Yu. Larin, *Voprosy krest'yanskogo khozyaistva* (M. 1923), p. 29, quoting *Pravda* for June 1923.

The revolution also had the effect of reinforcing and consolidating traditional features of peasant social and economic organisation in most of the country, and such trends were recognised in the revolutionary land decree (see above, p. 42). The basic social and economic unit amongst the peasantry was the household (*dvor*), usually, but not necessarily, of one blood-related family. This was a property-owning unit so that individual ownership of farm property was rare. The Stolypin reforms of 1906-11 had encouraged individual property ownership but they had been reversed in the revolution with few exceptions.[1] The household once again had legal recognition as an economic unit in the Soviet period.

Of greater significance was the continued influence of the commune (*obshchina* or *mir*). The peasant commune had enjoyed a peculiar legal position in old Russia until the Stolypin reforms had attempted to remove it. Most of the land taken during the revolution has been redistributed through the commune. And the 1922 land code recognised the legal position of the land society (*zemel'noe obshchestvo*) which, in nearly all cases, was the same as the traditional village commune. The land society was a community of households, usually within the same village, which performed an administrative function, exercised control over land use (including in some localities the periodic redistribution of land) and generally governed the farming programme. Government of the society was in turn in the hands of the gathering (*skhod*) of all members over the age of eighteen. In almost all cases this land society was synonymous with the old commune (*obshchina*). Exceptions were the small number of collective farms in existence in the early 1920s or freely united groups of individual farms (*khutora, otruba*) (Danilov, 1977, p. 95). The latter were most evident in western provinces. Voluntary collective farms were usually on land where there had not previously been a village commune, such as a former estate (Danilov, 1977, p. 96). In other words, effective local control over the land — the basis of the economy — was little different in structure from the position obtaining before the revolution. If anything the commune/land society was more extensive in the NEP period. Land formerly the property of the Tsarist state was for the most part taken over by land societies. In 1926, 83.4 per cent of such land in the Central Industrial region and 61.7 per cent in the Central Agricultural region was in land societies (Danilov, 1977, p. 99). The position was recognised and accepted by the Soviet regime and, in the early years, generally encouraged — as a barrier to individualism.

There was, however, growing official concern at some of the characteristics of this form of communal landholding. The principle of equalisation within the commune tended to foster the fragmentation of land into strips. This was a particular problem in the central provinces of European Russia. There was also a deal of concern with redistribution, which was practised in some areas. The fear was — in Soviet Russia as it had been in Tsarist Russia — that this encouraged negligence of land by households if they expected to have their landholding changed at some future date. It must be remembered that communal landholding did not mean communal land use. Farming was always undertaken by individual households and their income depended on their own efforts. Ironically, in 1925 the Peoples' Commissariat for Land (*Narkomzem*) of the RSFSR was actually encouraging redistribution of land within the commune, where it had not already occurred in the revolution, in order to reduce kulak landholding (Danilov, 1977, p. 117). In general, however, redistribution was discouraged — it was forbidden in the 1924 land code for Belorussia, for instance — though not always with conspicuous success.

Village organisation and agricultural production, which involved the great majority of the population was therefore little different from before the revolution. Government control was, in theory, manifest in the lowest organ of government, the rural soviet (*selsovet*); these were not only fewer in number than land societies — in 1926 there were 56,300 rural soviets in the RSFSR compared with over 300,000 land societies — but they were financially weaker too. Few rural soviets had their own operating budgets whereas land societies had an income from local taxation. In effect, land societies were organs of local self-government identical with the traditional commune.

Despite gains in landholding made at the revolution the peasantry in the early 1920s were suffering severe loss of income, principally because of market dislocation and the phenomenon of price scissors (see below, p. 54). Reports from Pavlov Volost, Tambov, in the rich black soil belt, in 1922-3 said that there were no markets or local fairs functioning (Ts. K.R.K.P. (b), 1923, p. 83). Low prices for agricultural produce prevented the purchase of agricultural machinery in Yaropol'sk Volost, Moscow province (Ts. K.R.K.P. (b), 1923, p. 48). In June 1923 the agricultural machinery syndicate, *Sel'mash*, reported unsold stocks of over 3,000 ploughs, 2,150 seed drills, almost 3,000 harvesting machines and over 12,000 threshing machines (Malafeev, 1964, p. 46). Local reports spoke of low prices for agricultural products destroying any stimulus for the development of the economy and alienating peasants from Soviet power.

A great gain made by the peasant population was the removal of interest charged by the peasant bank and rent charges to which they had been subject before the revolution. Malafeev has calculated that these amounted to 700 million gold rubles per annum. The revolution swept these away leaving the peasants better off despite lower prices for their crops. Malafeev claims that the peasantry could therefore accept up to 20 per cent lower prices and be no worse off (1964, p. 44). This precise calculation ignores the loss of side-earnings in crafts and trades (*promysly*) which, particularly in the northern provinces, had been a major source of money income before the war. The loss of urban or other 'off-farm' employment opportunities had seriously affected large sections of the peasantry as well as the proletariat. Many peasants had depended on such income to buy food on the local market. The civil war had therefore necessarily led to greater subsistence-orientation amongst peasants. It was only through the recovery of production and exchange that all sections of the population, including the peasantry, could improve consumption. NEP was designed to achieve just that end but it was not without problems.

Money and Inflation

Inflation affected all European nations during and after the First World War, and Russia was no exception. Printing money to help pay for the costs of war continued after 1917 and into the civil war. Under NEP, however, monetary stability was increasingly necessary and was achieved in 1924. Although there was inflationary pressure thereafter it was never to reach the levels of earlier years. The major single cause of inflation was the high level of government expenditure compared with income. Hence the government printed money to meet some of their obligations (Table 2.2).

Table 2.2: Notes in Circulation 1914-21

	Million rubles in circulation	Price index	
Mid-1914	1,530	1913 =	100
October 1917	17,175		
December 1918	57,391		
Mid-1921	2,347,164	1921 = 8,070,000	

Source: R.W. Davies, *Development of the Soviet Budgetary System*(1958), p. 9.

During the civil war ideas of a 'moneyless' economy were floated partly at least out of a genuine idealistic belief that the new society could dispense with this instrument of bourgeois economies. In effect, however, money went out of use simply because it lost value through hyperinflation. Later, under the market conditions of NEP, it was realised that money was the only possible medium of exchange. However, it was almost impossible for the government to get the budget into balance. State revenue remained too low because the tax system had all but broken down and because the level of production was so low. Government expenditure, on the other hand, remained relatively high because of the extensive role of the state in the economy.

In 1919 all state enterprises were placed on the budget, so that all their finances came from the central budget. By the same token, all revenue went to the state and all output was made available to the state. The system was gradually abolished from August 1921 and steadily removed through the following year, as more and more enterprises were permitted to sell their products. Indeed, they were forced to pay workers wages partly in cash, buy in raw materials and fuel and balance the books. Thus a system of commercial cost accounting (*khozraschet*) was introduced by the Peoples' Commissariat of Finance

(*Narkomfin*).[2] By the last quarter of 1922 all purchases and sales by state enterprises were made on the open market, and working capital was no longer made available through the budget. This reduced the strain on the state budget but at the same time reduced the degree of control over state enterprises. It also increased the need for a stable unit of account. Up to a point inflation was an important indirect form of government revenue but it was difficult to control, and although taxes on incomes and various excises were introduced and extended they were very far from closing the budget deficit. Rampant inflation and the ever-large issues of currency made budgeting and the course of trade difficult not just for government but also for the financially independent enterprises. Therefore, in October 1922 the state bank began to issue a new currency – the *chervonets* (the old ruble was known as the *sovznak*) – in large denominations as a stable unit of account. It was intended initially for commercial transactions in particular between nationalised enterprises. The new currency was equivalent to 10 old Imperial gold rubles, and its issue was backed by gold and foreign exchange (up to 25 per cent). Meanwhile the *sovznak* ruble continued in circulation, absorbing most of the inflationary pressure. However, the position could not continue. *Chervontsy* were more and more in demand, even in the countryside. Eventually the good money drove out the bad. Early in 1924 *chervontsy* were issued in small denominations and the *sovznak* suspended. The *chervonets* (once again called the ruble) became the only currency. One *chervonets* ruble was exchangeable for 50 milliard *sovznak* rubles.

Through a combination of increased taxation – the agricultural tax being levied in money, an urban property tax, increased excise duties – some recovery in production and economies in government expenditure the budget reached balance and the printing of money ceased to be necessary for this purpose. Inflation was now under control, but these crucial years before stabilisation had indicated two things. First, money was essential to the conduct of the economy. Second, market relations with the peasantry were more fragile than supposed. The latter was illustrated by the price-fluctuations concurrent with inflation known as the 'price scissors'.

The 'Scissors Crisis'

Price 'scissors' was a term used to describe the price differential between the products of industry and agriculture. This was to move severely in 1922 and 1923 and pose a political problem for the regime.

In 1922 the industrial trusts were forced to raise their own working capital, having been removed from the budget of VSNKh. As a result there was something of a rush to sell goods on the market. There was also a strong pent-up demand for agricultural products in urban markets. However, although the harvest of 1922 proved to be far better than that of 1921 (and indeed higher than 1920), when the rush of industrial goods on to local markets and bazaars (nicely known as *razbazirovanie*) took place in mid-1922 the harvest was not yet ready for sale. Ironically there was a mini-glut and sales crisis at a time of general shortage. If the market is seen on a simple plane of urban industry trading with peasant farmers (in fact, the real trading position was more complex than this) then the terms of trade at this time were firmly with the peasants — or at least those with a surplus to sell. Demand for agricultural products in the urban industrial sector was increasing but the supply of agricultural products was highly inelastic, so that however much industrial prices were reduced this was unlikely to attract a substantial increase in agricultural products in exchange.

The position was reversed the following year when the real 'scissors crisis' emerged. Before the end of 1922 industrial trusts began to organise syndicates to systematise their sales. Thus a relatively small number of large agencies appeared, putting state industry into a virtual monopoly position in the market with a mass of unorganised peasant producers. Through this monopoly power they were able to raise prices and restrict the flow of goods onto the market by building up stocks. They had been encouraged to do this by an 'instruction' from VSNKh to make profits. In addition, the 1922 harvest had indicated a significant recovery of agricultural production. In mid-1923, therefore, the prices of many industrial products went up while large parts of industry sat on stocks in anticipation of the harvest. Agricultural prices declined relatively and, in terms of pre-war gold rubles, absolutely. The average price for a pound of bread grain (in gold) in September 1922 was 74 kopeks; by February 1923 this had fallen to 44 kopeks (Larin, 1923, p. 58). It must be remembered that in terms of contemporary currency all prices were increasing with inflation. But the wholesale price index for industrial products increased steadily through 1923 and more rapidly than the index for agricultural products. The terms of trade had moved around very much in favour of industry and were considerably less favourable towards agriculture than they had been in 1913. But the hoped-for rush to the market by the peasants after the harvest did not occur. The 'scissors' continued to widen until October 1923.

There were several reasons for this phenomenon. First, as agricultural production had recovered more quickly than industry there was bound to be some change in market relation. By 1923 agricultural production had reached about 70 per cent of the 1916 level; a far higher recovery than industry but not enough to account for the price differential which reached almost 3 to 1 (Dobb, 1966a, p. 162) (see Table 2.3). Second, and more important, industry was attempting to exploit

Table 2.3: The Price 'Scissors' 1922-4: (ratio of the retail price index of industrial goods to agricultural produce)

Date	Ratio	Date	Ratio
October 1922	1.61	November 1923	2.49
November	1.51	December	2.02
December	1.67	January 1924	1.78
January 1923	1.84	February	1.59
February	1.80	March	1.60
March	1.80	April	1.41
April	2.21	May	1.27
May	2.23	June	1.47
June	2.19	July	1.37
July	2.11	August	1.22
August	1.87	September	1.29
September	2.80	October	1.41
October	2.97		

Source: A.N. Malafeev, *Istoriya tsenoobrazovaniya* (M. 1964), p. 386.

its monopoly position in the market by deliberately pushing up prices. Third, state policy played a part. This was a time of great inflation and when two currencies were in use. The government was attempting to have the burden of inflation borne by the *sovznak* ruble circulating in the countryside. But the peasantry were not ready to be fooled into disposing of their produce on such disadvantageous terms. The peasant response was perfectly rational. During very rapid inflation it made good sense to hold on to grain rather than exchange it for rapidly depreciating paper money. Alternatively, some peasants began demanding the stable *chervontsy* in exchange. At this time the agricultural tax was payable partly in cash, partly in kind, so peasants sought to maximise payments in cash and retain grain. The general response to the 'scissors crisis' amongst the peasantry showed that the peasantry as a whole was not ready to be fooled by the money illusion. Thereafter a more conciliatory attitude to the peasantry was demanded.

It seems unlikely that there was a conspiracy in government to exploit the peasant producers, for it was some time before government fully appreciated what was going on in the market-place and was able to separate the problem of price 'scissors' from the more evident problem of general inflation. When the problem was fully appreciated, action was taken. Nonetheless it is clear that sections of industry, combining through sales syndicates, were seeking to exploit their near-monopoly market position with the connivance of VSNKh. This was clearly a misreading of the market. The 'scissors' began to be closed after October 1923 largely through government action. First, the government forced down industrial prices by requiring banks to restrict credit which in turn forced industry to unload stocks onto the market. Second, maximum selling prices were fixed. Third, and possibly most important, was the policy of 'goods intervention' whereby government imported some consumer goods at low world prices and put them on the market in competition with home-produced items. As a result, prices fell by almost a third. Delivery prices to VSNKh for consumer goods fell on average by 29 per cent (in real terms) between October 1923 and October 1924: cotton piece goods by 37 per cent and leather by 42 per cent (Conjuncture, 1928, p. 20). Economies in production were thus forced on large sections of industry and a systematic programme of concentrating production in more efficient plants was adopted. Administrative costs, and the total number of trusts, were reduced.

Agricultural prices, on the other hand, were allowed to increase. The government abandoned its attempts to fix grain prices, replacing them with 'directive' prices. The agricultural tax became payable entirely in cash from 1924. There was a generally more conciliatory political attitude towards the peasantry, though the price 'scissors' were never finally closed. This is to say the terms of trade for the peasantry — what they could buy in exchange for their sales of agricultural produce — never returned to the pre-war level throughout the NEP period (Jasny, 1972, p. 19). The significance of the 'scissors crisis' and government perception of it was that an attempt, whether by accident or design, to 'cheat' the food-producing peasants or exploit the market did not work; that the peasants were able to exist, to an extent, independently of the market more readily than large-scale industry. Thus, after the uncertain and chaotic years up to 1923, the 'dictatorship of the proletariat' in effect gave way to the policy of 'face to the countryside'.

Labour

It was ironic that the industrial workers, in whose name the revolution had been made, were to bear the brunt of concessions to the peasantry made in the early 1920s. It was impossible, however, to draw a hard and fast line between peasant and proletariat. For generations peasants had undertaken short-term or seasonal work in urban or industrial centres. Further, many long-term urban workers had family ties in the village. The dislocation and confusion of revolution and civil war had resulted in a mass drift back to the land by millions of urban dwellers — now without work to do — and these numbers included many who had previously severed their connection with the land and the village. As a result not only was the urban proletariat in 1920-1 considerably smaller than in 1916-17 it was different in structure and of recent origin.

The advent of NEP brought relief for the workers after the misery and deprivation of war Communism, but the elements of capitalism manifest in NEP were to bring mixed fortunes. Wages increased initially and gradually payment in kind was replaced by money wages. In 1920 only 8 per cent of wages had been paid in money; by 1922 the proportion was 50 per cent. This, of course, gave greater spending discretion to wage-earners but it was accompanied by rapid inflation as well as by increasing wage differentials and growing unemployment. Officially the ratio of wages for skilled to unskilled workers increased from 1.04 in 1920 to 2.44 to 1 in 1922. But these official figures probably bore little resemblance to reality. The state was unable to regulate wages even in nationalised industry and a large proportion of workers were employed wholly outside the state sector.

The introduction of cost accounting (*khozraschet*) from 1921 dominated business practice. With few exceptions business organisations were required to make profits; and this affected workers' pay. The more successful industries, in particular consumer-goods industries, paid higher wages than those in producer-goods, which were slower to recover. Nationalised industry tended to pay less than industries where private ownership was significant, which in turn produced some anomalies in comparative incomes (Carr, 1969, p. 49). There was also a growing gap in income between the worker and the manager. Relatively high salaries for industrial managers became commonplace, often boosted by bonuses. In 1923 there was renewed government pressure for a reduction in differentials and anomalies. But of greater effect was the pressure to reduce costs after the 'scissors crisis'. This inevitably led to some real wage reductions and to redundancies. Thus, despite union opposition, urban workers suffered directly from the demands of the market-place and cost accounting in industry. In this respect the government and party were firmly in support of the industrial manager, the employer. Indeed the government was a major employer, albeit at some remove. The position of the worker was made worse by supply problems and the 'goods intervention' policy of diverting some consumer-goods to the peasant market.

In the face of this pressure trades unions were weak. Membership declined from a peak of 8.4 million in mid-1921 to 4.5 million in October 1922, recovering and levelling out at 5.5 million a year later. But unions had little power to bargain for wages, and only a few workers were covered by collective agreements. The key to their relative weakness was the spectre of unemployment. Urban unemployment was a real and large problem which was becoming apparent only slowly to central government. Labour exchanges and public works schemes introduced to try to cope with the problem proved inadequate, if only because of the size of the country. Public works schemes (from 1922) had barely any effect outside Moscow and Leningrad.

It was also uncertain how many unemployed there were. Recent arrivals from the village, former servants of the old regime and workers laid off by industry mingled together. Official figures for unemployment varied between one and one and a half million, but this was probably a gross underestimate; for one thing it excluded most unemployed women. Olga Narkiewicz estimates a real total in 1925 of at least 10 million unemployed (1970, p. 101). The problem was exacerbated by the growth in total population. The 1926 census recorded a total of 147 million people compared with 139 million for the same area in 1913. Industry was recovering quickly but not sufficiently to absorb the employable labour force. Indeed, the commercial capitalist organisation fostered to aid recovery was able to exploit the labour market by putting downward pressure on wages, in real terms. Improved employment, incomes and consumption depended on the recovery of industrial production.

Industry

Industrial development in the early 1920s was principally a result of recovery, whereby idle capacity was brought back into production, rather than new productive capacity being created. The 'recovery factor' was more effective with consumer-goods than producer-goods: the processes of production in the former case were more straightforward and less costly in terms of capital and energy, and in most years there was a ready market for the products. Between 1923 and 1925 cotton cloth production increased by 2.6 times in volume, wool cloth by 1.7 times (Gladkov, 1960, p. 420) (see also Table 2.4). Heavy capital goods industries demanded large investment and provided slow returns. A persistent problem was how and whence that investment was to be forthcoming. Market relations between industry and agriculture remained under some strain for most of the decade.

Table 2.4: Industrial Output 1921-5

Product	Unit	1913	1921	1925	1925 as percentage of 1913
Coal	million tonnes	29.1	9.5	16.5	57
Oil	million tonnes	9.2	3.8	7.1	77
Peat	million tonnes	1.7	2.0	2.7	159
Pig iron	million tonnes	4.2	0.1	1.3	31
Steel	million tonnes	4.2	0.2	1.9	45
Rolled steel	million tonnes	3.5	0.2	1.4	40
Electrical energy	million kWh	1,945	520	2,925	150
Cement	million tonnes	1.5	0.06	0.9	60
Tractors	(no.)	–	–	600	–
Paper	million tonnes	0.2		0.2	107
Sugar	million tonnes	1.3	0.05	1.1	85
Fish	million tonnes	1.0	0.3	0.7	70
Leather shoes	thousand pairs	8.3	3.4	8.2	98.8
All heavy industry	million rubles	10,251		7,739	75.5

Sources: V.T. Chuntulov, *Ekonomicheskaya Istoriya SSSR* (M. 1969), p. 230.
E. Yu. Lokshin, *Ocherk istorii promyshlennosti SSSR* (M. 1956), p. 129.

Although few industries had reached 1913 levels of production by 1925, industry as a whole had begun to be profitable — as demanded by the introduction of cost accounting. A few industries went ahead — peat, important as a substitute for coal which was in short supply, and electrical supply, resulting from the GOELRO plan. In 1922 a power station was constructed in Kashira, Tula province, to the south of Moscow, followed by others in the Urals, the Donbas and in Moscow in 1925. This development in turn called forth other new construction and new factories — a cement works in Moscow, an instrument factory and the '*Elektroapparat*' electrical equipment works in Petrograd

(Leningrad), *'Parastroi'* in Moscow and *'Krasnyi Kotelshchik'* boiler works in Taganrog. A car factory was opened in Moscow in 1924 (later to become *ZIL*), and tractors began to be produced in Saratov from 1922 and a year later in the former Putilov works in Petrograd.

Foreign Trade

A major obstacle to the growth of foreign trade was the reluctance of the new Soviet government to acknowledge the debts secured by and under the old regime. It therefore proved impossible to secure further foreign loans, despite repeated efforts. Understandably, the French government was most intransigent, for it had been Frenchmen and French companies which had lost most. The British government was more amenable, signing a trade agreement in 1921, but France and the USA effectively opposed negotiations for loans in Genoa and The Hague in 1922. The Treaty of Rapallo with Germany in 1922 was a turning-point, and trade increased significantly thereafter. The difficulty of securing export commodities put the Soviet Union into trading deficit in the early 1920s, though the position was alleviated by German credits.

The major demand within the USSR was for capital goods to aid recovery. Capital goods imports made up about two-thirds of the total. Another means of securing Western expertise was by granting concessions to Western companies to exploit natural resources (see pp. 192-3, below). These concessions were concentrated, but not exclusively, in forestry and mining and were originally conceived in long-run terms − forestry-concessions being offered for up to 24 years initially (*Concessions in the Far East*, 1925, vol. 1, p. 137). In the outcome, however, they proved to be short-lived and were of limited economic effect.

As exports the USSR offered timber, furs and, increasingly, oil and other mining products. But to cover the trade deficit it proved necessary also to sell gold and, on occasions, treasures of nineteenth-century art. In 1922-3 agricultural exports were only one-fifteenth of their pre-war level (Krzhizhanovskii, 1927, p. 33); a lack of recovery in agriculture was restricting foreign earning power. The position of the Soviet Union was made more difficult by currency instability. The ruble had virtually lost international exchange value, though the new *chervonets* ruble was convertible and even bought on foreign exchange markets for a short time. The tightly controlled state monopoly of foreign trade, introduced in 1917, was necessary to govern the use of scarce foreign exchange resources. As Western economies recovered from the war and stabilised the exchange values of their currencies there was a gradual, if short-lived, return to the gold standard (by Sweden in 1924, Britain in 1925 and France in 1928). But the ruble was removed from international exchanges in 1926 and has remained so ever since.

NEP was broadly successful in generating economic recovery. The state maintained extensive control in the industrial economy and some beginnings of planning were evident. The hunger and shortages of the civil war had been largely remedied and rapid inflation had been brought under control. Yet deeper problems remained. State control over agriculture, which constituted the greater part of the economy, was limited and these limitations were later to result in constraints on industrial policy. More particularly, economic objectives were unclear and there was inconsistency in policy. From 1925 policy had tended to favour the peasantry with price-concessions and other measures. This was to change, markedly, in subsequent years.

Notes

1. Individual farms were reduced substantially with the exception of some western provinces, notably Vitebsk and Smolensk, where they increased slightly.

2. This system nominally required all costs to be covered and profits to be made, but it was possible, in some cases, to build in a subsidy.

3 CHANGE OF COURSE

Industry, agriculture and trade continued to recover, 1926 being roughly taken as the year when 1913 levels of output were re-achieved. There were, however, lags in the expansion of agricultural marketings which set great problems for policy-makers. The year 1926 also marked the zenith of the policy of conciliation to the peasantry, which had been adopted after 1923. In the late 1920s more forthright policies towards the peasantry to aid industrialisation were adopted. Before the end of the decade the whole structure of NEP was to be dismantled and a general plan replace the market. The late 1920s were thus vital, tempestuous years of radical redirection in the economy of the USSR.

After Lenin's death in 1924 the minor vacuum was filled by a triumvirate of Kamenev, Zinoviev and Stalin. Lenin had left a 'testament' in which he expressed reservations about, and opposition to, the succession of either Stalin or Trotsky to individual power. Each may have been regarded or have regarded himself as a natural successor, and there would seem no logical reason why Lenin's will should continue in some quasi-monarchical style after his death. Nonetheless, Lenin was greatly revered and Stalin had his testament suppressed to safeguard his own position. Hostility between Stalin and Trotsky was already evident, and Stalin was eventually to triumph. His 'victories' began immediately, for, from 1924, the era of 'Socialism in One Country' emerged. The basis of this policy was that a socialist society could be created in a single country, in contradiction to the earlier expectation that the Russian revolution would be the spark to ignite the fires of revolution elsewhere in Europe. This was a realistic appraisal by Stalin, for clearly there was no chance of other European revolutions by this time. Thus Stalin became associated with a form of socialist nationalism. Trotsky with international socialism. Political conflict continued and centred largely around economic policy. In this vital area it was Trotsky and his supporters on the left who were defeated. Trotsky himself was dismissed from the party in 1927, exiled in 1928 and deported in 1929.

The Industrialisation Debate

By the mid-1920s the 'recovery factor' — the re-absorption of existing capital resources into production — was largely, if not entirely, exhausted. Future growth would depend on the creation of new productive capacity, and it was on this assumption that serious and extensive discussion on the future of industrial development, the rate and method of capital accumulation, took place. It came to be known as the 'industrialisation debate'. There was not a single debate, though the best-known arguments were voiced in the Fourteenth Party Congress in 1925. Contributions and opinions were expressed before then and continued thereafter. The debate was to call forth a variety of views, some original and farseeing economic ideas and considerable conflict. It is worth while reminding ourselves that this economic debate took place in a context of economic knowledge and understanding far less sophisticated than the post-war world of Keynesian demand-management and development economics, at a time when minimal government economic activity was accepted as the norm in Western Europe. But the debate over economic affairs went beyond mere economics. It was closely bound up with, and an extension of, political rivalry and jockeying for power within the party.

In the early years of Soviet power there was some opposition expressed to the idea of a priority for industrial development. There was good reason for it. It was simply more sensible and economically rational to exploit Russia's resources and earning power within the world economy; to be consistent with the principles of comparative advantage. Optimum returns to investment could be secured from agriculture. Agricultural products (grain and timber for the most part) could be exported and industrial products imported. There were here shades of the populist-Marxist debate of the 1890s; a streak of anti-industrialisation, most associated with the neo-populist and brilliant economist Nikolai Kondratiev. These ideas proved quite unacceptable to the party. Industry meant strength; and socialism was dependent upon industrialisation. Yet the ideas had some advocacy even within the party. Sokolnikov, the Commissar of Finance, favoured a short-run dependence on agricultural exports, using them to pay for imports of capital goods thereby effecting industrialisation without heavy direct investment. Sokolnikov published these ideas in 1925, at about the same time as Shanin (the director of Gosbank, and an acolyte of Sokolnikov) made a similar submission. His was a criticism of the heavy emphasis on capital goods contained in the control figure forecasts. As financiers, Shanin and Sokolnikov were clearly concerned with optimising returns to investment. These would be best fulfilled by giving more emphasis to consumer-goods and agriculture which, with a lower capital-output ratio than heavy industry, would produce better returns and thereby enable savings. Although not acceptable as they stood, these ideas were to have some influence, for it was the advocates of a heavy emphasis on producer-goods industry who had little influence before 1926.

It was Trotsky and his economic spokesman Preobrazhensky who most fully represented the views in favour of large-scale investment in heavy capital goods industry, though they were supported by Kamenev and Zinoviev within the party and some within VSNKh. They came to be known as the Left Opposition, and the defeat of these ideas meant the political defeat of Trotsky and his supporters.

The ideas of the left were expressed most cogently and originally by Preobrazhensky. His *New Economics* was published in 1926, though many of the ideas contained therein were publicised in lectures and speeches in earlier years. At the basis of his ideas was the assumption that potential savings exceeded actual savings within the economy as a whole. Further, the only effective way to create modern, technologically advanced capital-intensive industry was to go ahead and build it, rather than rely on some indefinite accumulation through the sale of consumer-goods. It also required a much larger increase in producer-goods output in the early period in order to produce an increase in consumer-goods in a later period – by a factor of four or five to one. This therefore required large investments on fixed capital. How was the accumulation to be effected? On this point Preobrazhensky drew a parallel with the idea of primitive or primary accumulation in a capitalist economy as deduced by Marx. According to Marx, early capitalist economies (in particular Britain) had accumulated capital through the exploitation of colonies. In contrast, Soviet Russia had no colonies to exploit; indeed the whole notion of colonial exploitation was anathema to the makers of the revolution, whose motivation had been one of liberating subjected peoples. For the new socialist state, therefore, sources of accumulation would have to be found internally in the non-socialist bourgeois branches of the economy that were remaining.[1] Above all, this meant the peasantry. Thus Preobrazhensky formulated a law of primitive socialist accumulation:

The more backward economically, petty bourgeois, peasant a particular country is which has gone over to the socialist organisation of production, and the smaller the inheritance received by the socialist accumulation fund of the proletariat of this country when the social revolution takes place, by so much the more, in proportion, will socialist accumulation be obliged to rely on alienating part of the surplus product of pre-socialist forms of economy.

(Preobrazhensky, 1965, p. 124)

Accumulation at the expense of the non-socialist or 'pre-socialist' sectors in the economy was not the only means of obtaining funds. The important objective was to extend the state economy in what was a mixed economy of NEP.

> This process of extending and consolidating the state economy can proceed both at the expense of its own forces and resources, that is the surplus product of the workers in state industry, and at the expense of the private, including peasant (itself including middle peasant) economy. (Preobrazhensky, 1965, p. 226)

Thus Preobrazhensky was not singling out the peasantry. The point was that the peasants made up the largest part of the population and accounted for the largest proportion of the economy.

The accumulation of capital could be brought about in a number of ways: taxation, especially of capitalist profit (i.e. the state taking over what the capitalist is accumulating); inflationary printing of money (shades of 1920-4); through the banking system and the market. The state could exploit its monopoly position in banking by passing on as credits to state organs deposits received from private producers. But most emphasis fell on the market and price policy. By the state exploiting the advantages of a real or virtual monopoly position in the market it could fix prices so as to obtain an inequitable rate of exchange with the capitalist sector – and this meant, in effect, the peasantry above all. Thus the socialist sector (the state) could obtain super-profits which would provide the capital for investment, and that investment would be directed to capital-intensive heavy industry.

A parallel requirement was careful protection of the economy to prevent wasteful imports of consumer-goods. It was also ideologically necessary to protect the industrial working class from exploitation. Increases in real wages were essential, and they would be forthcoming as production increased (in the longer term) and by shifting the burden of restraints on consumption to the peasantry (in the short run) (Erlich, 1967, pp. 49, 57). Out of concern that the peasant population be alienated it was not proposed that direct taxes be raised unduly but that indirect taxes be used in discriminatory action against the peasantry. In advocating a diversion of resources away from agriculture to heavy industry Preobrazhensky's proposed policies were deliberately not optimal, for they encouraged capital-intensive techniques where

capital was scarce. However, there was no suggestion that the market
structure of NEP be destroyed; rather the market was to be exploited.

But as a policy these ideas were not acceptable to the party. Deliberate discrimination against the peasantry would have posed a threat to
the *smychka* and thereby the whole basis of NEP; discriminatory
price policy threatened a revival of the price scissors, the effects of
which the government was still at pains to correct. Indeed,
Preobrazhensky had had some influence over VSNKh in its pricing
policy of 1922-3 which had contributed to the scissors crisis.
Preobrazhensky was not unaware of this danger in his ideas, though he
was a little unclear as to how to avoid it.

There were some good economic reasons for not accepting the
governing principle of the left, though political motives were probably
at least as important. Bukharin was the major critic of the left's economics, and Rykov, Kalinin and Stalin joined him in opposing their ideas.
There was equal criticism, however, of the idea of postponing
industrialisation as advocated by Shanin and Sokolnikov. The Fourteenth Party Congress resolved to pursue a policy of heavy industrial
development as 'the economic corollary of socialism in one country'
(Carr, 1970, p. 378). Industrialisation, to develop the means to
produce the means of production, was necessary to ensure economic
independence — and therefore full political independence. But the
mode and tempo of industrial development advocated by
Preobrazhensky and Trotsky were not acceptable because of the risks
involved. The party line followed the ideas of Bukharin. Stalin
announced at the Fourteenth Party Congress in 1925 that 'we are and
we shall be for Bukharin'.

Nikolai Bukharin was a young intellectual who for some time had
been recognised as the creative genius of ideology. In 1921 he had been
a close collaborator with Preobrazhensky in writing *ABC of Communism*. Now they were opponents. Bukharin's criticisms of the 'left opposition' were by no means totally dismissive; they were rather concerned
with tempo. The state, he acknowledged, would certainly have to divert
resources from agriculture to industry but not at a rate to jeopardise
internal stability. He said in July 1926:

> Our state industry cannot obtain the means for its expansion solely
> from the labour of the working class . . . The peasantry must take its
> share in helping the state to build up a socialist system of industry
> . . . The whole question is: how much can we take away from the
> peasantry . . . what are the limits of the pumping over? Comrades of

the opposition are in favour of an immoderate amount of pumping over and want to put so severe a pressure upon the peasantry that in our opinion the result would be economically irrational and politically impermissible. (Quoted by Dobb, 1966b, p. 203)

The crucial element in Bukharin's ideas was his concern with *optimality* and balanced growth. He was concerned that there should be an optimal combination of producer-goods and consumer-goods, and that both industry and agriculture should grow together at an optimum rate. Industry should not, indeed could not, grow at the expense of agriculture. Industry was dependent upon agriculture as a source of supply of raw materials (timber, cotton, flax, etc.) and on peasant demand. Similarly, agricultural development was dependent upon industry — for the supply of agricultural machinery, artificial fertilisers, consumer-goods and as a market for agricultural produce. It was therefore essential for agricultural incomes to increase so that more savings could be obtained from agriculture in future. Rather than be exploited the peasants should be encouraged. He even went as far as using the words 'enrich yourselves' in April 1925. He was, however, forced to withdraw the statement soon afterwards as an unacceptable encouragement to kulaks. But it was upon the richness of peasant demand that industry depended. Industrial development might be gradual or slow (even at a 'snail's pace') but it would be steady and its rate would be governed directly by the growth in agricultural output and exchange. A faster rate of growth would be enabled by a faster turnover in trade between industry and agriculture, and this in turn implied an increase, not a decrease, in peasant incomes. Savings could be channelled (voluntarily) through savings banks which would, of course, be under state control. The state could certainly channel resources from the private capitalist sector to the socialist sector. Socialism would eventually overcome private enterprise because of its greater efficiency. A crucial aspect of Bukharin's view here, though, is his conception of the peasantry. Unlike his fellow Bolsheviks, including Lenin, Bukharin did not see the peasants as petit bourgeois or capitalist. To him the family economy of the peasantry was peculiar; neither capitalist nor socialist. This was by no means a unique estimate, though one unusual for a Marxist in Russia at the time. Prevailing doctrine tended to regard the peasantry as including small-scale capitalist or (at best) pre-capitalist producers, of whom some were exploitative (the kulaks). A minority of peasants were comparable to the proletariat — the poor (*bednyak*) or landless (*batrak*) — and exploited. The imposition of inappropriate class notions on the peasantry at this time was one of the greatest conceptual errors of the 1920s.

Careful and detailed analyses of the peasant economy had been made and were published in the 1920s. Many suggested that the peasant economy was a peculiar form of production and consumption unit neither pre-capitalist nor petty-capitalist but different from capitalist whose scale, operation and behaviour were not determined by commercial capitalist motives and considerations. The best-known advocates of such views, Makarov and Chayanov (the latter better known in the West since a translation of his major theoretical work in 1966), were colleagues of Kondratiev. Bukharin — a political opponent — was a long way from them in his thinking, but he was, similarly, an advocate of the co-operative movement. Thus the peasantry were not simply to be treated as capitalists (and thereby real or potential opponents) but as real or potential allies, to be encouraged slowly and surely to join co-operatives voluntarily. Political and economic favours could be granted to co-operatives so that eventually even the kulaks would join. Preobrazhensky, on the other hand, had little time for co-operatives, not seeing them as contributing to the transition to socialism.

Bukharin's ideas had most influence over economic policy in the mid-1920s as the more extreme and untenable notions of Preobrazhensky were rejected. Concessions to the peasantry reached a high point in 1925, in which year peasants were permitted to employ hired labour. Bukharin was not simply pro-peasant. He was in no sense a neo-populist, but he argued strongly against exploiting the peasantry and in favour of balanced growth between industry and agriculture and between producer-goods and consumer-goods. Within the party Stalin supported Bukharin. At the Fifteenth Party Congress in 1926 he noted that 'industry must not be promoted through neglect or violation of the interests of agriculture' (quoted in Carr and Davies, 1974, p. 308). Stalin, of course, was to change his attitude some years later, but at this time, by supporting Bukharin, he could direct criticism against the left opposition headed by Trotsky. There was also some support at this time for the Bukharin line from VSNKh, of which Felix Dzerzhinsky was head. When he died in 1926 there was to be more pressure within VSNKh for stronger priority to producer-goods.

Bukharin, long an advocate of gradualness, was to find himself more and more isolated as greater emphasis was put on extending the stock of industrial capital. The capital stock had actually been run down to this date, which was one reason for Preobrazhensky's great concern with big increases in investment (Erlich, 1967, p. 106). At no time, however, was there any suggestion that the essentials of NEP be undone. All participants in the debate retained the notion that a stable currency would be maintained, rising living standards (for the proletariat) would be aimed at and, above all, the market would remain. The most important element in the market that dominated contemporary thinking was the relations between the industrial sector and the agricultural producers.

Industry and the Beginnings of Planning

As we have seen in Chapter 2, planning evolved in the 1920s as a unique feature of the Soviet economy. The idea of a long-term (10 to 15 years) general plan was evident in GOELRO dating from 1920. Annual plan forecasts were drawn up as Control Figures from 1925. In 1923 Gosplan drafted a perspective plan covering a five-year period for industry as a whole, and there were other five-year plans made by industrial commissariats and even local authorities. From 1926 various drafts of prospective five-year plans were made both by Gosplan and VSNKh. The significance of this development was twofold. It marked the beginning of a commitment to industrialisation and state direction of that development through a comprehensive plan; and it adopted a medium-term five-year period to put it into operation.

Thus, although 1928-9 can properly be seen as the first year of full central planning, it was in 1926 that the political commitment to planning became evident. It was from that year that a definite policy of creating a self-sufficient industrial economy was firmly established. Plans for the creation of new industries, involving high capital-investment with a long gestation period, were made. In 1926 approval was given to building the Turkestan-Siberia railway and the Dnepr dam HEP project. The following year it was decided to launch the building of the Stalingrad tractor factory, the Sverdlovsk engineering works and new iron and steel plants in the Krivoi Rog (in the Ukraine) and the Kuznetsk basin. Such projects were extremely expensive in terms of investment capital and would be slow to produce returns to that investment. As Professor R.W. Davies has succinctly put it: 'The crux of the economic problems of 1926 and after was the need to achieve, in an agrarian environment, a substantially higher level of investment in industry and to direct this investment towards the construction of new factories' (Carr and Davies, 1974, p. 296). Ultimately the problems of funding investment, especially as projects became more ambitious, were to lead to the destruction of the market economy of NEP. For the time being, however, the contemporary commitment remained the preservation of the *symchka*, or link, with the peasantry and the pursuit of balanced growth between producer-goods (group A) and consumer-goods (group B). VSNKh, however, put forward proposals with greater priority to producer-goods. In Gosplan there was even talk of 'forcing' the pace of industrialisation, though proposed investment levels were more modest.

The major anticipated source of new investment in large-scale 'census' industry (for which VSNKh was responsible) was expected to be internal accumulation, or profits. To this end the 'regime of economy' was launched in 1926 to foster cost-saving and efficiency in state-controlled industry. It aimed to rationalise production and the utilisation of labour and reduce labour costs to combat a renewal of inflationary pressure which was becoming evident (*Resheniya*, vol. 1, 1967, pp. 530-3). Subsequently, VSNKh advocated greater rationalisation of production, more mass production and standardisation. Price-reductions were made in June 1926 to reduce the gap between wholesale and retail prices and the difference between industrial and agricultural prices. *Narkomtorg*, the Peoples' Commissariat for Trade, and STO reduced prices by 10 per cent, but the real effect was more on wholesale prices than retail (Malafeev, 1964, p. 103), and industrial profits were disappointing. Industrialisation required higher prices to increase profits. The campaign to reduce industrial prices was not generally successful, but the attempt illustrated increasing administrative controls within the then market economy (Carr and Davies, 1974, p. 731).

As it turned out, capital investment in 1926-7 was higher than planned and VSNKh industry grew by 20 per cent (some of which was attributable to re-absorption of existing equipment). The following year, 1927-8, also showed continued growth. Large-scale industry was growing at a faster rate than small-scale, and group A goods at a faster rate than group B (Carr and Davies, 1974, p. 334 and table 3.1). Small-scale, private industry did not show the same pattern of growth, even though Gosplan, in its control figures, had assumed that private industry would increase. VSNKh was neglecting small-scale industry, which included workshops and artisans, both because of the belief in the superiority of large-scale industry, especially in future industrialisation, and because of ideological hostility to private capital (Carr and Davies, 1974, p. 415). Figures for industrial development 1925-8 are shown in Tables 3.1 and 3.2.

State-owned enterprises accounted for most 'census' industry. 'Census' industry included enterprises employing more than 16 workers, if mechanised, or 30 workers, if unmechanised. Private enterprises were more significant in consumer-goods than producer-goods. In 1925-6 private industry accounted for 4.6 per cent of consumer-goods production, in 20.1 per cent of enterprises. But even here the share of private capital fell to less than 1 per cent of production in 1927-8. According to contemporary accounts, from probably incomplete statistics, there were 3,342 million workers employed in small-scale industry in 1926-7 and 3,858 million in 1927-8 (*Industrializatsiya*, 1926-8, 1969, p. 261).

Table 3.1: Industrial Production 1925-8 (thousand rubles at current prices)

	1924-5	1925-6	1926-7	1927-8
Gross production,				
census industry	6,760,798	9,955,991	11,438,948	13,618,352
including group A	2,153,311	3,215,068	3,968,283	4,674,096
group B	4,607,487	6,740,922	7,470,665	8,944,256
Small-scale industry I[a]		4,185,000	4,603,000	4,748,000
Small-scale industry II	–		2,752,000	3,112,000

Notes: a.I = small-scale industry from control figures given in Carr and Davies.
II = non-census small-scale industry (predominantly handicraft and artisan) in 1926-7 prices given in *Industrializatsiya*, p. 261.
All figures for small-scale industry are rounded.
Sources: *Industrializatsiya SSSR 1926-28 gg. Dokumenty i materialy* (M. 1969), pp. 261, 262, 270, 276: E.H. Carr and R.W.D. Davies, *Foundations of a Planned Economy* (1974), p. 1004.

Table 3.2: Industrial Products in Physical Terms

	1925-6	1926-7	1927-8
Coal (million tonnes)	25.4	32.1	35.4
Crude oil (million tonnes)	8.5	10.3	11.8
Electric power (millions kWh)	3.2	3.9	5.2
Pig iron (million tonnes)	2.2	3.0	3.3
Crude steel (million tonnes)	2.0	3.0	4.2
Rolled steel (million tonnes)	2.2	2.8	3.3
Cement (million barrels)	8.5	9.7	11.9
Sugar (thousand tonnes)	1,063	870	1,340
Cotton yarn (thousand tonnes)	240	277	322

Source: Carr and Davies, *Foundations* (1974), p. 1008.

It was not until 1930 that there was a severe decline of artisan industry, but even before then, from 1926 to 1929, there was evident pressure on this sector. This, coupled with the growing priority to producer-goods, was disturbing the notion of 'balanced growth'. It was in

September 1928 that Bukharin published his 'Notes of an Economist', criticising VSNKh proposals. In the following month he in turn was criticised, first in the press and then in the party. In November 1928 Stalin defended the rapid rate of industrialisation to the Central Committee of the Communist Party. There had, then, been a marked change in basic policy away from 'balanced growth' and gradualness. In April 1929 the party gave formal ratification to the first five-year plan, which had been technically operative since October 1928. The plan marked the effective end of NEP; the market was replaced. The forecasts and directive plans of earlier years were superseded, by a plan for five years — long enough to cover harvest fluctuations and to give sufficient time for new construction to come into operation.

Gosplan prepared two variants of the plan for consideration and approval in late 1928. The basic variant suggested a feasible or realistic, but nonetheless ambitious, estimate of growth potential. The second, optimum, variant was, as its name implies, based on the most optimistic assumptions, being the maximum possible achievement. The basic variant demanded increases in total investment of 250 per cent; the optimum variant of 320 per cent (Zaleski, 1971, p. 61). In drafting the optimum variant of the plan Gosplan had assumed favourable circumstances: no harvest failure; a general growth in foreign trade with more foreign credits forthcoming; no change in the international terms of trade; rapid improvements in crop yields and in general industrial productivity to reduce costs; and armaments expenditure to be no higher than in the basic variant. Few of these conditions were to be met: there was a famine of disastrous proportions; the terms of trade moved markedly against the USSR in the depression after 1929; crop yields and labour productivity did not increase as expected; and industrial costs rose. While few of these changes could have been foreseen by the planners (e.g. the movement in terms of trade and the calamitous results of collectivisation which was introduced without the plan), they illustrate the fragile basis of the optimum variant.

Yet it was the optimum variant which was adopted and formally approved as the official five-year plan by the Sixteenth Party Congress in April 1929. Significantly, the assumptions underlying the optimum variant were not published in the party resolution which approved the plan. It was wholly unrealistic to accept the most optimistic plan forecasts during a serious grain-procurement crisis, which immediately preceded the launching of the collectivisation campaign. Nonetheless, the plan was adopted in an atmosphere of tension and excitement about the future and, of equal importance, at a time when the main advocate of 'balanced growth', Bukharin, was under attack. And there was a further dimension. The international political position of the country had deteriorated. Britain broke off diplomatic relations in 1927 and potential allies in China were lost with the massacre of most Chinese Communists in 1926. By 1929 the political priority had therefore become that of catching up with the West and doing so quickly. The need for rapid industrialisation to strengthen the encircled 'fortress Russia' was a growing mood which lay behind the approval, notionally after it had gone into operation, of a wildly optimistic plan. In such circumstances it could hardly hope to succeed.

Agriculture and the Market

The central problem of the economy in the 1920s was the relationship between industry and agriculture. While the state had succeeded in extending and consolidating control over the greater part of industry, agriculture remained beyond its governance. And this inability to govern, fully, the supply and distribution of foodstuffs was a real constraint on overall economic policy.

The harvest of 1925 marked a real recovery in agricultural production: gross grain production exceeded the pre-war average and yields were the highest of the decade (Table 3.3). Although grains were far from being the only significant branch of agriculture (flax, hemp and cotton were important industrial raw materials, for example) they made up the largest part of total production and provided the basic foodstuff. Agricultural statistics, however, present great difficulties. The size of harvest, yields and, in particular, the volume of marketed produce were the subject of varied estimates at the time and indeed since. Research in this area is still proceeding, so the figures presented should be treated with appropriate caution. Allowing for such difficulties, it may reasonably be accepted that total production recovered but that the volume of marketings fell short of the planned level to accord with state demands – to feed the army and the urban population and provide some margin for export. For the next few years it was the problem of procurement, rather than production, which was to dominate policy. There is far less certainty about the reasons for the shortfall in grain supplied to the state. They were hotly debated at the time and have been the subject of controversy ever since.

In the economic year 1926-7, after the 1926 harvest, state grain collections were not disappointing and there was no 'procurement crisis'.

This appears to have encouraged the optimistic investment plans made in that year. But this proved to be exceptional. In the autumn and winter of 1927 there were serious shortfalls, and further decline in 1928. The persistence of shortfalls in anticipated or planned state procurements of grain marked the immediate background to the breaking of the market mechanism, the virtual seizure of grain and the eventual implementation of mass collectivisation. The 'solution' to the crises, together with the adoption of central planning at the same time, marked a profound revolution in the Soviet economy.

Table 3.3: Agricultural Production and Sales

Year	Average yield (centner per hectare)	Gross harvest (million tonnes)		Amount sold on market
1909-13	7.2	72		
1917	6.4	54.6		
1919	6.2	50.5		
1921	5.5	42		
1923	7.2	56.6		
1924	6.2	51.4		
1925	8.3	72.5		
1926	8.2	76.8	(1925-6)	9.4
1927	7.6	72.3	(1926-7)	9.8
1928	7.9	73.3	(1927-8)	8.3
1929	7.5	71.7	(1928-9)	8.3
1924-8 average	7.6	69.3	(1923-7)	8.4
1925-9 average	7.9	73.3		

Notes: The amount sold refers to that sold outside rural areas, i.e. for the army, urban population and other industrial workers, or for export.
   Pre-war figures and those for 1921 have been revised upwards as a result of research by Wheatcroft (1977).
Sources: V.P. Danilov, *Sovetskaya dokolkhoznaya derevnya* (M. 1977): Yu. A. Moshkov, *Zernovaya problema* (M. 1966), p. 20: S.G. Wheatcroft, 'Grain Production Statistics in the USSR in the 1920s and 1930s', *CREES Discussion Papers*, SIPS No. 13 (Birmingham 1977), p. 9: Carr and Davies, *Foundations*, 1, (1974), pp. 997-8.

One contemporary explanation for the procurement crises, and one employed by Stalin, was that of agricultural structure and the levelling effect of the revolution. This had had the effect of wiping out the commercially most successful element – the gentry and kulaks – and producing a larger number of small peasant farms oriented to subsistence rather than producing for the market. There is no doubt that the revolution did result in levelling, and the removal of the small but highly successful commercial estate sector had a marked effect on exports in particular. Yet before the revolution the peasantry had provided over 75 per cent of total grain marketings (Koval'chenko, 1971, p. 190). The loss of the 25 per cent gentry estates was a serious and substantial one, particularly for exports, but not sufficient in itself to account for the procurement crises. Further, the increase in the number of peasant farms was not as great as suggested by Stalin. Official figures show that, for the territory of the USSR, the total number of peasant households increased from 21 million in 1916 to a peak of 25 million in 1927 (Ts.S.U., 1930, Table 1, p. 2) declining to 24.5 million in 1929 (Danilov, 1958, pp. 94-5). At the same time the average size of peasant households fell slightly from 5.67 in 1916 to 5.10 in 1927 (Ts.S.U., 1930, Table 1, p. 3; there was a decline in all republics of the union). More significantly, the average land-holding per farm (in the RSFSR only) increased from 10 hectares in 1916 to 13.22 hectares in 1927 (Danilov, 1977, p. 219). Such averages obscure regional and local variations but they show beyond doubt that the 'average' peasant was better off in terms of landholding after, than before, the revolution. He was eating better too. In the late 1920s average per capita meat consumption was more than double the pre-war level, at 40 kg (84 lb) in 1926 compared with 16 kg (33 lb) in 1914. Each kilo of meat took 5 kilos of grain to produce — one reason why less grain was sold. But this does not explain why it was more attractive to feed grain to pigs than sell it on the open market. A serious, if partial, explanation put forward by some Soviet historians is that peasants were making up for the years of deprivation before the revolution, and famine immediately after, by eating more while they had the chance.

A real problem was that there was more than one market. The state agencies and the co-operative network were able only to account for part of the overall market in grain and other foods. In part this was because a large proportion of total sales never went beyond the village or locality. The non-rural market, to which the figures refer, accounted for only part (but in this context the crucial part) of total sales. As there were different markets there were also different price levels, so that it was more advantageous for peasants, with a surplus, to sell at a higher price rather than a lower one. On average, private traders were prepared to pay more for agricultural products than the state, and the gap widened between 1926 and 1929. An index of prices (1913 = 100) paid by official agencies moved from 146 in 1925-6 to 157 in 1928-9. In the same years the private market price index moved from 159 to

183 (Carr and Davies, 1974, p. 1022).At the same time, overall demand for foodstuffs was rising as population grew, especially the urban/industrial population, and as urban incomes increased. Urban industrial incomes were higher relative to 1913 than peasant incomes, despite the concessionary policies made to the peasantry after 1923, and part of this income was being spent on foodstuffs.

It is on this point that pricing policy becomes crucial, for at a time of rising demand it was clearly inept to aim to reduce prices paid for grain, especially as there were alternative outlets for peasant producers. Official or state prices were reduced in 1926 because there was a good harvest and as part of a general price-reduction policy at the time (see above, p. 71). Agricultural wholesale prices were reduced from 1925/6 to 1926/7, as were state retail prices. The prices of the private market continued to increase, however. The object of the price-reduction campaign was to reduce costs to industry and improve urban living standards. But at a time of shortage and of excess demand it flew in the face of economic rationality to reduce prices. In this sense, therefore, government policy aggravated the procurement problem.

Despite price differences, the private trades, the *Nepman*, took a decreasing share of the non-rural total of trade. Co-operative trading organisations took the major share (Table 3.4). State trading organisations were more important in wholesale than retail trade. In 1923 about 60 per cent of all bread had been sold by private traders and 16 per cent by co-operatives. By 1926 the respective figures were 30 per cent and 56 per cent (Arskii, 1927, p. 96).

Table 3.4 Shares of Internal Trade (percentage handled by various organs)

Year	Private	State	Co-operatives
1925-6	27.1	31.6	41.3
1926-7	18.5	30.9	50.6
1927-8	15.8	29.2	55.0

Source: R. Arskii, *10 let bor'by na khozyaistvennom fronte* (Leningrad, 1927), p. 83; quoting figures published by *Narkomtorg*, the commissariat for trade.

In later years Stalin was to hold up the private trader as the 'class enemy' and accuse him of creating shortages. These figures make nonsense of that claim. The fact that private trade did not increase its share of the total, despite differences in the price level, suggests that state price reductions were not the only cause of 'procurement crises'.

A further explanation can be found in the disincentive to trade in urban markets because of the poor quality and availability of consumer goods. The 'goods shortage' was very evident in 1925 and 1926 when industrial production had not yet fully recovered, but it did not disappear thereafter (Gladkov, 1960, p. 420). The 'goods shortage' was a function of repressed inflation, again made worse by the government attempting to reduce prices for industrial goods after 1926. It further illustrated the dilemma of industrialisation policy. Industry (represented in particular by VSNKh) needed a favourable exchange to make profits for future investments, especially in producer-goods. Consumers (peasants *and* workers) wanted more consumer-goods. From 1926, as we have seen, there was a marked shift to heavy industrial investment rather than substantial increases in consumer-goods. The 'goods shortage' itself, then, was a result of central government policy, and it became more severe from 1927. There were even local reports of peasants coming to market with grain to sell, looking around at the stalls and, seeing that there was nothing worth buying, loading up the grain again and taking it home. The increasing demands on the economy put strains on the market equilibrium of NEP, which in turn resulted in the 'procurement crises' we have been considering. The ambitious and optimistic five-year plan was launched in the middle of a procurement crisis, with the result that the market mechanism of NEP was finally destroyed.

Collectivisation

As pressure for greater investment grew in 1928 there was widespread concern at the increasing conflict of interest between a large proportion of the peasantry and the state. Agricultural economists, well acquainted with peasant behaviour, could foresee the dangers. Even within the party there was opposition, with Bukharin, so long the favoured ideologist, speaking against the policies which would produce unbalanced growth and aggravate disequilibrium in the market. But the objectives did not change. Bukharin came under attack. Yet the government was in an impasse. Already in 1928 investment plans had been reduced and grain exports cut back, as peasants with grain to sell appeared to be holding on to supplies in anticipation of a price increase. Food shortages in towns and in some rural areas forced government into buying a margin of grain at high open-market prices. There was also some diversion of manufactured goods to grain-producing areas to attract a marginal addition to the sales volume. The industrialisation plan, and thereby the very basis of economic policy, was under threat.

Early in 1928 a system of direct procurement, bypassing the market, was adopted, initially in the Urals and western Siberia. It thus became known as the Urals-Siberian method. The basic notion was that grain was to be delivered to the state as a form of voluntary self-taxation. In fact, it meant that local officials coerced or forced unpaid deliveries from peasants. As legal backing, article 107 from the penal code was used. This had been introduced in 1926 to guard against hoarding and provided for prison sentences for those causing prices to rise. It was now used as a 'catch-all', nominally against the kulak.

The kulak was presented as the class enemy in the countryside. The kulak was the rich peasant, the one with a horse and cart who could carry grain to a market for a better price; the one with sufficient land to live well even when times were bad; the one with money to lend at usurious rates of interest; the one whose voice was heard at the village gathering, who was able to exercise influence over neighbours to his own advantage. There were no consistent criteria to define a kulak, though size of landholding was commonly adopted. In fact, the definition of kulak in the late 1920s was an arbitrary decision made by local officials. Public criticisms of the kulak were made by Stalin to suggest that it was this rich peasant stratum which was responsible for the grain-procurement crisis. This was clearly impossible. In 1928 less than 5 per cent of households were regarded as kulaks. If the peasants were holding back grain then it was not simply the kulaks who were responsible but large sectors of the middle peasants (*serednyaki*) also (Lewin, 1968, p. 220). Government attempts to unite poor peasants (*bednyaki*) against the kulaks failed. Kulaks may often have been hated in the village, but the government — or at least their local agents or armed militia — were hated more. Often, indeed, those labelled kulaks were well-respected village leaders or successful farmers. Attacking the kulaks, designed to divide the peasantry, had the opposite effect of uniting them against the representatives of the state.

From 1928 in effect there was a general attack on the peasantry. The market was no longer fundamental to the relations between town and country. The *smychka* was smashed. NEP was dead. Stalin, in public speeches, began to leave out the crucial references to the kulaks as being responsible for procurement crises. From now on it was the peasantry as a whole which was under attack — though the kulak was still used as a scapegoat in the countryside. The Urals-Siberian method began to be generally applied, but the policy was essentially one of procurement. Mass collectivisation, as a policy, dated from April 1929, but collectivisation was concerned with the process of agricultural production.

There were no plans for mass collectivisation immediately prior to its introduction. The five-year plan envisaged only 15 per cent of households in collectives with 90 per cent of production still in private hands. When the decision to introduce mass collectivisation by force was made it was done quickly and without legal backing. Compulsory procurement, or forced seizure of grain, led some peasants to destroy produce or even engage in terrorist attacks. Yet the plan demanded more procurement. It therefore became necessary to gain complete control over the peasantry to break their resistance once and for all. According to Lewin, collective farms were seized on as a way of doing so (1968, pp. 516-18). The history of the period, documented in much detail by Lewin, suggests that decisions were made hurriedly and in panic, with little thought of the outcome, apart from the immediate objective. Thus, he claims, mass collectivisation was a panic measure taken to cope with the strains in turn imposed by the effects of the Urals-Siberian method of grain seizure.

But it would be mistaken to suppose that there were not long-term objectives of introducing collectivised agriculture before 1928. There had always been some commitment, if a vague one, to collective or socialised agriculture as there had been in industry. Even a former SR and critic of Bolshevik agrarian policy, P. Oganovskii, writing in 1917 had spoken of a form of collectivised agriculture being the long-term objective of agricultural evolution (Oganovskii, 1917, p. 100). The policy was considered and advocated by the party central committee early in the 1920s. In 1922 a report to the central committee from Kiev province on agricultural conditions noted that: 'The small (*malomoshchnoe*) farm would have nothing against the organisation of agricultural collectives . . . but they would need far more equipment' (Ts.K.R.K.P., 1923, p. 26). Indeed there was already a number of voluntary collective farms before 1928 and even before the revolution. In September 1924 a statute was published to give more aid to collective farms (Danilov, 1977, p. 160). On 24 October 1924 *Narkomzem* issued a local circular designed to reduce the number of independent farms (*khutora*) and open the way for collectivised landholding (Danilov, 1977, p. 158). However, by the eve of forced collectivisation voluntary collectives were insignificant in number though their numbers were increasing rapidly. In June 1927 there were 14,832 collective farms, a year later already 33,285, or a total of 416,700 households on

5,383,200 hectares of land (Danilov, 1977, pp. 175-6). So the collectivisation campaign did not invent a new structure or system. Until 1929 it had been widely supposed that collectivisation would be a gradual and essentially a voluntary process. Throughout the 1920s it was assumed that collectives would be encouraged and would act as an example of progress to other peasants who would therefore join voluntarily. This assumption was built into the first five-year plan. Even as late as April 1929 Stalin was speaking of the primacy of the private sector in agriculture.

During the collectivisation campaign the agricultural *artel*[2] was adopted as the norm. All collective farms were co-operatives, and not strictly therefore part of the state sector. In the *artel* most of the productive capacity was in collective ownership and could be subject to control, while at the same time member-households could retain some land to maintain themselves. To emphasise the arbitrariness of the procedure there was no systematic analysis of collective farms, no research into collective agriculture and the collective *artel* had no proper constitutional definition until the collective farm charter of 1935, after the major campaign.

The state sector proper in agriculture before 1928 was almost negligible. Although all land was nominally nationalised, in effect it was in peasant hands. In 1925 in the RSFSR (excluding autonomous republics) total state holdings were 15,487,800 hectares of agricultural land compared with peasant holdings of 233 million (Danilov, 1977, pp. 81-2). The state holdings included a state fund (*gosfond*) in various provinces, which was available for rent by peasants. In Nikolskoi village, Tambov province, in 1923 peasants rented 375 desyatinas (410 hectares) from the state fund, or almost exactly the same as they had rented from gentry landowners before the revolution, though at a lower rent (Larin, 1923, pp. 49-50). In 1925 2,593,300 hectares of state land had been in state farms (*sovkhoz*). Unlike collective farms, state farms were state-owned units and their members state employees.

There was a firmly entrenched ideological belief that state farms were more productive than collective farms, which in turn were more productive than private farms. There was some statistical evidence to support this view. Before 1928, in European Russia, average rye yields on collectives were 21 per cent higher than in individual peasant farms (Danilov, 1977, p. 311; see also Table 3.5). However, before 1929 socialised farms were the exception rather than the rule and their apparent superiority was not maintained in later years. Further, recent detailed research has suggested that the earlier statistical differences may have been exaggerated by local officials anxious to support the 'blind official dogma' (Wheatcroft, 1977, pp. 2-3). Discrepancies cannot, however, simply be attributed to statistical distortion. Collective and state farms, because of political bias, owned and used more machinery than ordinary peasant household farms. They were also more likely to receive expert advice and aid. Collectivisation on a mass scale could not produce the same advantages simply because the number of collective and state farms grew so quickly. Average yields declined after 1928.

There were clearly also political reasons for collectivisation. It was anathema to allow potential political hostility to develop in the countryside which would, after all, affect the greater part of the population. The Bolshevik Party had never enjoyed widespread political support in the countryside and during the consolidation of power in the 1920s there had remained a political gulf between the party and the peasantry. This is clearly demonstrated by the ineffectuality of the rural soviet, which had less effective power in the countryside than the traditional commune. The commune had even been sanctified in law as the land society (*zemel'noe obshchestvo*) (see above, pp. 50-2). As such it was no part of the apparatus of state though it enjoyed effective local self-government. The commune thereby had more independence from the state than it had before the revolution (Male, 1971, p. 211).

Table 3.5: Crop Yields on Private, State and Collective Farms (centners per hectare: all grains)

Year	USSR average	Private farms	State farms (*sovkhozy*)	Collective farms (*kolkhozy*)
1927	7.6	7.6	10.4	8.6
1928	8.0	7.9	10.3	8.7
1929	7.5	7.4	8.6	8.0
1930	7.8	7.9	8.5	7.6
1931	6.5	7.3	5.7	6.1
1932	6.7	7.4	6.9	6.5

Note: In 1927 state and collective farms together accounted for 1.7 per cent of the area sown to grains; by 1932 it had risen to 78.5 per cent.
Source: Wheatcroft, 'Grain Production Statistics in the USSR', p. 18.

Collectivisation swept away the old commune structure and practices. The land society was abolished by a law of 1930. Thus collectivisation achieved administrative control over the peasants, which had not been achieved by the rural soviets (Male, 1971, p. 213). Collective farm chairmen were party appointees or appointed with the agreement of the party. Real or potential leaders amongst the peasants, the successful and respected ones, were amongst the kulaks dispossessed and deported.

There has been considerable debate about the necessity or otherwise of collectivisation; whether it was possible to accommodate the demands of the state for industrialisation within the structure of NEP. NEP was conceived as a transitionary stage but there were never any suggestions within the party, from any faction, that it be brought to an end. As it turned out, there was an effective necessity to create a new system. Thus collectivisation became necessary in contemporary political terms. But to many this necessity was in itself a function of the failure of government policies. In Lewin's view the regime failed to make NEP work; it failed to consolidate its political position in the countryside (1968, p. 516) and failed to provide sufficient incentive and capital for agriculture. The grain-procurement crisis, which lay behind the decision to collectivise, is attributed by Karcz to government ineptness in policy — particularly the price-reduction campaign (Karcz, in Millar, 1971a, pp. 41-2). Further, the regime remained ignorant of the real nature of peasant society, being obsessed with Marxian class analysis which was simply inappropriate for the Russian peasantry. It is difficult to accept that a body of thinking people in the party could fail to understand the social and economic nature of the peasantry in the country of their birth, especially when the peasantry had been the subject of such extensive research and discussion for generations beforehand and into the 1920s. Nonetheless it does seem that critical discussions and warnings from expert and experienced agricultural economists (including Kondratiev, Makarov and Chayanov) were ignored. It is significant also that the discredited and exiled leader of the left opposition, Trotsky, writing from abroad in 1930, condemned forced collectivisation and the hurried 'liquidation' of the kulak class. The policy was too extreme even for Trotsky.

A contrary view is that collectivisation was forced on to government by the impasse of the procurement crises. The investment plans, which, rightly or wrongly, were drawn up in the late 1920s could not be accommodated within NEP. An alternative policy, which involved collectivisation, was therefore necessary. Such a policy involving force was never publicly advocated before its institution, though it has had its apologists since. Whichever set of views has more credibility there is no doubt that collectivisation was perceived as an economic necessity at the time, despite the risks to the regime that it entailed. Stalin later admitted to Churchill that he felt the regime to be threatened at this time. But there was a crucial political dimension also. In forcing through collectivisation Stalin was able to weaken (but not yet totally destroy) his opponents on the right — Rykov, Tomsky and Bukharin in particular. The left had already been removed. Collectivisation was certainly not a device for continuing political power by Stalin but it was an occasion for consolidating his position and it marks the beginning of his unchallenged personal power.

Collectivisation was a pragmatic decision made in an atmosphere of great uncertainty and virtual panic and designed to overcome short-term obstacles. Yet it had long-term consequences and marks a bloody period in history which remains largely taboo in Soviet historiography.

Notes

1. Accumulation through foreign trade, by the state exploiting its foreign trade monopoly, was also a feasible policy but in the early 1920s there was a persistent balance of payments deficit (Arskii, 1927, p. 109).

2. Before 1929 voluntary collective farms took one of three main forms, the *kommuna* (commune, but not to be confused with the *obshchina*) wherein all property and income was pooled; the *Toz* (Association for the Joint Cultivation of the Land) which allowed for private property, with co-operative purchasing or marketing and the *artel*. The *artel* had commonly owned arable fields with a household plot retained by each member. Work on the common holdings were shared with income distributed according to work. The *Toz* was the most frequent type, but from 1929 the *artel* was adopted as basic model in mass collectivisation.

4 THE ADVENT OF CENTRAL PLANNING

Central planning and control have come to characterise the Soviet economy and it was through such means that rapid growth and industrial development were achieved. The first decade of planning, 1928 to 1937, saw the creation of the Soviet economic system. It saw also the extension of state control to all aspects of life, the elaboration of a totalitarian system wherein Stalin exercised considerable personal power. This power was, however, very far from absolute. The decade of the 1930s was characterised by the incidence of elaborate measures to consolidate Stalin's position. Before 1930 non-Bolsheviks were removed from responsible positions and later put on trial;[1] the 'Reign of Terror' was initiated after the murder of Kirov, Leningrad Party Secretary, in 1934. Trials of party members began in 1935 and the great purge of 1937-8 saw the removal of thousands of opponents, real or imagined, in all walks of life, including the armed forces. In 1938, the most noteworthy opponent, Bukharin, was put on trial. Terror, at the hands of the political police, became the hallmark of Stalinism. It is impossible to claim that such terror was essential to economic tasks; indeed it may well have been counterproductive. On the other hand, central control did emerge as an essential aspect of Soviet economic management.

It is doubtful if Stalin occupied a position of absolute individual power, despite the purges, both because there were always those who supported him and exercised some influence upon him and because absolute power and control would have been more effective, in economic terms, than the history of the period suggests. Obviously, such a large economy demanded an elaborate and complex control structure (given that the market was replaced), and this implied a large number of responsible personnel at various levels. Further, it is noteworthy that the commands of the command economy, as it emerged, were not always successful. Plans were far from being as smoothly operating as ideally hoped for.

Planning was a complex and pioneering experiment, for which there was no example to follow. Drafting a five-year plan took a long time; drafts for the first five-year plan were made over four years, though subsequent plans were drawn up a little more quickly. A plan made for a five-year period could not accommodate exogenous factors and influences, so constant readjustments were necessary. In many respects the first five-year plan fell short of its targets. The second plan (1933-7) was more successful according to its own criteria, but it was the first plan above all which established a system, a structure which affected the whole of the subsequent decade and, in many respects, post-war years. The first years of central planning signalled a strong and over-whelming commitment to growth. In principle the object was to achieve balanced growth, but in reality the development was unbalanced, with heavy priority to producer-goods and shortfalls in agricultural and consumer production and real incomes. There was an effective departure from the notion of optimising given resources. Thus there was heavy emphasis on capital intensity, in contradiction to the factor-endowment in the economy where capital was expensive and labour relatively cheap. However, it was assumed that the real costs of accumulation would fall as industrial profits and labour productivity increased. As it turned out, those crucial indicators failed to reach expectations. There was also a heavy emphasis on introducing the most up-to-date technology, which was usually imported. New industrial centres were established — Magnitogorsk perhaps being the best known — both to exploit recently discovered sources of energy and raw materials and for strategic reasons. Military considerations were important not so much in that there was a large element of military expenditure but rather that the plan was to build the industrial base for future military as well as civil needs. There were thus strong long-term commitments in the plans. The object was the creation of a new industrial base; not simply making more of the same, but a transformation of the economy.

Yet, despite these long-term considerations, the need was for urgency, to build quickly, to undergo the transformation with almost panic-like rapidity. The emphasis on speed was reinforced by Stalin in a speech to the All-Union Conference of Managers in Socialist Industry, in February 1931:

> It is sometimes asked whether it is not possible to slow down the tempo, to put a check on the movement. No, Comrades, it is not possible! The tempo must not be reduced! On the contrary, we must increase it as much as is within our powers and possibilities . . . To slacken the tempo would mean falling behind. And those who fall behind get beaten . . . One feature of the history of old Russia was the continual beatings she suffered for falling behind . . .
>
> We are fifty or a hundred years behind the advanced countries. We must make good this distance in ten years. Either we do it or

they crush us. (Stalin, 1947, pp. 355-6)

Stalin greatly exaggerated the degree of industrial backwardness in the USSR at the time. He was much nearer with his forecast; Germany invaded in June 1941. The speech illustrates current thinking; the need to drive for growth at a hitherto unmatched pace, in virtual siege conditions. To achieve such a rapid rate of industrial growth demanded huge levels of investment, ever-tighter central controls to check leakages, ever-growing restrictions on individuals and clearly determined priorities. In the first five-year plan the priorities emerged as sources of energy — coal and electric power (much of which was generated through coal-burning), steel and heavy engineering. Increases in agricultural production were expected (45 per cent increase in grain output, 34 per cent increase in livestock numbers) but failed to materialise. Consumer-goods output fell below plan and much small-scale handicraft industry, which had served local consumer markets, was closed down. Thus, although the plan was comprehensive in its nature, in effect it became a glorious form of rationing, directing scarce resources to tightly controlled and politically determined priorities. It is debatable and debated as to whether or not the plan targets were themselves internally compatible (Hunter, 1973; Davies and Wheatcroft, 1975). In fact, the plan proved to be impossible to achieve *in toto*, and this was, at least in part, caused by the unplanned turmoil and famine resulting from the collectivisation campaign and the consequences of the international price depression. The plan was thrown off-course and much within the plan was sacrificed in order that the main priorities could be achieved. One authority has even observed that planning as such disappeared in the years of the first five-year plan (Lewin, 1973).

It must be emphasised that there was no blueprint to follow. The nature and principles of planning were worked out by trial and error. There was no theory; practice came first. The Great Leap Forward was a leap in the dark. The system that emerged involved detailed statistical analysis and arbitrary political imposition. On the basis of information gathered from the main organs of the economy Gosplan drafted an outline plan. Many such drafts were made in the 1920s, as we have seen, and VSNKh was also closely involved, though this body was abolished in 1932. Industrial commissariats (they were later renamed ministries) also supplied information and their own sectional plans to compare with Gosplan. The overall plan was drawn up as a general growth target, what Zaleski has called a 'vision of the future' (1980, p. 482). It did not become operational until it was broken down into component elements and passed through the commissariats, eventually to the productive enterprise. Each level in the hierarchy of control added details which became orders to the level below. Details of necessary new material and component supplies to fulfil individual plans were then resubmitted up the ladder of control to Gosplan, which then faced the task of co-ordinating and resolving the various elements in the plan. It is on this point that the recent work of Zaleski is of interest, for he suggests that co-ordination was not so important in Stalinist planning as determination of economic goals. Thus maintenance of equilibrium or balance was less important than growth.Of course, there had to be some plan co-ordination but this was carried out after the plan had been initiated and after the details of carrying out the plan had been worked out at lower levels of control (the commissariat, *glavk* or enterprise) (Zaleski, 1980, pp. 482-3). Both the first and second five-year plans were formerly approved after they had come into operation. The principles of planning, expressed here very simply, suggest two clear points. First, the system or structure was necessarily hierarchical, because different levels had important functions in working out, as well as implementing, the plans. There were thus bureaucratic elements built into the whole planning process from early days. Second, as a corollary, there was some element of consultation by the centre with lower levels. It is not apparent, however, how much consultation was involved. It is clear that, for the first plan, targets were established and required inputs calculated to meet them. Improvement in efficiency and productivity were thus residual figures. It is also evident that agricultural interests were underrepresented in drafting the plan.

With approval by the party and government the plan became law. The elements of the plan, as they affected the enterprises, were directives, and to contravene them was a criminal offence. This was a long way from the forecast plans of the 1920s. The overall five-year plan gave broad targets and their detailed application was contained in annual or quarterly operative plans. This enabled revision during the course of the plan, which was undertaken in the first five-year plan when some targets were raised. Periodic revision was also needed to maintain cohesion in the overall plan.

Planned output was expressed in physical units. Plan fulfilment was achieved by producing the requisite number, size, weight or volume of production. Value or price were less important but not unimportant. The inputs in terms of allocation and supply to the enterprise were measured in physical units just as was the output, but there were parallel financial flows. The overall and disaggregated financial plans were used as a constraint ('control by the ruble') within the plan and as a means of regulating demand within the economy. Financial discipline was increasingly necessary after uncontrolled inflation developed in the early years of the first five-year plan. Wage-inflation and a very much larger recruitment of labour than planned, together with a serious shortfall in consumer-goods production, led to excess purchasing power and inflationary pressure. Indirect taxes, on the one hand, and greater financial constraints for employers, on the other, were used to try to reduce the inflationary pressure after 1930 and to ensure that the total wage fund was below the value of goods on the market. This balance was never achieved in the 1930s because wage costs rose faster than planned and generated inflation. The consequent disequilibrium in supply and demand was one reason for the use of rationing until 1935. Inflation was also (necessarily) used by the state as a means of financing state expenditure. The amount of money in circulation increased from 1.4 milliard rubles in 1927 to 5.7 milliards in 1932, to 11.2 milliards in 1937 (Malafeev, 1964, p. 404) though it was deliberately reduced in 1933 in an attempt to curb inflation.

Expenditure was running ahead of plan and of revenue — a danger that had been foreseen by some economists, including Bukharin and Sokolnikov, when the first five-year plan was drafted. It had clearly become necessary to increase state revenue and yet it was practically impossible to do so adequately from direct taxes. Thus the tax reform of 2 September 1930 established turnover tax and deductions from profits as the major sources of state revenue. Since that time, direct taxes have played a negligible role in revenue, being used primarily for some discriminatory redistribution from the private sector. Thus the average agricultural tax per household in a collective farm (*c*. 1932) stood at 13.7 rubles, compared with 27.5 rubles for individual arms and 350 rubles for kulaks employing labour. Such discriminatory taxes against private or non-socialised income (for example, the clergy) still obtain. The maximum income tax in the early 1940s for manual and clerical workers was 3.5 per cent.

Until 1935 turnover tax and profit deductions were to make up 55 per cent of total budget revenue. Of these, turnover tax was the more important, as profits were small. The turnover tax was levied on the transfer price of goods from one enterprise to another but more importantly on the retail margin. In other words, turnover tax *was* the retail margin after allowing for necessary retail expenses. Thus the tax burden was much higher on consumer-goods and therefore provided a means of reabsorbing much of the excess purchasing power in the economy. It also meant a high effective and non-progressive tax burden on the Soviet citizen. Taxes on profits were levied at 10-20 per cent for industry and 50 per cent for banks. In some cases, however, the tax was negative, there being substantial subsidies used to counteract inflation. These applied to coal, iron ore, steel, cement and some other key industries. Other indirect taxes included transport revenue, excise duty on vodka and other items, and social insurance. Local taxes were of minor significance (though collective farm taxes were used for local purposes) as was a small inheritance tax. In 1935 rationing was ended and retail prices of former rationed goods increased substantially. Turnover tax revenue increased as a result (from 27 milliard rubles in 1933 to 66 milliards in 1936) to account for 70 per cent of budget revenue in 1936. The very large increases in food prices also meant that food sales provided the bulk of turnover tax revenue (see below, p. 107). Also in 1936 subsidies to industry were phased out, and the agricultural tax was replaced by a mildly progressive income tax which continued to discriminate against the non-collectivised farmer.

Although not taxes in the strict sense of the term, the purchase of state bonds by the population amounted to much the same thing. In effect, bond purchases were a direct tax, with contributions often being levied at the place of work — compulsory in all but name. Initially, issues were made annually for a period of ten years, with a rate of interest of 10 per cent. Until 1934 they provided for 20 per cent of budget expenditure which was used directly for financing industry; the loans were raised specifically for that purpose. However, the issue was not redeemed — being converted to 4 per cent stock after the ten-year period. Bond sales continued, and yet they have never been redeemed.

Budget expenditure was primarily on the economy, with social and cultural facilities taking second, and defence third, places. Capital investment in industry by 1930 was 285 per cent of the 1926-7 level, and by 1933 was 449 per cent, though this is measured at 1926-7 prices, which inflates the rate of increase. The second five-year plan made for a 250 per cent increase in investment over the level of the first plan. Of this planned investment, in the second five-year period 52 per cent was to be in industry, 11.4 per cent in agriculture, 19.7 per cent in transport and 13.5 per cent in housing and public services. The real results of such plans are tempered by statistical method (see below, pp. 91-2) but nonetheless the plans in the first and second five-year periods indicate clearly that industry would have a far higher priority than agriculture; producer-goods would come before consumer-goods.

Defence expenditure increased substantially after 1936, though there is evidence to suggest that before this date the real level of defence expenditure was higher than revealed in budget statistics (see Chapter 5). The clear implications of Stalin's famous speech of 1931 were that defence demanded more investment. Throughout the first years of planning the major source of finance for rapid industrialisation came from constraints on consumption, particularly from heavy taxation on basic consumer-products and foodstuffs. In the outcome, the plans were in effect far more concerned with priorities than with balance, with specific targets rather than general ones.

Results

There has been much dispute over the achievements of the first two five-year plans and in particular over the rates of growth of output in these years. Not surprisingly, Soviet estimates have tended to err on the generous side; those of many Western observers, in the other direction. In part, such discrepancies can be explained by statistical quirks. Throughout the 1930s Soviet statistics (at least published statistics) used 1926-7 prices as a constant measure. This has the effect of greatly inflating industrial production. Many goods made at high cost in 1926 (or not at all) were made on a larger scale in later years and unit-cost reductions were not allowed for. This common tendency with base-year pricing (the so-called 'Gerschenkron effect') was exaggerated in the Soviet case. There is then a built-in over-emphasis in the Soviet practice of using 1926-7 prices. Further, in the compilation of index numbers differential rates of inflation for different products can produce markedly different results when using base-year or end-year prices. Similarly, differences in weighting in compiling index numbers can lead to varying results without any distortion or dishonesty involved. This is not the place to go into the niceties of statistical method, which are more fully explored elsewhere (Nove, 1969, appendix). Such problems of precise measurement are always evident but in the case of the Soviet Union, 1928-37, they are writ large.

Resultant estimates of rates of growth vary considerably therefore according to whether base-year or end-year price weights are adopted. Soviet GNP (based on official data) can be seen to have increased substantially (Table 4.1).

Table 4.1 also compares Soviet figures for industrial production with those estimated by Western observers. A further Western estimate, by

Table 4.1: Indices of Growth 1928-37

	GNP (1937 100)		
	at 1928 prices		at 1937 prices
1928	30		62
	Industrial production		
	1928 100	1932	1937
Soviet official:	gross	202	445
	net	237	585
Seton		181	380
Nutter		140	279

Note: Seton's figures from 'Soviet Industrial Expansion', *Manchester Statistical Society* (1957): Nutter's from *Growth of Industrial Production in the Soviet Union* (1962).
Source: R.W. Davies, 'Planning for Rapid Growth in the USSR', *Economics of Planning*, 5, 1965, pp. 81-2.

Abraham Bergson (1961), shows the growth rate for GNP to vary between 4.8 per cent per annum at 1937 ruble-factor cost to 11.9 per cent at 1928 prices (3.8 per cent to 10.8 per cent per capita). Soviet figures for gross industrial production are 19.2 per cent per annum in the first five-year plan and 17.1 per cent during the second (*Istoriya*, 4, 1978, p. 125). A reasonable (and convenient) deduction − precision remains elusive by the nature of the subject − is to settle on a figure somewhere in between. Soviet estimates have tended to exaggerate aggregate growth by overestimating consumer-goods production. Consumer-goods were subject to far greater price inflation than producer-goods in this decade. Some Western estimates, on the other hand, have tended to underestimate the overall real rate. There is much less uncertainty when dealing with physical indicators (weight, numbers, etc.), but the use of 1926-7 prices for gross figures, as explained, does tend to bias the figures upwards (Table 4.2).

Despite contemporary claims, it is clear from the unit-output figures (Table 4.2; see also Zaleski, 1971, appendix Ai for complete results) that the first plans were not fulfilled in all criteria. Consumer-goods and agricultural output fell far short of target. Thus consumption declined. And yet it was claimed that the first plan had been achieved ahead of schedule. The urban labour force exceeded expectations, thus putting greater strains on urban services at a time when housing remained hopelessly inadequate. Building-materials went to make dams and factories before workers' flats. The optimum variant of the first five-year plan proved too optimistic, and yet in the midst of it all in 1930, some output targets

Table 4.2: Achievements of the First and Second Five-Year Plans (selected indicators)

	1928	1932/3 (plan)	1932 (real)	1937 (plan)	1937 (real)
National income (milliard rubles at 1926-7 prices)	24.4	49.7	45.5	100.2	96.3
Gross industrial production (milliard rubles at 1926-7 prices)	18.3	43.2	43.2	92.7	95.5
Group A	6.0	18.1	23.1	45.5	55.2
Group B	12.3	25.1	20.2	47.2	40.3
Gross agricultural production (milliard rubles at 1926-7 prices)	14.5	22.6	13.1	26.2	20.1
Number of workers in state employment (millions)	11.3	15.8	22.9	28.9	27.0
Electricity (million kWh)	5,050	22,000	13,540	38,000	36,200
Coal (million tonnes)	35.4	75	64.4	152.5[b]	128.0[b]
Oil (million tonnes)	11.7	21.7	21.4	46.8[b]	28.5[b]
Steel[a] (million tonnes)	4.0	10.4	5.9	17.0	17.7
Pig iron (million tonnes)	3.3	10.0	6.2	16.0	14.5
Machine tools (thousands)	2.1		19.7	40.0	45.5
Tractors (thousands)	1.8		50.6	166.7	66.5

Notes: a. Ingots and castings, excludes rolled steel. b. Includes natural gas.
Sources: *Industrializatsiya SSSR 1929-32* (M. 1970), pp. 342-6; *1933-37* (M. 1971), pp. 382-92:
Istoriya Sots. Ekon., IV (M. 1978), pp. 11, 12, 23:
Resheniya partii, 2 (M. 1967), p. 445: E. Zaleski, *Planning for Economic Growth (1971)*, Appendix.

were further increased, even though the original targets had proved illusory. This was wholly unrealistic intervention which helped create further bottlenecks. It helps to illustrate an atmosphere of wild excitement and unreal expectation. There was some relaxation, however, with the liberalisation of the private market in 1932. The outcome of the first five-year plan was far from negative. The essential achievement of these bloody and tempestuous years was to lay the groundwork for later production and growth. It was during the first five-year plan that many new productive establishments were built which could come into operation in later years. The capital-intensive projects were bound to be slow at producing returns because so much was involved in building factories which were not yet making anything. It was only in later years that they began production.

More than half the machine tools in use at the end of the first five-year plan had been made or installed during the plan period; one-quarter of the coal output came from new mines; electricity-generating capacity was doubled. Vast new construction projects were built from virtually nothing. Best-known was the Ural-Kuznetsk combine in the Urals region, built to exploit deposits of coal and iron ore. This, albeit marginal, shift of industry to raw materials was designed both to reduce demands on transport and to relocate industrial centres away from vulnerable borders, east and west. In the 1930s industrial production increased in the Urals at a faster rate than anywhere else, and at the end of the second five-year plan period, Magnitogorsk (at the southern end of the Urals) and Stalinsk (in the Kuznets basin) between them had an iron- and steel-producing capacity equivalent to the entire country before 1914. Magnitogorsk had the largest iron and steel works in the country. It was built from scratch in the first plan period. The largest tractor factory was built at Chelyabinsk and a motor works at Gorky. Such factories were built specifically to be readily adaptable to military production in the event of war. The Dnepr dam HEP project, designed to generate 756,000 horse power, was opened in 1932 (though operating below capacity), serving new industrial centres. Such enterprises took years to complete and come into operation.

This was one reason why the second major plan was more successful in detail than the first. The output of steel, coal and machinery was much nearer target. As well as this was the fact that forecasts were more realistic after 1932. Through 1933, which was officially the first year of the second five-year plan, there was no full plan but merely a fairly modest one-year directive. The second plan proper was approved by the Seventeenth Party Congress in January 1934 (*Resheniya*, 2, 1967, p. 342). The severe financial restrictions which had been imposed on enterprises began to restrict inflationary pressure. The year 1933 also marked an improvement in agricultural production, and the beginnings of some improvement in the international terms of trade. During the second major plan period 4,500 new industrial enterprises were opened compared with 1,500 in the first (*Istoriya*, IV, 1978, p. 22), so that by 1937 more than 80 per cent of all industrial products were manufactured in new or wholly reconstructed enterprises. In almost all respects the second five-year plan was much nearer target than its predecessor. One reason for this was the great improvement made in labour productivity, which improved, on average, more than expected. The labour input was below plan (Table 4.3). Such productivity increases, and imposed financial discipline, helped to reduce unit costs and enable internal financing of capital investment without state subsidy (*Istoriya*, 1978, p. 25). There was particularly heavy emphasis on the production of machine tools, which exceeded plan. This helped to reduce imports and produce the means of producing future construction and growth.

Table 4.3: Labour Productivity 1932-7 (percentage increases)

	Plan	Real
Industry	63	82
Railway transport	43	47.9
Construction	75	83

Source: *Istoriya Sots. Ekon.*, IV, 1978, p. 25.

Two hundred new types of machine tools were brought into use; non-ferrous metals — particularly aluminium, which was first produced in 1932 — had a higher priority. Nickel, tin and magnesium production were initiated in the second five-year plan. Production of tractors doubled, automobiles (cars, lorries and buses) increased eight times and new industries, in particular in chemicals and non-ferrous metals, grew from nothing. Without question, the first decade of planning was one of spectacular growth and outstanding industrial achievement.

It was far from smooth, however; consumer-goods fell below target in the second as well as the first five-year plans. The real successes were in large-scale industry; the output of small-scale industry declined during the first five-year plan, by 2 per cent according to Jasny, against a planned increase of 50 per cent (1972, p. 44).

There were further problems. Ironically, the policy of industrial relocation aggravated rather than alleviated transport bottlenecks, as equipment and labour was shipped to virgin construction sites. Inadequacies in railway investment were shown up as bottlenecks developed, and accidents to overworked rolling stock were numerous. Dobb estimated that in 1937 freight traffic was five times greater than in 1913, but the length of the track only 50 per cent more (1966a, p. 274). In the midst of this there were anomalies. Trains shipped thousands of dispossessed kulaks to the east while there were hold-ups in the movement of goods — a curious comment on contemporary priorities.

It is significant that expert commentators, Jasny and Lewin, pay scant regard to the five-year period as a planning basis in real terms, Lewin by emphasising the incidence of 'administrative measures' in the one-year directive plans and Jasny in his pattern of 'three good years' and 'three bad years'. In the 'good years', 1934 to 1936, industrial development was helped by some improvement in agriculture. Then followed the bad years of 1937-9, following the poor harvest of 1936 and other setbacks. In reality, the planners were working more in the short term than the five-year plan concept might suggest. The very levels of investment forecast inevitably caused problems. A breakdown in one element of the plan caused strain throughout. For example, labour productivity failed to increase as planned before 1932, so that costs increased and more labour was demanded. Excess demand for labour in turn led to non-economic controls through the system of internal passports. Slower than anticipated rates of construction demanded that the government specify construction priorities (Lewin, 1973, p. 276). The use of plans was far from a smoothly functioning system. The pioneers of central planning were still groping along an ill-lit tunnel.

Collectivised Agriculture

The collectivisation campaign adduced a generally negative response by the peasantry and a generally negative effect upon them. Terrorist attacks on collectives and party personnel were reported from Smolensk (Fainsod, 1958, p. 253n). They were presumably not confined to that province. More serious, and evidently more wide-spread, was passive response, in particular the wholesale slaughter of livestock. Peasants slaughtered their animals on such a scale that cattle and sheep numbers and total meat production did not reach their 1929 levels until after the Second World War (Table 4.5). There seem to be three reasons for this slaughter. First, there was a feeling that as the animals were to be taken anyway it was better to eat meat while it was still available (the process is graphically described by M. Sholokhov in *Virgin Soil Upturned*); second, and more likely, was a stubborn refusal to let the collective take them away even if it meant slaughter; and third, it was simply impossible to keep so many animals when feed-grain was being confiscated. Such passive response caused great anxiety to government, for there was a fear that the spring sowing in 1930 would be seriously affected. It was therefore in March 1930 that Stalin issued his famous 'Dizzy with Success' statement, in *Pravda*. In this statement he claimed that the plan for collectivisation had been over-fulfilled by 100 per cent by February 1930 as over 50 per cent of farms were collectivised. He went on to criticise excesses and to blame irres-ponsible local party elements for being carried away with enthusiasm.

The party's task was 'to wage a determined struggle against these sentiments, which are dangerous and harmful to our cause, and to drive them out of the Party' (Stalin, 1955, p. 198). In other words, Stalin was shifting the responsibility for excesses (and implicitly violence), which he himself had instituted, onto party officials.

The result was a temporary withdrawal. The proportion of households registered as being in collective farms fell to 23 per cent. The spring sowing campaign was a success and was followed by a renewed offensive. By July 1934, 71.4 per cent of households were officially collectivised (ranging from 80 per cent in European Russia to less than 50 per cent in the Caucausus). By 1937 private agriculture was virtually eliminated (Table 4.4). The renewed campaign was accompanied by

Table 4.4: Collectivised Agriculture 1928-40 (pre-1939 borders)

	1928	1932	1937	1940[a]
Percentage households collectivised	1.7	61.5	93.0	96.9
Percentage sown area collectivised	2.3	77.7	99.1	99.9
Number of kolkhoz (thousands) (agricultural only)[b]	33.3	210.6	242.5	235.5
Member-households (millions)	0.4	14.7	18.1	18.7
Average	12	70	75	79
Number of state farms (thousands)	1.4	4.3	4.0	4.2
Number of MTS (thousands)		2.4	5.8	7.1

Notes: a. The real figures for 1940 were smaller as, by that year, Baltic and east Polish areas had been absorbed into the Soviet Union but their agricultural holdings were not yet collectivised. b. In addition to these were relatively small numbers of non-farming collectives involved in fishing, etc.
Source: *Narodnoe khozyaistvo v 1958 g.*, (M. 1959), pp. 346, 349.

less force and terror. Individual farmers were, in many areas, left unmolested though they suffered severe tax-discrimination and were subject to tough procurement demands. The campaign had broken the back of peasant resistance. Families, labelled kulaks, were dispossessed ('liquidated as a class'), and thousands of them exiled before 1933. According to official data on the eve of collectivisation 4-5 per cent of households, or 1-1.1 million, were kulaks (*Nar. khoz. 1958 g.*, p. 347). The terror and chaos created by the policy during the campaign led to severe famine which afflicted much of the country. The number who died is uncertain but it probably exceeded 5 million (see pp. 168, below).

Thus the overall consequences of the collectivisation campaign were serious for production (Table 4.5), particularly for livestock products.

Grain production also declined after 1930, though with fluctuations. There was a serious shortfall in 1936 (a figure which remained unpublished until 1978), followed by a bumper harvest in 1937 (it fell back again thereafter). At the same time, demand was increasing with the growth in population and capital input increased substantially. But if the effects on production were negative they were successful in increasing state procurements.

Compulsory procurements, with echoes of War Communism, had been initiated from 1928. This amounted to confiscation. Gradually a system emerged whereby fixed deliveries were made by collectives, and others, in return for fixed prices. The prices were low and deliveries remained compulsory but were less arbitrary. Anomalies remained, however, with farms sometimes being obliged to deliver goods they were not producing. The contract system, involving state purchasing of an agreed quantity of crop in advance, was faded out and scapped in 1932. The following year a system of bonus purchases (*zakupki*) was introduced, under which the state paid a higher price for deliveries above the compulsory minimum. Nonetheless, compulsion remained at the basis of the relationship between collective farms (which were not part of the state or socialist economy, let it be remembered) and the state. Prices paid for the bulk of deliveries were notional and totally determined by the state. As they remained essentially unchanged until the early 1950s, while other prices rose, they lost virtually all significance.

It was in 1933 that a further means of obtaining agricultural supplies outside the market was introduced. From that date, payments made to the machine-tractor stations (MTS, see below) for provision of machinery (for ploughing, harvesting, etc.) were to be in kind. By the end of the decade these payments in kind to MTS were the major sources of grain procurements by the state. Total state procurements of grain are shown on Table 4.6. Despite the fall in production the state was able to obtain an increasing quantity of grain, and by far the greater part of this was met by the collective farm sector. State farms increased their share substantially, but overall the state sector in agriculture remained unimportant. State farms (*sovkhozy*) were a state enterprise employing wage labour and thus had fixed wage costs. They were not a conspicuous success in the 1930s; indeed their numbers fell a little (Table 4.4). Many had been conceived originally as specialist 'grain factories', but as the decade progressed they were to be more successful in livestock farming or in specialised crops like sugar-beet. Many, however, operated below cost so that, in effect, the state sector was subsidised by the co-operative sector in agriculture.

Table 4.5: Agricultural Production 1928-37

	Gross Production Index 1913 = 100		Grain[a] (million tonnes) Total	from collectives	Meat[b] (million tonnes) Total	Livestock numbers (millions)			
						Cows	Pigs	Sheep	Horses
1928	124		73.3	0.9	4.9	29.3	22.0	97.3	32.1
1929	121		71.7	2.7	5.8	29.2	19.4	97.4	32.6
1930	117	(77.4)	83.5	21.3	4.3	28.5	14.2	85.5	31.0
1931	114	(67.6)	69.5	37.2	3.9	24.5	11.7	62.5	27.0
1932	107	(67.1)	69.9	44.9	2.8	22.3	10.9	43.8	21.7
1933	101	(68.8)	68.4	49.0	2.3	19.4	9.9	34.0	17.3
1934	106	(72.0)	67.6	53.7	2.0	19.0	11.5	32.9	15.4
1935	119	(77.5)	75.0	62.5	2.3	19.0	17.1	36.4	14.9
1936	109	(59.2)	55.8	49.6	3.7	20.0	25.9	43.8	15.5
1937	134	(98.2)	97.4	86.9	3.0	20.9	20.0	46.6	15.9
1940			95.6						

Notes: a. Total grain production figures are subject to varying estimates. Recent recalculated figures by Wheatcroft (1977) are shown in brackets. However, the 1936 figure was published officially only in 1978 and it is, significantly, lower than Wheatcroft's estimate. All figures for production on collectives are from Wheatcroft. b. Meat is carcass weight and includes fat and hides.

Sources: *Sel'skoe khozyaistvo SSSR stat. sbornik* (M. 1960), p. 79: *Sel'skoe khozyaistvo SSSR v 1958 g.* (M. 1959), p. 350: Moshkov, *Zernovaya problema* (M. 1966), p. 226: Zelenin, *Istoriya SSSR*, 5, 1964, p. 14: Malafeev, *Istoriya tsenoobrazovaniya* (M. 1964), p. 128: *Vesnik statistiki*, 1978, no. 2, p. 92: Wheatcroft, 'Grain Production Statistics in the USSR', p.22.

The organisation of collective farms and state farms was to achieve (or provide the potential for achieving) an objective which had hitherto eluded Tsarist and Soviet governments alike. By taking over arable land formerly in peasant control it was possible to abolish the customary mode of land tenure (*zemlepol'zovanie*) which divided fields into a mass of intermingled strips. To eliminate such strip farming had been one of the aims of the Stolypin reforms which had met with such limited success in the years immediately before the First World War. Now with household tenure of arable land removed, strip farming could go, boundaries be redrawn and the way opened for mechanisation (*Resheniya*, vol. 2, 1967, p. 519). This had indeed been a long-term objective of Soviet policy, and reflected a near-obsession with the power of the machine and technology in general. It is unclear, however, how far this was a strong motive for compulsory rapid collectivisation after 1929. Certainly to accommodate the tractor and machinery (or at least make their use practicable) would require a substantial readjustment of field patterns in much of the country. Yet the need for tractors was in turn created by the mass slaughter of horses, itself a response to the collectivisation campaign. Collectivisation became, if only in the long run, a glorious exercise in land-use measures (*zemleustroistvo*), a reordering of land structure and layout to suit a new age. As an aspect of policy during the campaign this can only have been incidental. Nonetheless, Lenin's dream of 100,000 tractors was more than fulfilled. By 1932 there were 148,500 in use; by 1935, 379,500 (Zelenin, 1964, p. 4). Two-thirds of these were in machine-tractor stations (MTS).

The MTS were, as the name suggests, service stations providing machinery for ploughing, harvesting, haulage (usually with drivers or operators) for hire to collectives. Any MTS served a large number of collectives (Table 4.6) and, there was great regional inequality in the provision of equipment.

The MTS was, in theory, a reasonable way of providing scarce machinery and trained manpower to collectives, though, of course, there were often pitfalls in operation. As we have seen, the state was able to exploit their monopoly position in the provision of capital to collectives via the MTS by demanding heavy payments, which had second call on the collectives' assets after compulsory state deliveries. Further, political control was extended through the political department (*polit-otdel*) of the MTS.

Details of the structure of the collective farm and its legal rights and obligations were worked out piecemeal as the first two five-year plans progressed and as collectivisation was consolidated throughout

Table 4.6: State Procurements of Grain (million centners)

	Total	From state farms	Collective farms	Individual farms
1929	160.8	3.9	15.1	
1930	221.4	13.4	65.3	
1931	228.4	18.0	141.1	53.9
1932	187.8	17.0	128.4	27.5
1933	232.9	20.6	169.4	23.2
1934	260.7	22.2	170.1	18.1
1935	296.0	30.2	202.2	10.2

Source: Moshkov, *Zernovaya problema* (M. 1966), p. 225.

the country. The collective farm was only finally defined in law under the collective farm (*artel*) charter of 1935 (*Resheniya*, vol. 2, 1967, p. 519). The charter essentially codified established practice. Payment to peasant members of the collective was made according to the number of labour days (*trudodni*) performed in the year. Various tasks had different labour-day values, so that difficult or skilled work was rewarded more highly than routine tasks. The average working year in labour days (not necessarily corresponding to ordinary days) was 118 in 1932, 166 in 1934 and 180 in 1935 (Zelenin, 1964, p. 21). Payment for these labour days had the last call on the resources of the collective (after obligations to the state, MTS, provision of seed, food for the old and sick, provision for cultural facilities, insurance, etc.). It was thus a residual payment rather than a wage proper. Payment was, in the 1930s, usually in kind, on average 2.3 kg of grain in 1932 per labour day and 2.9 kg in 1933-4 (Zelenin, 1964, p. 21). There were, of course, great regional variations, the poorer collectives sometimes being left with nothing to distribute. Karcz claims that in 1939 3.6 per cent of collective farm households received no grain at all. In 1940 the proportion was even higher (Karca, in Millar (ed.), 1971a, p. 55). Subsistence in such cases, and indeed for most collective farm households, was maintained through the private plot.

Under the charter member-households were able to retain a private plot of between a quarter and half a hectare (or up to one hectare in exceptional cases). They could also keep some tools and equipment (Articles II and III). The permitted livestock holding varied regionally and according to the predominant type of farming. In agricultural regions, where arable farming was important, households were allowed to retain 2-3 cows, 2-3 sows and litter, 20-25 sheep and goats and unlimited poultry or rabbits. They could not keep a horse, for a horse — the major draft animal — gave the owner an unwelcome degree of independence. In areas where livestock farming was more important households could own draft animals (horse, mule or camel) and more live-stock (4-5 cows, 30-40 sheep and goats). This applied to much of central Asia, the Caucausus and part of Kazakhstan. In the nomadic regions (Mongolia, the Nagai region and elsewhere) households were allowed up to 10 horses, plus 8-10 cows, 100-150 sheep and goats, 5-6 camels (Article III, *Resheniya*, 2, pp. 520-21). It is noteworthy that, in all cases, rights and obligations were vested in the household rather than individuals — just as they had been in the traditional commune. This still holds true today.

Thus the bulk of Soviet agriculture was based on a compromise. The state established and maintained political control in the countryside — through the MTS political department to an extent and through influencing the choice of collective farm chairmen. The state could also determine what and how much was produced, and control the distribution of the major arable produce through compulsory deliveries and, to a lesser extent, the bonus purchase system.

At the same time all financial responsibility remained within the collective. The state had no wages to pay, no budget to finance. Labour-day payments were often inadequate, so the means of subsistence, the private plot, was built into the system. But the compromise went further than that, for private sales provided an essential element not only in peasant consumption. A resolution of 20 May 1932 by the Central Executive Committee and *Sovnarkom* permitted the sale of agricultural produce on collective farm markets (and local bazaars and railway stations) by collective farms and by their members selling the products of their private plots, after meeting their other obligations (*Resheniya*, 2, p. 388). These sales at free market prices provided essential food supplies. As late as 1940 private sales (which were principally from the private plots) accounted for 54 per cent of all potatoes consumed, 18 per cent of other vegetables, 61 per cent of milk and 55 per cent of meat (*Nar. khoz.*, 1970, p. 283). An element of private enterprise was essential to maintain sustenance for the population as a whole. Only those who grew the food themselves were able to sell. Middlemen and traders were not tolerated. In fact, the private sale of foodstuffs had been going on through the years of the first five-year plan — for the most part, it must be assumed, from those peasant farms as yet remaining outside the collective farm system, though there were also some illegal sales on the black market by collective farmers. Indeed, local markets were an essential means of supplementing the inadequacy of the state mechanism of distribution.

Just as the necessity for collectivisation prior to its introduction has been debated so has the economic value of the policy in funding industrial investment in the first five-year plan. The main views are considered briefly in the Appendix to this chapter. The arguments rehearsed there are not finally resolved, though the essential problem can be framed simply. Resources to finance investment, which was planned to grow by enormous amounts and without foreign borrowing, could come from only two sources: they could be newly created from industrial profits, which in turn rested on productivity improvements; or they could be transferred from consumption. As we have seen, profits and productivity in industry were disappointing, though positive in the first five-year plan. Thus constraints on consumption became more important than planned or anticipated. The plan, indeed, was one means of achieving this transfer as it involved the virtual elimination of the market mechanism. It can be argued with equal force that the agricultural policy initiated from 1928, which culminated in collectivisation, was a further means of constraining consumption and transferring real resources to investment in a way that the market economy could not have accommodated. It seems clear also that the 'sacrifice' of foregone consumption did not fall entirely on the peasantry. The mass-collectivisation programme both forced resources from the peasantry (at prices which were nominal and, in the circumstance, irrelevant) and consolidated state control over the peasantry. In so doing, the regime of the early 1930s created new problems as it solved old ones, so that the negative outcome of the campaign persisted long after Stalin died.

Summary

Many volumes have been written on the economic history of the 1930s and the emergence of the Stalinist economic system. It is difficult, indeed, to characterise the overall results of this decade briefly. As we have seen, the plans did not succeed in detail. Growth was uneven and unbalanced; living standards were sacrificed, not through cynical disregard for the populace but because private consumption was bound to take a low priority. At the same time communal services were greatly extended. The great success was to create a major economic power, though the relative position of the Soviet economy was aided by the setbacks of recession that had affected the capitalist world. By 1937, 53.1 per cent of national income (by Soviet definition) was produced by industry compared with 41.7 per cent in 1929. Industry accounted for 77.4 per cent of aggregate (*sovokupnyi*) production (*Istoriya*, IV,

1978, p. 117). Industry laid the foundation for defence and military production. The need to catch up with capitalist economies and to do so quickly, so urgently demanded by Stalin, was, in large measure, answered.

But it had not been done without cost. The agricultural sector remained large and inefficient, continuing to employ 54 per cent of the labour force in 1937. The mass of the peasantry remained in squalor, as alienated from their Soviet masters as they had been from the Tsars. Above all, terror was employed as an economic weapon. At one level, forced labour was used in some areas for particular projects, but more generally coercion, backed up by the real threat of imprisonment or worse, was used to implement policy. The system of planning as it emerged was so highly centralised that a small error could result in great problems, without there being any balancing mechanism as in a market economy. Only terror and coercion could control the crises created by the demands put on the economy. Coercion became an essential part of the system of control (Lewin, 1974, p. 115). It would be difficult to maintain, however, that the terror was cynically employed to meet economic ends. The purges of the mid-1930s removed many able minds from factories to central committees. This had a real, if unquantifiable, debilitating effect on economic management and the setbacks to the economy experienced after 1937 are no doubt linked with them. What the purges achieved was a wholesale clearing out of the previous control mechanism, so that anyone in any position of authority or responsibility by the end of the 1930s had been put there by Stalin directly or under his patronage. The exercise was effected to maintain and protect the position of Stalin even though it involved economic cost. Any criticism, however constructive, became intolerable. All truth came from the top. The notion of public debate, weak enough in Russian culture, was crushed. Public comment was confined to adulation for Stalin. Even economics as a questioning analytical science was destroyed. But Stalin's dictatorship was not absolute, his command not perfect.

First, there were ideological constraints. Although ideology was overtly based on the principles of Marx it was inevitably compromised by circumstance under Stalin, as under Lenin. In building, as they claimed, socialism the Soviet leaders were breaking new ground, so that practice generated a new creed like some perverse atheistic church. Political intention could be fulfilled, it was supposed, by the strength of political will, the new equivalent of the power of prayer. Nonetheless, despite evident pragmatism, Zaleski has stressed the importance of political and ideological objectives in the planning process, above all in acting as a constraint on policy alternatives (1980, p. 484).

'Second, there were practical constraints. The economy could only produce according to its capacity. No amount of mathematical brilliance or central command could produce gold from base metal. Hence planned objectives could not be perfectly fulfilled. Planning did not signify a unilinear development; there were competing demands. Periodic increases in defence expenditure set back 'civilian' development (see pp. 113-16) while the passage of collectivisation and the purges clearly disturbed the plans, even though they were a means of extending Stalin's control. Control from the centre strengthened; governance of the economy became hierarchical, and these features, coupled with the intolerance of dissent, were characteristic of centuries of Russian history.

Yet command and coercion were not merely traditional. That they became essential to the economy indicates that planning as a system had not created a smoothly operating method of management but rather lurching unsteady progression. The system could not manage itself for, as well as the incidence of 'administrative measures', there were channels of communication and control expressed through the party and, though less certainly, through the political police. But even this did not always succeed: it was often necessary, particularly at the micro-level, to contravene one aspect of the plan in order to meet another. In the first five-year plan period especially the finance plan was broken. Wage payments were exceeded out of necessity to meet physical output demands. Illegal dealings to obtain supplies were commonly resorted to by enterprise managers rather than underfulfil their output plans. Such was the importance of these illegal measures that specialist dealers or 'pushers' (*tolkachi*) emerged. Thus parallel markets emerged without the plan in order to make the plan succeed.

The great success was to achieve an unprecedented rate of growth, though at exactly what level remains a matter of dispute and statistical discretion. Yet even the low estimates for 1928 to 1937 have virtually no parallel in history. This growth was achieved by huge increases in the input of labour and capital. The growth of industrial labour went far ahead of plan, 1928 to 1932, because productivity increases were so poor. They improved from 1932 to 1937 and were negative 1937 to 1940. Labour was often used wastefully. More significant, however, was the inefficient use of capital. The marginal capital-output ratio increased so that the growth of GNP per capital unit was negative, at -0.1 per cent to -6.1 per cent per annum (depending on price weights) from 1928 to 1937. Thus 'Soviet growth has depended more on inputs of factors than on the increased efficiency of their utilization' (Cohn, 1970, p. 328). In other words, growth depended on a high level of investment— up to a quarter of GNP — a relatively high proportion, and, uniquely, a huge ratio financed totally from internal accumulation. The high rate of capital utlisation suggests wastage, a danger reinforced by the fact that capital bore no effective cost, in the form of an interest charge. There was much wastage through damage to farm tractors and other machinery. It remains an open question as to how far terror and political repression, and indeed collectivisation, were necessary to achieve such a high rate of saving, but there can be little doubt that it could only have been achieved by the action of the state. But the inefficiency of the plan meant that the comprehensive aims of the plan could not have been achieved, for such a high rate of investment necessarily meant a diversion from consumption. Growth was dependent upon restraining personal consumption, and that in turn meant ever tighter state controls. As internal accumulation from profits fell short of expectation, more demands were put on the population and more state intervention and further 'administrative measures' were required. The broad outlines of the five-year plan came to have less significance and the annual plan directives to have greater consequence as periodic adjustments to cope with problems generated within the plan. There was therefore greater centralisation. Marx had forecast that under Communism the state would wither away, its function rendered superfluous. In the USSR in the 1930s it was clear that more state intervention was constantly required to maintain direction and momentum to the economy. The state did not diminish but grew; far from withering away, the state became ever more absolute.

Note

1. In the trial of the Mensheviks in 1930-1 there were fourteen defendants, among them V.G. Groman, who had been purged from Gosplan in 1929.

Appendix

Did Agriculture Finance the First Five-Year Plan?

Collectivisation created such problems with production that the wisdom of the policy — from an economic point of view — has been seriously questioned by Western commentators and indeed, though not in print, by some Soviet observers. The immediate economic objective of collectivisation was to secure control over agricultural production and supplies for the urban population, the army and for export at a price to the state that would facilitate a high rate of investment. Table 4.6 indicates a marked increase in state procurements. Further, the manipulation of prices, or rather the absolute control over procurement prices by the state, and the state determination of minimum production and delivery levels therefore enabled the state to accumulate funds at the expense of the agricultural sector— by underpaying the producer. Nove quotes the following figures. In 1933 the procurement price for rye was 5.70 rubles per centner; the price it sold to mills was 22.20 rubles, the greater part of the difference going to the state as turnover tax. In 1934 turnover tax per centner of rye was 66 rubles from a selling price of 84 rubles; that for wheat 89 rubles out of 104 rubles selling price (Nove, 1969, pp. 210-11). With the abolition of rationing, food prices were increased so that revenue from foodstuffs provided the major share of turnover tax, which in turn made up 70 per cent of budget revenue (see above, p. 90). Taxes on agricultural products, in providing a third of state revenue, thus made a vital contribution to the cost of industrialisation. The low prices paid to the peasant producer were, in effect, a form of taxation. Here we have, so it has been claimed, the implementation of the notions of primitive or primary accumulation, as advocated several years earlier by Preobrazhensky. Collectivisation, in other words, established the means for the state to extract surplus product from the peasantry. However, there are clear flaws in regarding this programme as the implementation of Preobrazhensky's theories. Preobrazhensky never advocated mass, forced collectivisation; he based his theories on market exchange and assumed a steady improvement in (urban) working-class living standards. Stalin's policies destroyed the market-place (at least as an area of price-determination) and brought declining living standards. Collectivisation was not simply an implementation of the economic programme of the left opposition; and it was a long way from the moderation of Bukharin and the 'right wing'. It was a pragmatic policy, introduced out of real or perceived necessity. Thus, it is argued, because market exchange could not provide the investment demands of the first five-year plan, collectivisation was introduced. However horrific in execution, collectivisation might be seen as essential to achieve the aims of industrialisation as indicated by the plan. Such an assertion rests on the assumption or deduction that the 'forced saving' from agriculture was both positive and, implicitly, more than could otherwise have been achieved through the market.

Such a deduction was long assumed to be the case but even this has been subject to question and academic controversy. 'It may well be one of those myths which are often repeated but which explode when they are more carefully checked' (Fallenbuchl, 1967, p. 7). The role of agriculture in the financing of industrial investment in the early 1930s – particularly in the years of the first five-year plan, 1928-32 – has been subject to careful scrutiny. Ironically, the debate began with Soviet publications by A.A. Barsov (1968, 1969) in which he concludes that, far from being a net contributor of capital, the agricultural sector was actually a net recipient of capital in these years. The argument has been taken up and developed by Millar (1970, 1971b, 1974) and Ellman (1975). The arguments produce two main conclusions. First, the flow of capital out of agriculture was no greater than and probably less than the flow of capital into agriculture. Second, much of the burden of low procurement prices borne by collective farmers was passed on to the urban population through the free market (i.e. uncontrolled prices).

The destruction of capital stock (in particular, working animals) by the peasantry in response to the collectivisation campaign in turn demanded substantial replacement – through the input of tractors and machinery to the MTS (Millar, 1970, p. 89). The input of machinery increased by 2.2 times between 1928 and 1932, at 1926-7 prices (Barsov, 1969, p. 186), while total net industrial production little more than doubled. In other words, agriculture received large amounts of capital equipment from industry, though this equipment was transferred to the state sector of agriculture – the MTS and state farms – rather than to collective farms directly. Where peasants were able to obtain direct 'benefits' was through the 'free' or private market. The urban population depended on the private market to supplement rations, though to what extent is impossible to say. Until 1932 private sales were subject to local restriction and not recorded, though the rate of price-increase suggests supply fell far short of demand. Malafeev's figures show an increase in all private market retail prices (not food alone) from 100 in 1927-8 to 769.3 in the first half of 1932, and a further increase thereafter (1964, p. 402: index weightings suggest a 15-20 per cent share of total sales in the private market). The restraint on consumption required by the low procurement prices to meet the costs of investment in heavy industry was shifted, to some extent, to the proletariat through the free market. Barsov thus draws the astonishing conclusion that 'the greater part of this major accumulation for industry was created by the labour of the working class' (1969, p. 195). It is Millar's view that the transfer of this cost to the working class – which in turn meant that the agricultural surplus was negative – was in itself determined 'not by the requirements of rapid industrialisation but instead by the need to offset the economically disastrous consequences of collectivisation itself' (Millar, 1971b, p. 306). Thus, he concludes, collectivisation was counterproductive.

The debate hinges on the measure of value of the capital flows between industry and agriculture – which prices to use. Free market prices by definition only applied to the uncontrolled market and were subject to rampant inflation. The crucial element is the adoption of a constant price level, but this itself can lead to distortions (see p. 91). Barsov uses 1928 prices as a constant measure for the flow of funds between agriculture and state industry. Ellman has further examined the Barsov thesis on the basis of 1913 prices as well as 1928 and found that in principle the assertion remains sound (Ellman, 1975, pp. 852-3); that the value of capital from state industry to agriculture (MTS and state farms) was greater than the flow from agriculture to state industry. The 'surplus', whether measured in 1928 or 1913 prices, was negative. The main counter-argument put forward by Alec Nove (1971) again rests on prices. Because prices were arbitrary they cannot be taken as a realistic measure. It is impossible, he asserts, to measure the price of agricultural goods which were obtained by force, as procurement, or which were delivered as payments *in kind* to the MTS (Nove, 1971, p. 399). In fact, collectivisation was intended to extract a surplus and was the mechanism whereby the peasants were deprived of foodstuffs, whatever the notional price may have been. Table 4.7 illustrates changes in physical terms.

Table 4.7: Grain-forage Balance of the USSR (million centners)

Year	Agricultural population	Personal consumption Non-agricultural population	Cattle feed	Demands of industry	Export
1928	312.2	53.7	204.0	15	1.1
1929	303.5	55.0	202.6	15.5	2.8
1930	299.1	70.2	186.6	16	48.7
1931	284.4	83.1	149.3	18.5	51.8
1932	260.0	92.5	138.0	16.5	22.0

Source: Moshkov, *Zernovaya problema* (M. 1966), appended.

If one of the 'problems', from the point of view of the industrial decision makers in the mid-1920s, was that peasants were eating more and not selling enough (see p. 76, above) then collectivisation enabled peasant consumption to be reduced (Nove, 1971, p. 397). Further, the burden of the famine (1932-4 and, strictly, after the first five-year plan) which was the result of the collectivisation campaign was shifted on to the peasantry.

Can such contrasting views be resolved? In part they concentrate on different points of emphasis and there are areas of agreement. Quite obviously, agriculture cannot have paid for all the increase in investment in the first five-year plan, for that increase exceeded total agricultural production (Ellman, 1975, p. 844- again using constant prices). But agriculture can have provided an essential marginal contribution. The agricultural sector provided labour for expanding industry, crucial exports (if very much smaller than in 1913) and some import-substitution (e.g. in cotton and tea). Above all, perhaps it provided a *minimum* supply of subsistence at negligible cost (Ellman, 1975, p. 858). As for the transfer of capital resources, it was the state sector of agriculture (MTS and state farms) which received the capital equipment. This was then rented by the co-operative collective farms. There is thus a distinction between the agricultural sector in aggregate and the peasants within collective farms and indeed operating as individual household farms (collectivisation was incomplete by 1932). This distinction is important in this context for until 1932, when collective farm free markets were established, it was the individual farms which were able to benefit most from the rapid increase in free market prices — above all, though not exclusively, one must assume, in those regions where collectivisation had made least headway, for instance in the Caucausus.

There is little doubt that the massive increase in investment, both in the first and second five-year plans, was made possible only by (unplanned) reductions in average levels of consumption, and that this decline was felt both by peasants and workers. Collectivisation imposed the reduction (in some cases to a terrifying extent) on the peasants. Through the free market some peasants were able to shift part of the burden onto the working class. As early as 1961, Naum Jasny claimed that between 1928 and 1937 per capita real income fell by 19 per cent for peasants, compared with 40 per cent for non-agricultural wage-earners (Jasny, 1961, p. 446). Even without the benefit of subsequent debate, Erich Strauss suggested that 'the proportionately biggest contribution to the forced industrialisation of the country was being extracted from the workers rather than from the peasants' (Strauss, 1969, pp. 121-2). Barsov's main discussion, and the evidence he adduces, is concerned with the first five-year plan to 1932, but he notes also that in 1937 the peasants' exchange position was almost the same as in 1928 (98.5), and in 1940 slightly better (104.1) (Barsov, 1969, p. 186).

There is, however, a further qualification to Barsov's case. He uses a two-sector analysis: 'agriculture' and 'industry'. During the period 1928 to 1932, he claims, the terms of trade moved in favour of agriculture. Ellman elaborates this to a three-sector model: agriculture, the state and a 'proletarian sector'. In his analysis, both the agricultural and the state sector's terms of trade improved while those of the proletariat deteriorated (Ellman, 1975, p. 850). However, this appears to be a simplification. It has already been pointed out above that the 'agricultural sector' and 'peasantry' were not equivalent. Similarly, at least before 1932, there was considerable overlap between peasant and proletarian. Internal mobility was relatively free until 1932, when the internal passport system was reintroduced, and millions of peasants moved to industrial work. A large proportion of industrial workers, and virtually all new workers, were themselves peasants who had just left the land. Further, and more important, the private market was far more extensive than agriculture (the peasants) exchanging with industry (the workers). There was widespread and long-established trade between villages and between agricultural regions. The mass of peasants in the northern provinces of European Russia, for example, customarily depended on the market for their food. Throughout the country poor peasants were often net purchasers of food on the market, earning their living by other occupations. Barsov claims that the poor peasants were better off as a result of collectivisation, but, even so, there can be no doubt that many thousands of peasants were adversely affected by the great increase in free-market prices of agricultural products. There can thus be little doubt that everybody (bar a privileged few) went without, that consumption in general was held down or declined (see pp. 184-5, below). It is, however, significant that in the workers' state it was the industrial workers who bore more than their fair share of deprivation. To declare, as Barsov does, that 'this is one of the clearest manifestations of the *avant garde* role of the working class in the construction of socialism' (1969, p. 195) seems little more than a semantic device.

Does this suggest, as Millar does (1971, p. 300, 1974, p. 764), that collectivisation was counterproductive and therefore unnecessary to the first five-year plans of the 1930s? From the foregoing evidence there would seem to be much to support such a view. But although collectivisation had serious negative effects on production it enabled government control over minimum procurements, a supply of exports and indeed control over the supply and allocation of large numbers of peasants. If it can ever be measured satisfactorily (which is doubtful) it may be possible to show that collectivisation was not *objectively* necessary. Nonetheless it was seen to be economically necessary at the time of its implementation. There is far more agreement that compulsory procurements were necessary to meet the demands of the plan after 1928. The harsh enforcement of the emergency procurement measures and the peasant response to them in turn signalled the forced collectivisation of peasant farms. Collectivisation thus became a necessity within the political environment of 1929. That it failed in its objectives in later years does not alter this assertion. The contemporary environment was determined by three major characteristics: the investment demands of the first five-year plan (as unrealistic as they were); the political limitations of the Bolshevik regime (in particular its lack of a power-base in the countryside); and the power struggle within the party. Collectivisation was in many respects an economic failure which brought disaster in the short term and debilitation in the longer run. But it is difficult to see an alternative strategy: the Bolsheviks could not allow flourishing capitalism in the countryside while they sought to build socialism in industry. Collectivisation was Stalin's victory both over the peasantry and over his political opponents. It signalled both the consolidation of party control in the countryside and of his power within the party.

5 WAR AND RECOVERY

The German invasion in June 1941 brought the most severe test to the resilience of the Soviet economy. The ensuing hostilities can, with every justification, be termed the 'Great Patriotic War'. The danger of war had long been feared by the Soviet leadership and, as it happens, the invasion came ten years and four months after Stalin's famous prediction in 1931 (see pp. 86-7). Later in the 1930s the Soviet government had tried to elicit joint resistance, with Britain and France, to German expansion, but at the price of allowing effective Soviet penetration into much of eastern Europe. Western powers were unprepared to allow such expansion, nor to take a strong line against Hitler. Rather they followed a policy of 'appeasement' until, that is, the German invasion in 1939, in response to which Britain and France declared war. Ironically, it was in 1939 that the Soviet government became the biggest appeaser of all by signing a trade treaty and non-aggression pact with Nazi Germany. The way was open for the German invasion of Poland, following which Soviet troops moved west, through the Baltic states and into eastern Poland. Such moves were a holding operation, designed primarily to secure western frontiers from attack. Indeed in 1940 Soviet troops invaded Finland in an effort to push the border further from vulnerable Leningrad. The resistance of the Finns, who were greatly outnumbered, indicated Soviet weakness to the Germans and to Soviet military planners.

After the invasion of Poland, Germany and her allies swept across Europe, reaching the North Sea coast in 1940. At this time Britain stood alone in the war against Hilter. Germany and the USSR were never in formal alliance; they had signed a non-aggression pact and trade treaty, and Soviet-German trade increased substantially. When the invasion came it took the Soviet defences very much by surprise, and the invading forces were able to make rapid headway, until meeting strong resistance at Moscow in November 1941. German occupation of Soviet territory was the most terrible of the war. Millions were killed or imprisoned; early military engagements resulted in Soviet troops being captured by the thousand. The scale of the war, in terms of the numbers of men and machines involved, was unmatched anywhere on the western front. As late as 1944 there were twice as many German infantry and tank divisions on the eastern front as on the western seaboard. Soviet resistance began at Moscow and was perhaps most power-fully symbolised by the siege of Leningrad, which lasted from 1941 to 1943. Counter-attack, and a major turning-point in the war, was evident at Stalingrad in 1943. German and other Axis forces were then gradu-ally pushed back and were virtually in full retreat from the country well before the Allied landings in Normandy in 1944.

The war caused destruction and loss of life in the Soviet Union unmatched in Europe,[1] in part because of the barbarity of the occupy-ing forces. Prisoners of war were employed as forced labourers under the most brutal of conditions;[2] the Slavs were regarded as lesser beings. However, in counter-attack the Soviet forces were little more merciful. German prisoners of war were harshly treated and many, indeed, held long after the war had ended. Brutality was by no means exclusive to the German forces.[3] Victory in the war, which was achieved at such cost, also brought Stalin to the forefront of world politics and the USSR to the status of world power. The map of Europe was redrawn by the world leaders, Stalin among them, even before the ending of hostilities. As a result, Soviet influence was extended to neighbouring states in eastern Europe, states which quickly became military allies and, later, important trading partners. Soviet territory was extended also to embrace most of the area in the western borderlands that had previously been in the old Empire.

Although much of the pre-war policy had been concerned with possible military conflict there is uncertainty about the levels of mili-tary and economic preparation. Military expenditure as such did not figure greatly in the first two five-year plans but was of a higher order in the third five-year plan from 1937. It is important to consider this before an examination of the war economy itself.

The Third Five-year Plan

The third five-year plan was launched in the midst of the great purges, which had a debilitating effect on its implementation. Ironically, how-ever, one result of the purges was to bring to prominence Voznesensky, who was to prove such an able chairman of Gosplan through the war years. In many respects the third plan was a more co-ordinated and balanced exercise than earlier plans. It aimed for an increase in industrial output of over 90 per cent, averaging 14 per cent per annum. Priority was again given to group A (producer) goods (15.7 per cent per annum) over group B (consumer) goods (11.5 per cent); much of this growth was to result from increases in labour productivity, in turn a result of better organisation of production and tighter labour discipline. The need to match the strength of Western economies was maintained and, accordingly, some emphasis was put on industries which had been relatively neglected, such as chemicals and non-ferrous metals. Electric power generation was also to increase substantially, though with coal rather than oil remaining the prime source of energy (Table 5.1).

Table 5.1: The Third Five-Year Plan

Indicator	1937 (Actual)	1940 (Actual)	1941 (Actual)	1941 (Plan)	1942 (Plan)
National income (milliard rubles at 1926-7 prices)	96.3	128.3	118		173.6
Gross industrial production (milliard rubles at 1926-7 prices)	95.5	138.5	135.7	162	184.0
Gross agricultural production (milliard rubles at 1926-7 prices)	20.1	23.3	14.5		30.5
Number of workers[a] (millions)	27	31.2	27.4	31.6	32.0
Wage fund (milliard rubles)	82.2	123.7		133.7	137.0
Retail trade (milliard rubles at current prices)	126.3	175.1	152.8	197.0	206.0
Coal (million tonnes)	128	165.9	151.4	190.8	
Crude oil (million tonnes)	28.5	31.1	33.0	34.6	
Steel[b] (million tonnes)	30.7	31.4	30.5	38.2	
Cement (million tonnes)	5.4	5.7	5.5	8.0	
Mineral fertiliser (million tonnes)	3.2	3.2	—	—	
Electric power (million kWh)	36.2	48.3	46.7	54	
Leather shoes (million pairs)	182.9	189.5		221.6	
Cotton cloth (million m^2)	3,448	3,954	3,824	4,338	

Notes: a. Workers and wage fund refer only to state economy, excluding collective farmers. b. Steel includes ingots, castings and rolled steel.
Sources: *Istoriya sotsialisticheskoi ekonomiki SSSR,* V (M 1979), p. 20:
E. Zaleski, *Stalinist Planning for Economic Growth 1933-52* (1980), pp. 550-65, 578-93.

This was a plan of austerity because of the much higher expenditure on armaments. Further, the increase, over plan, on arms expenditure was at the cost of civilian production. Thus although the plan was cut short by the war in 1941 it was short of target before that time largely because of the diversion of resources to military needs. 'Civilian' engineering and metals industries fell short while military output in such industries grew apace. Between 1938 and 1940 armaments increased by 39 per cent compared with 13 per cent for all industry (Zaleski, 1980, p. 189). Defence expenditure increased in 1939 and

1940 (39.2 milliard rubles and 56.7 milliard actual expenditure, respectively) and further increases were budgeted in 1941. In 1940 defence goods made up 26 per cent of gross industrial production, and the defence sector accounted for 15 per cent of national income (Tupper, 1981, p. 1). The third five-year plan was in effect a war-preparation plan. It was, of course, imperfect as well as incomplete, and it is a matter of debate how well prepared the country was for war.

War Preparation

On the eve of war no European nation was prepared for a lengthy war of attrition. German strategy became one of *blitzkreig*, which led to outstanding military success. By 1941 Germany, her allies and occupied territories included a population of 250 millions, compared with 175 millions in the USSR; per capita production exceeded that in the Soviet Union. The comparative ease with which Germany had established this position, losing only 200,000 men, suggested a strong military ascendancy over the ill-prepared Soviet state. Soviet budget expenditure on defence (Table 5.2) was low in the 1930s, increasing markedly after

Table 5.2: State Budget Expenditure on Defence (per cent)

1923-4	16.7	1933	3.5
1925-6	14.5	1937	18.6
1927-8	12.0	1933-7 average	14.1
1928-9	10.9	1938	18.7
1932	4.2	1940	32.6
1928-32 average	6.3		

Source: J. Cooper, 'Defence Production and the Soviet Economy', *CREES Discussion Paper*, SIPS, 3 (Birmingham 1976), pp. 35-6.

1936. Further, the military was seriously weakened by the purge of officers. German superiority in the quality of military hardware, particularly aeroplanes, in 1940-1, was generally acknowledged. There can be no question that Soviet authorities were caught by surprise when the attack came on 22 June 1941, and this was despite advanced warning from at least three intelligence sources, including the British government. There had been further indications of German mobilisation for an attack, yet deliveries under the trade treaty were accelerated. Immediately after the attack Stalin reacted with disbelief and panic. Khrushchev, in his memoirs, claims that Stalin gave orders not to return fire at first, not believing that it was a full invasion (1977, vol. 1, pp. 192-3). Stalin made no public statement until 3 July, the state of war having been broadcast by Molotov. Public morale was low. There was little effective resistance and the invading forces were even welcomed in much of the Ukraine as liberators from Russian oppression.

Yet there is much evidence to show a far greater degree of war preparation than this might suggest.[4] Strategic considerations had been built into the five-year plans; the limited relocation of industry was an indication of this. New factories, particularly for tractors, had been built with the purpose of ready conversion to military production. Tank and tractor productive technology developed in parallel. The experience of the Spanish civil war and war with Finland had demonstrated the need for improved armour for tanks, and from 1938 the heavy KV tank and the lighter T-34 tanks were produced. Before the oubreak of war their production was well advanced, and already there had been some relocation of production to Chelyabinsk and Stalingrad (Cooper, 1976, p. 14). Aeroplanes were less well developed, but here again there was marked acceleration in production before the invasion (Table 5.3). Further, there had been a degree of hidden expenditure

Table 5.3: Military Production 1930-41 (numbers built each year)

	All Tanks[a]	Military aircraft	All guns
1930	170		952
1932	3038		2,574
1937	1559	1,612[b]	5,473
1941	6590	12,516	42,300
(including first half)	1800	3,950	9,100

Notes: a. These include some small tanks. b. 1935.
Source: Cooper, 'Defence Production', pp. 46-8.

on defence not revealed in the budget figures in Table 5.2. In December 1936 a commissariat of defence production was established. Before then, defence industries had been within the control of the commissariat for heavy industry and many 'civilian' factories had already been engaged in defence production, a feature that was to grow after 1936. Periodic shortcomings in civilian plan fulfilment through the 1930s had, to an extent, been the result of coincident increases in military production. Defence industries always had the top priority for materials, fuels and skilled manpower. In effect, the burden of high defence production was borne by the civilian sector. The relocation of industry, which proceeded rapidly in the war, was planned before 1940 (Hutchings, 1971, p. 216), and controls over labour had been introduced from 1938. Ironically, however, because civilian factories had been incorporated into defence production the strategic relocation of the defence industry was slowed down. In 1941 most defence production was in strategically vulnerable western locations (Tupper, 1981, p. 14). On the eve of war the Soviet defence industry was well developed and limited by the general resources of the economy rather than by the particular resources of the defence sector. The Soviet army had numerical superiority overall; during the war it was able to match the Germans for quality. Liddell Hart estimates that in July 1941 the Soviet Union had a total of 24,000 tanks against 3,550 Panzers on the Russian front (1970, pp. 158-9).

The War Economy

The invading forces made rapid headway, reaching the outskirts of Moscow by November 1941. By December, Nazi forces had laid siege to Leningrad and Sevastopol; they held all other territory west of a line from Rostov-on-Dov to the Finnish border. *Blitzkrieg* had all but succeeded; but they went no further. The response was to stand firm and fight out a war of attrition. Stalin and his war council stayed in Moscow, while the 'diplomatic' capital moved to Kuibyshev in the Urals. Yet now the main resources of pre-war industry were in enemy hands. The invading forces occupied areas which, prior to the invasion, had accommodated 40 per cent of the total population, 32 per cent of all workers; 33 per cent of all industrial enterprises and provided 33 per cent of gross industrial production including 68 per cent of pig iron, 58 per cent of steel, 57 per cent of rolled steel, 71 per cent of iron ore, 74 per cent of coke, 35 per cent of manganese ore, 63 per cent coal, 42 per cent of electrical energy, 57 per cent of tractors and 52 per cent of cement. This area had also produced 38 per cent of the gross grain harvest, 87 per cent of sugar, 60 per cent of pigs and 38 per cent of cattle (Kravchenko, 1970, pp. 123-4).

In response, people and productive capacity were evacuated; Marshall Zhukov was put in charge of Moscow forces and the German army was held up in the winter. The initial advance on Moscow was delayed while some forces were diverted south to the Ukraine and north to Leningrad. Having learned from intelligence reports that Japanese forces would not invade in strength from Manchuria, the Soviet Command was able to move reinforcements, from the east, to defend Moscow, and Hitler's delay had given them time to do so. The Axis powers, on the other hand, had huge occupied territories vulnerable to seaborne attack from the west. In December the Red Army was able to counter-attack. From then, the main German attack was in the south, towards the Caspian oil-fields. They never reached them. Hitler became obsessed with taking Stalingrad and squandered resources on seeking the town which had far less strategic significance than the oil-fields. Stalingrad was saved, the German armies being defeated in February 1943. At the same time large forces besieged, and never took, Leningrad with consequences of terrible suffering for the population.

Control over the economy took on a quasi-military style. Military discipline over labour was extended and all production was diverted to military needs. By November 1941, 1,523 enterprises had been evacuated from western regions, 667 to the Urals, 244 to western Siberia, 78 to eastern Siberia, 308 to central Asia and Kazakhstan and 226 to the Volga region (*Istoriya*, V, 1978, p. 234). Even state and collective farmers were evacuated, together with machinery from MTS (Shigalin, 1960, p. 47). Whole factories were dismantled, put on trains and taken east to be reassembled in hurriedly converted or constructed shelters. Often this was achieved amazingly quickly. In three weeks 5,800 metal-working lathes were taken from the Kirov works in Leningrad to new buildings in the Urals. They began producing tanks even before the building had a roof, and by 8 December the first 25 T-34 tanks produced there were at the front (*Istoriya*, V, 1978, p. 173). Tank production was stepped up in the converted tractor factories, in Gorky and Stalingrad and diesel production was transferred to the Chelyabinsk tractor factory making the heavy KV tank (Kravchenko, 1970, p. 117).

Non-military production fell. Between June and December 1941 iron output declined by three quarters, steel by nearly two-thirds and total industrial production by more than half. Military production and output on the 'new areas' increased. In 1942, which had the lowest overall wartime production levels, industrial output in the Urals exceeded 1940 levels by 2.8 times, in western Siberia by 2.4 times and in the Volga by 2.5 times. A recovery in production occurred after 1942, and the Red Army began to push westward once more, though, because of the systematic destruction undertaken by the retreating German army, it was not easy to bring recovered capacity back into production (Table 5.4). Factories were destroyed, crops burned, villages decimated, even wells poisoned.

Table 5.4: War Economy 1941-5

(Items measured as a percentage of the 1940 figure)	1941	1942	1943	1944	1945
Number of workers and employees	88	59	62	76	87
National income	92	66	74	88	83
Gross industrial production	98	77	90	104	92
including military	140	186	224	251	–
Gross agricultural production	62	38	37	54	60
Transport goods turnover	92	53	61	71	77
Retail trade turnover (state)	84	34	32	37	45

Source: Kravchenko, *Ekonomika SSSR v gody* (M. 1970), p. 358.

Allied Aid

As an ally of the Western powers the USSR was provided with aid and lend-lease deliveries. Although of great value, these deliveries made what was probably little more than a marginal contribution to the war effort, especially in armaments provision. They were, however, enormously important in overcoming bottlenecks, particularly in transport. Official figures show that allied deliveries provided 2 per cent of artillery, 12 per cent of aircraft, 10 per cent of tanks and made a major contribution to the provision of food, petrol and lorries, as well as raw materials — aluminium, zinc and nickel (*Istoriya*, V, 1978, p. 541). The total value of military supplies shipped from Britain, which included some Canadian deliveries, exceeded £300 million together with over £120 million worth of food and raw materials. The Allied run to Murmansk taking such deliveries was one of the most risky of the war, with high losses. American deliveries, for the most part, were sent overland through Iran. Khrushchev in his memoirs has paid tribute to the Allied deliveries and indeed emphasised Soviet dependence upon food and transport equipment. Foodstuffs from Canada, USA and Britain totalled 2,545,000 tonnes (Shigalin, 1960, p. 191) including inevitably, but vitally, 'Spam'. Other sources put less emphasis on such deliveries, pointing out that armaments deliveries fell short of agreed levels (*Istoriya*, V, 1978, p. 541). Little could be exported in return and the balance of trade moved into severe deficit (see below, p. 195). The great bulk of military equipment, guns, tanks and aeroplanes were Soviet-made and the destructive demands of war, in the perverse way of history, brought forth enterprise and technical innovation. The superiority of Soviet tanks (notably in the T-34) was consolidated, and aeroplane design was improved. Military production exceeded German levels but in some respects civilian production remained behind (Table 5.5).

Table 5.5: Soviet and German Wartime Production

	USSR July 1941- July 1945	Germany 1941-4
Pig iron (million tonnes)	31.5	98.1[a]
Steel (million tonnes)	45.4	113.4
Coal (million tonnes)	441.5	1,321.4
Electrical energy (million kWh)	147.3	334.0[a]
Tanks (numbers)	95,099	53,800
Military aircraft (numbers)	108,028	78,900
Guns (medium and large calibre) (thousands)	188.1	102.1
Mortars (thousands)	347.9	68

Note: a. These figures include German-occupied territories.
Source: G.S. Kravchenko, *Ekonomika SSSR* (M. 1970), p. 359: A.S. Milward, *War, Economy and Society 1939-1945* (1977), p. 79.

The Soviet economy was thus much more of a total war economy than Nazi Germany. The extensive controls over the economy which had been developed under the planning mechanism facilitated wartime controls but this is not to say that conversion to a war economy was undertaken without difficulty. The war years were ones of intense sacrifice and suffering by the population of the USSR.

Agriculture

Agricultural production declined seriously, the biggest losses being in livestock products (Table 5.6). Much stock was lost through confiscation and systematic destruction in the German retreat. Seventeen million head of cattle were lost and seven million horses; 1,876 state farms, 2,890 MTS and 98,000 collective farms were destroyed or 'plundered'. Tractors numbering 137,000, 49,000 combine harvesters, 46,000 seed-drills and other equipment were destroyed or confiscated (Shigalin, 1960, pp. 189-90). After 1942 the sown area of crops, and from 1943 livestock numbers, began to recover, though never to pre-war levels (Kravchenko, 1970, p. 263, and table 5.6). The gross harvest of all grains was 95.5 million tonnes in 1940 (*Sel'skoe khozyaistvo*, 1960, p. 26) and only 47.3 million tonnes in 1945 (Kravchenko, 1970, p. 266). Yet there was real progress in agricultural production during the war years as a result of bringing new areas into cultivation and increases in labour productivity. Vegetables and potatoes increased in area in Kazakhstan and western Siberia and the cotton area was extended in Azerbaidzhan, Turkmenistan and Kazakhstan. Despite the loss of manpower, many collective farms were able to increase yields

Table 5.6: Agriculture in the War Years

Sown area (million hectares)	1940		1942		1944	1945
All grains	110.4		67.3		82.0	85.0
Technical crops	11.8		5.9		7.5	7.7
Vegetables and potatoes	10.0		5.0		10.0	10.0
Feed crops	18.1		9.5		10.4	10.1
	150.4		87.7		109.9	113.6

Livestock numbers (million head)	1941		1943			1946
Cattle	54.5	31.4	28.4	33.9	44.2	47.6
of which cows	27.8	15.0	13.8	16.5	21.6	22.9
Pigs	27.5	8.2	6.0	5.6	8.8	10.6
Sheeps and goats	91.6	70.6	61.8	63.3	70.2	70.0
of which sheep	79.9	–	–	52.0	57.9	58.5
Horses	21.0	10.0	8.1	7.7	9.9	10.7

Source: G.I. Shigalin, *Narodnoe khozyaistvo v period velikoi otechestvennoi voiny* (M. 1960), pp. 197, 208.

(Shigalin, 1960, p. 191), a tribute to the strength and resource of womanpower. The common goal of defence, in this case, appears to have brought forth increased effort and sacrifice.

Not all was left to community of spirit, however, for the war also brought greater controls over agriculture. Compulsory labour days on collective farms were increased and payment reduced. In some areas there was no effective labour-day payment at all. The political departments in MTS, which had been dropped in the 1930s, were reintroduced. There were limits on the size of private holdings and increased taxes on income derived therefrom. Some peasants were able to benefit by the enormous increase in free market prices for foodstuffs. A price index reached 12.6 times the 1940 level in 1943 for non-livestock products and 13.2 times for livestock products. Thereafter, with recovering production, it began to fall (Malafeev, 1964, p. 229). Many peasants depended on such sales to buy bread for themselves, but it was also evident that some were able to accumulate substantial hoards of paper money. There were also suggestions that private plots were unofficially extended, presumably in occupied areas or where farm chairmen turned a blind eye. Measures to reverse the process were adopted soon after the war. There was a massive extension of urban allotment-type plots and of farms subsidiary to factories.

The Budget

For most of the war years the government was able to maintain a nominal budget surplus, in proudly declared contrast to the substantial deficit run by her major allies, the USA and Britain. State income was increased through greater taxes on the population, especially direct taxes, including a 'bachelor tax' and a small family tax. This was a substantial reversal of pre-war financial policy, which had relied little on direct taxes. It was impossible, however, to depend on turnover tax when heavy industry was largely receiving subsidies and when retail turnover was at such a low ebb. Direct taxes were therefore a necessary wartime contingency. In fact, credits from the state bank were also required to cover expenditure. Even so, a small deficit in some years contributed to inflationary pressure (Table 5.7). To combat this, prices of heavy industrial goods and armaments were subsidised and ration prices were kept low. Most inflationary pressure came from excess demand, and was manifest in the free market for foodstuffs, so that much of the increase in money wages was transferred to the peasantry.

Table 5.7: Wartime State Budget (milliard rubles)

	1940	1941	1942	1943	1944	1945
Total income	180.0	191.4	165.0	202.7	268.7	302.0
Turnover tax and profits tax	127.6	116.7	81.7	91.1	116.3	140.0
Taxes from population	9.4	10.8	21.6	28.6	37.0	39.8
Loans	11.4	11.0	15.3	25.5	32.6	29.0
Expenditure	174.3	191.4	182.8	210.0	264.0	298.6
On economy	58.3	51.7	31.6	33.1	53.7	74.4
Socio-cultural measures	40.9	31.4	30.3	37.7	51.3	62.7
Defence	56.7	83.0	108.4	125.0	137.8	128.2

Source: Kravchenko, *Ekonomika SSSR* (M 1970), p. 230.

Labour

Labour supply was seriously affected by mobilisation – and the most serious effects were in rural areas where sometimes whole villages lost their adult male population. The total number of workers and employees fell from 31.2 million in 1940 to 18.4 million in 1942. As most men were conscripted, there was substantial labour-dilution with the drafting of women into the industrial labour force. Rapid training of labour proceeded, 7.6 million newly trained workers becoming available in 1942 (Kravchenko, 1970, p. 111). The disturbance to the labour force and the relocation of industry and people caused difficulties to the economy — the most serious results being in agricultural production. Nonetheless, in key areas labour productivity was substantially increased (Table 5.8).

Table 5.8: Labour Expenditure on Military Equipment (thousand man-hours)

	1941	1943
Aeroplane IL-4	20.0	12.5
Aeroplane IL-2	9.5	5.9
Aeroplane PE-4	25.3	13.2
Large-calibre machine gun (100)	64.2	32.9
T-34 tank	8.0	3.7

Source: Malafeev, *Istoriya Tsenoobrazovaniya* (1964), p. 227.

The sacrifices made by the population were almost inestimable. Labour was subject to military discipline, holidays abolished, consumer-goods simply not available, direct taxes increased and food rationed. Accommodation was poor, and evacuees often had to camp out before building their own shelter. Over ten millions were evacuated east but the construction of dwellings took a low priority. Each evacuated worker was allowed to take 100 kg of belongings and each family member only 40 kg. All effort was for the front.

Soviet Victory

This is no place to attempt to discuss military strategy; it is, however, worthy of note that the contrary military tactics adopted by the invading Germans contributed to their own downfall. Ill-equipped for winter, they were delayed in the initial drive on Moscow and then faced the harshness of the elements as well as Soviet reinforcements (Liddell-Hart, 1970, p. 265). The strategy of *blitzkrieg* clearly failed, and the German forces were eventually defeated in a war of attrition. Added to this was the crude brutality of the occupying regime which alienated local populations, some of whom had initially displayed support. There was widespread guerrilla fighting by partisans. It is an irony also that a feature of backwardness helped the Soviet Union. The German army was mobile and depended on wheeled transport: most Russian roads could simply not accommodate this traffic, and much of it became literally bogged down.

Nonetheless, the fact remains that the Soviet people withstood deprivation, sacrifice and cruelty and fought back. The endurance of their soldiers and civilians was a source of amazement to German commanders. In creating a war-machine there is no doubt that the development of industry in the preceding years of planning was a vital contribution. Guns, tanks or aeroplanes cannot be made without engineering, metallurgical and related industries. However, it is also true that much of the real construction took place during the war years. The policies of Stalin in the 1930s evidently weakened Soviet resolve at the start of the war — the purges are an obvious case in point. Equally Stalin's leadership and resolve were a crucial example during the war. More significantly, there were necessary policy changes in the war years. The thrust of propaganda was nationalist rather than socialist; the appeal was to defend the motherland of Russia rather than the homeland of socialism. There were concessions to the Orthodox and other churches and their leaders gave their blessing to Stalin. There can be no doubt that the weight lent by such spiritual leaders had a profound impact on public morale and unity of purpose. Stalin, as commander-in-chief, became the great war hero. The cult of personality, and its attendant power, reached a zenith.

Most of the country was liberated by 1944. The Red Army advanced to Berlin and the areas annexed after 1939 were consolidated into the USSR. In addition, the Soviet 'sphere of influence' was now extended to include countries bordering the USSR in the west. Wartime losses were enormous. The occupied zone had been subject to confiscations and systematic destruction. In all 1,710 towns and 70,000 villages were wholly or partially destroyed. Other losses included 82,000 industrial enterprises, 3,000 MTS and 1,300 railway bridges. Fifty-five per cent of steel-producing capacity was lost, 50 per cent of electrical generating capacity and 60 per cent of coal output. There were more than 20 million dead. Soviet military losses exceeded those of any other nation.

Post-war Recovery

At the end of the war victory was tempered by the massive task of reconstruction. The fourth five-year plan aimed to make good war-losses, and do in five years (1946-50) what would have been done in ten (1940-50). The plan thus took 1940 as a base, though production in 1945 was below the pre-war level. It aimed for an increase in industrial output of 48 per cent (60 per cent for group A, 29 per cent for group B); this represented a planned increase over 1945 levels of 61 per cent (43 per cent group A, 119 per cent group B!). As we shall see, the plan was fulfilled overall but once again consumer-goods output fell short of target. In setting out on the road to recovery the Soviet Union had certain 'advantages'. First, the political position of the government and party had been consolidated in victory so that the system of over-all management and control was already firmly established. Second, to a limited extent, recovery had been initiated before 1945 as the country was reoccupied. Third, the 'post-war recovery factor' came into play, so that idle capacity brought into production produced very rapid initial growth. Fourth, the physical area of the country was extended to include the annexed Baltic states, Bessarabia (Moldavia) and eastern Karelia as well as some former Polish or German territories. Further, political control over much of eastern Europe, beyond Soviet frontiers, added to the productive assets over which it had command. Against these, of course, must be set the enormous levels of losses to popula-tion and productive capacity.

Reparations demands were imposed upon defeated Axis powers and their allies. These included some deliveries made from western Germany and Italy but overwhelmingly from those countries where the Soviet Union was able to exercise direct political pressure: Hungary, Rumania, Finland and, above all, eastern Germany. Further, some 'political deliveries' of coal at giveaway prices were made from Poland, and the Soviet Union took control of former German assets in east Europe, including Czechoslovakia and Austria. It is impossible to be precise about the contribution to Soviet recovery made by such deliveries. Zaleski quotes a figure of an average of 5 milliard rubles per year trans-ferred to the USSR (as reparations or other assets) from 1945 to 1956. This was in total less than 8 per cent of the Soviet estimated capital losses (Zaleski, 1980, p. 346). It may reasonably be concluded that such resources would have been more productive left where they were. Oil from Rumania, coal from Poland, timber and steel from Finland and a mass of industrial equipment from the Soviet zone of Germany helped to overcome bottlenecks in the early post-war years. Plans and equipment to build aeroplanes, motor vehicles and optical instruments were confiscated from Germany. The USSR was clearly exploiting its dominant position to the detriment of the subject-countries. On the other hand, food supplies were sent into eastern Europe. The demands on all countries were reduced between 1948 and 1950, and finally abolished in 1954. Only Finland met all demands in full, by 1952. The advantage to the USSR was that she had been able to obtain scarce supplies of capital resources, a process aided, in western Europe, by the Marshall Plan, in which the USSR took no part.

The fourth five-year plan set out to re-establish pre-war consumption levels by reconverting to peacetime production. The high forecasts of consumer-goods production were thus to be achieved by diverting resources from military and defence expenditure. However, in the outcome, consumer-goods output was below plan, and this despite the introduction of new, expensive consumer-durables. Producer-goods (group A) took a larger share of output in 1950 (68.8 per cent) than in 1937 (57.8 per cent) (*Promyshlennost' SSSR*, 1964, p. 37). Recovery to pre-war levels for producer-goods was achieved in 1948, that of consumer-goods in 1951. The growth of industrial production overall was almost spectacular, though it was inflated by the continued use of 1926-7 prices.

Industrial production was boosted by the re-employment of new workers (demobilised soldiers and workers in new territories) but more particularly by substantial improvements in productivity. The number of workers of all types (clerical, manual and technical) in industry increased from 9.5 million in 1945 to over 14 million in 1950. From 1940 to 1950 average productivity for all workers increased by 45 per cent, that of manual workers alone by 37 per cent (*Promyshlennost' SSSR*, 1964, pp. 56-7). Improvements in labour productivity were boosted by the return to material incentives with the abolition of rationing from 1947, though more particularly by new technology. More attention was paid to mechanisation and automation in production, especially with the extension to civilian production of some of the techniques developed in the war. William Beddell Smith, the US ambassador from 1946 to 1949, reported production methods at a motor plant he visited to be no different from those in the USA (Smith, 1950, p. 131). There was also more technical training, both on the job and in vocational 'labour reserve' schools. The number of apprentices, however, actually fell from 1945 to 1950. The experience of war and the technological advances made therein demonstrated the need for properly acquired scientific and technical skills for industry.

In 1950 national income reached 118.9 per cent of plan target, that for gross industrial production, 116.9 per cent, producer-goods 127.5 per cent and consumer-goods 95.7 per cent at 1926-7 prices (Table 5.9) (Zaleski, 1980, p. 525).

Thus, in most respects the fourth plan was overfulfilled, though it was short of the planned 17 per cent annual average increase in consumer-goods. Lokshin claims a real increase of 73 per cent in indus-

Table 5.9: Growth of Production 1945-50

Product	Unit	1940	1945	1950
Pig iron	million tonnes	14.9	8.8	19.2
Steel	million tonnes	18.3	12.3	27.3
Rolled steel	million tonnes	13.1	8.5	20.9
Oil	million tonnes	31.1	19.4	37.9
Electrical energy	milliard kWh	48.3	43.3	91.2
Mineral fertiliser	million tonnes	3.2	1.1	5.5
Metal-cutting lathes	thousands	58.4	38.4	70.6
Automobiles	thousands	145.4	74.7	362.9
Tractors (15-hp units)	thousands	66.2	14.7	242.5
Combine-harvesters	thousands	12.8	0.3	46.3
Cement	million tonnes	5.7	1.8	10.2
Cotton cloth	milliard metres	3.9	1.6	3.9
Leather shoes	million pairs	211.0	63.1	203.4
All grains	million tonnes	95.5	47.3	81.2

Sources: Lokshin, *Promyshlennost' SSSR, 1940-1963* (M. 1964), p. 150: *Sel'skoe khozyaistvo SSSR* (M. 1960), p. 24.

trial production 1940-50 (1964, p. 152). Although this figure is inflated by the use of outdated price levels there was significant progress in total output. Such were the advances made, especially in productivity and consequent cost reductions, that subsidies to heavy industry were removed in July 1948. Consumer-rationing was formally abolished by the Council of Ministers on 14 December 1947. At the same time there was a substantial currency reform which was designed to eliminate idle cash balances in the economy, and was therefore a pre-requisite to the ending of rationing. Hoarded cash was converted at a ratio of 10 to 1, state bond holdings at 3 to 1 and saving bank deposits below 3,000 rubles at par. There was no change in price or income levels as a result of this reform; rather the effect was virtually to wipe out the value of hoarded money at a stroke. Above all, this affected the peasants who had been able to accumulate funds from private sales during and after the war. It also substantially reduced state bond payments. Although this reform was necessary to take excess cash out of circulation (fundamental currency reforms designed to stabilise money values and reduce inflationary pressure were widely adopted in Europe at around this time), it can hardly have been calculated to win friends, particularly in the countryside. In the following years, 1947-50, there were regular and systematic price-reductions on consumer-goods with the object of improving (urban) real incomes (Lokshin, 1964, p. 156). This was, indeed, the measurable effect, but in real terms no amount of price-reduction could make up for shortages in supply; rather it aggravated them. However, productivity increases enabled supply to be maintained, so that the 40 per cent reduction in retail prices between 1947 and 1952 did not result in increased shortages (Davies, 1958, p. 318). Price-reductions followed – or perhaps forced – cost-reductions in industry. It is significant that, although shortages remained, there was a deliberate policy of improving real incomes.

The industrial economy grew sufficiently to fund increases in military expenditure brought on by the advent of the 'cold war'. The outbreak of the Korean war disturbed plans for further growth after 1950, and this was one possible reason why there were no plan forecasts published until 1952. However, there is evidence of some deeper internal differences in plan priorities between those favouring the continued dominance of producer-goods, such as Stalin himself, and those favouring more consumer-oriented production, such as Malenkov (Dunmore, 1980, p. 114). The long-run commitment to improving the lot of the consumer, necessarily reversed in the war, was once again evident in the post-war plan, though the outcome was disappointing. Stalin's established dogma was that heavy producer-goods industry would always grow more quickly than light industry. When Voznesensky, head of Gosplan, appeared to question this he found himself on trial, and executed in 1949. Plan-figures for post-1950 development once again emphasised the producer-good sector over consumer-goods (group A to grow by 13 per cent per year, group B by 11 per cent), though after Stalin's death there were some rapid adjustments in favour of consumer-goods.

It is significant, then, that Stalin did not go altogether unchallenged, though the basic structure and priorities of the economy were not substantially changed in his lifetime. Nowhere was this more evident than in agriculture.

Agriculture after the War

Agriculture was the poor relation of the Soviet economy. Although there is considerable uncertainty as to how far the peasants (or some peasants) suffered for the sake of industrial growth there is no doubt that in many respects they remained second-class citizens. They were denied internal passports, most of the social welfare provisions that had been developed for the urban population and even a proper return for their labours. The collective farmers were ultimately dependent for their own incomes on their limited private holdings. It is also beyond dispute that the collective-farm structure was resented by the mass of the peasantry. At the end of the war the excesses of the forced collectivisation were still within living memory. After the war, however, the position was not to get any easier but rather the reverse. In September 1946 a decree on 'measures to liquidate violations of the Kolkhoz charter' was published, to claw back illegal extensions of private holdings of land and livestock (*Resheniya*, vol. 3, 1968, p. 336). Taxes on income from work on private plots were increased in 1948, 1950 and 1951 to discourage too much time being spent on them. Work on the collective holdings was emphasised, yet without reward. Procurement prices for deliveries to the state saw no general increase after 1933, during which time industrial prices multiplied. Prices paid for beef, pork and grain were actually lower in 1952 than in 1940. Cotton and sugar-beet, on the other hand, bore much higher prices, though these crops were largely grown in specialised state farms. And it was on such receipts that payment for labour days ultimately depended. Compulsory deliveries were also levied on the product of the private plot, though most was left for free disposal by the peasants. The lot of the peasants was not alleviated and this in turn had adverse effects on the supply of foodstuffs. The per capita urban supply of bread grains in 1952 was still below 1940 levels, and the urban consumer depended on the free peasant market for almost 50 per cent of meat and milk. In addition to this, marginal supplies of vegetables, especially potatoes, were obtained from urban allotments.

There was not a complete neglect of agriculture, but there was an apparent disregard for peasant interests, and only after Stalin's death could remedial (and urgent) action be taken. In the meantime, administrative measures were adopted. The council for Kolkhoz affairs was established in 1946 to co-ordinate and reinforce political control in the countryside; there were moves towards amalgamating collectives to exploit economies of scale (see below, p. 145), and in 1948 the grandiose scheme for the transformation of nature through large-scale planting of forests. It came to nothing. Perhaps most indicative of Stalinist agrarian policy after the war was the extension of collectivisation to the new Soviet areas in the Baltic, Moldavia and western Belorussia. The collective-farm structure was introduced in these areas with force and, apparently, brutality between 1948 and 1952. There was a cruel logic to the process. It was clearly impossible politically to allow private agriculture to continue in the new areas without threatening the stability of the structure elsewhere. Yet the economic rationale which had been the basis for collectivisation after 1929 was totally lacking twenty years later. Collectivisation had by now become part of Soviet economic ideology and was therefore bound to be imposed with Soviet control. It was extended even to Eastern Europe after 1948, though without universal success. The process was, for example, reversed in Poland.

Stalin died in March 1953. The country was plunged into mourning and his erstwhile colleagues into a scramble for power. There was an immediate consensus, however, that Stalin's henchman, Beria, should be removed before he made a real bid for power himself. He was shot. Stalin left behind him a well-established industrial base, a strong country, a powerful nation in the world. From 1949 it even had the ultimate power of the atom bomb. The country had thus been dragged from its backwardness through a cruel industrial revolution to victory in the Great Patriotic War and virtual parity in the then current cold war. In achieving this Stalin had employed, cruel, dictatorial, arbitrary methods, so long a feature of Russian history. He had been no more tolerant of debate and dissent than the most reactionary of the Tsars, yet had more effective methods for countering such dangers. The analogy with the rulers of old Russia is not inappropriate, for parallels have frequently been drawn between Stalin and autocratic forbears. In pursuit of industrialisation for national aggrandisement Stalin had common objectives with, if radically different methods from, Sergei Witte, Minister of Finance to Tsar Nicholas. Under Witte there was no social ideology of economic growth and development; indeed the social structure and institutions provided many obstacles. Stalinism, as a mutation of Marxism, provided the ideology of rapid industrial growth, and in this prime objective it was successful. Stalin's position, however, had not been absolute. The course of Soviet history in his period of office cannot be explained solely in terms of Stalin's personal power. There were numerous interest-groups and competing agencies. The planning system could not have been put into effect in the way that it was without significant power and influence at the various levels of command, from the ministries (until 1946 they were known as commissariats) to the enterprise. It was the heavy industry faction, which Stalin supported, which had enjoyed most influence. The planning system which had developed was therefore unbalanced, giving excessive priority to producer-goods. Capital was often wastefully employed, whereas light industry was usually more efficient in terms of returns to capital investment. Debates over relative efficiency and plan priorities were to re-emerge, openly, in subsequent years. Above all, under Stalin, agriculture was a seriously neglected sector. Stalin's successors thus faced tasks of continuing development and of correcting distortions from the foregoing regime.

Notes

1. The proportionate destruction was comparable in Poland.

2. At first the Germans were reluctant to employ Russians, as they were regarded as inferior. After 1942, however, orders were given to the effect that Soviet prisoners of war were to be treated as slave labour with absolute minimum of expenditure, and that the Soviet population be exploited to the greatest possible extent. Otherwise there was little by way of true 'exploitation' of Soviet territory by Germany. The net resources taken by Germany from the USSR was considerably less than from other occupied territories (Milward, 1977).

3. The USSR had never adhered to the Geneva Convention.

4. The comments here are based very much on unpublished research by Julian Cooper and Stephen Tupper, which I would like to acknowledge, with gratitude.

6 KHRUSHCHEV IN POWER

When Stalin died he left a power vacuum more intense than that left by Lenin. For a short time Malenkov became both party secretary and Prime Minister, though within weeks, he relinquished his party post to Khrushchev, who then used this position to secure full power. With the ending of the Korean war and a reduction in military demands Malenkov announced price-reductions and production increases of consumer-goods. Khrushchev used this as a platform to attack Malenkov and the latter was forced to resign, in 1955, for 'administrative incompetence'. His post of Prime Minister was taken by Bulganin.

Subsequent years were marked by significant changes. Khrushchev travelled widely at home and abroad and ushered in a period of relative liberalism. In 1956, at the Twentieth Party Congress, he attacked Stalin in the famous 'secret speech'. But the liberalisation was limited. Popular revolt in Hungary was crushed by the Red Army and more modest risings in the GDR in 1953 and Poland in 1956 resulted in changes in government. At home there was concerted reaction to Khrushchev and an attempt to remove him from office in 1957. In resisting this Khrushchev was able to consolidate his own power, replacing his opponents, the 'anti-party' group, with supporters. A year later he took on the position of Prime Minister. None of his opponents was executed, though they were relegated to minor positions.

In October 1964, while Khrushchev was on holiday, there was once more a move against him. A special meeting of the Central Committee of the Communist Party was held, and Khrushchev summoned to appear before it and face his critics. This time he was unable to rally support and was forced to resign, officially on grounds of ill-health.

It is noteworthy that Khrushchev had never been able to establish himself in a position of unrivalled power in the intervening years. The reasons for his fall from grace can be attributed in large measure to failures in economic policy and performance as well as political rivalry. His years in office, however, had also seen some international embarrassment with the Cuban blockade and the ideological rift with China. Under his control the economy had continued to develop but had disappointed the high expectations of the leadership.

Industry and Planning

Khrushchev inherited an atrophied system of economic control and priorities. The changes he made were marginally to affect the priorities but made little ultimate difference to the system of controls, notwithstanding a variety of administrative measures designed to achieve such an end. After his early criticism of Malenkov, Khrushchev was himself to put more emphasis on consumption in the economy of which an increase in food supply was the most essential aspect. However, his interest in agriculture went beyond the question of food supply, for he had a real concern for the peasantry whose miserable condition he had witnessed at first hand. It was significant indeed that Khrushchev made such efforts, while in power, to travel widely within, as well as without, the country. Stalin rarely travelled beyond his own quarters and was accused (by Khrushchev) of being ignorant of real conditions in much of the country. Increases in farm prices and reductions in taxes on private plots marked a change in political attitude to the peasantry and agricultural sector in the economy. These early measures were not of Khrushchev's making, but he continued and extended a generally ameliorative policy to the agricultural population.

Khrushchev's early years were generally successful in dealing with the economy and gave rise to unduly optimistic expectations and, unwisely, forecasts. The sixth five-year plan was approved by the Twentieth Party Congress in February 1956, the occasion of the famous 'secret speech'. It forecast a 65 per cent increase in industrial production (70 per cent group A, 60 per cent group B) and a 60 per cent increase in national income. Real wages for workers were to rise by 30 per cent, and collective farm incomes, in cash and in kind, by 40 per cent. The plan was not fulfilled and was abandoned in favour of a seven-year plan from 1959. Nonetheless real advances were made in the years to 1958. (Table 6.1). Between 1953 and 1958 GNP grew by 6.7 per cent per annum, a rate exceeded only by Japan and West Germany among industrial countries. The industrial economy was continuing to make progress as it had in previous years, with particular success in the producer-goods sector, but consumer-goods output increased also. Real incomes had been boosted by retail price reductions, though this was partially offset by the virtual doubling of compulsory bond sales to make up for falls in turnover tax revenue. Although higher money incomes were not fully matched by increases in the availability of consumer-goods, there was a substantial increase in the volume of retail trade turnover (Table 6.1), including food purchases. The use of 1950 prices, when foodstuffs especially were expensive, exaggerates the increase shown by the retail trade index in Table 6.1, but nonetheless the changes were real and the relative share of the private market in total retail trade declined.

Table 6.1: Main Economic Indicators 1950-64

	1950	1958	1963	1964
National income (Index)	100	229	311	339
Gross industrial production (Index)	100	249	393	421
of which group A	100	263	487	475
group B	100	225	320	332
Gross agricultural production	100	158	157	179
Retail trade turnover	100	248	341	359
Labour productivity: industry	100	180	235	244
agriculture	100	184	206	244
Major products				
Pig iron (million tonnes)	19.2	39.6	58.7	62.4
Steel (million tonnes)	27.3	54.9	80.2	85.0
Mineral fertiliser (million tonnes)	5.5	12.4	19.9	25.6
Electrical energy (million kWh)	91,226	233,371	412,418	458,902
Oil (million tonnes)	37,878	113,200	206,069	223,603
Natural gas (million m^3)	6,181	28,084	89,832	108,566
Coal (million tonnes)	261.1	495.8	531.7	554.0
Cement (million tonnes)	10.2	33.3	61.0	64.9
Automobiles (thousands)	362.9	511.4	587	603
Tractors (thousands) 15-hp units	246.1	419	683.5	715.3
Cotton cloth (million m^2)	2,745	4,308	5,071	5,371
Leather shoes (million pairs)	203.0	355.8	462.7	475

Note: Automobiles include cars, lorries, buses.
Sources: *Narodnoe khozyaistvo SSSR v 1958 g.* (M. 1959): *Narodnoe khozyaistvo SSSR v 1964 g.* (M. 1965): *Narodnoe khozyaistvo SSSR v 1970 g.* (M. 1971) *passim: Razvitie sotsialisticheskoi ekonomiki SSSR* (M. 1965), p. 442.

However, these years were not without problems. Technological innovation and the development of new products were slow. The substitution of plastics for more traditional materials and oil and gas for coal was proceeding at a pace much slower than in the West. More priority was given to these areas in later years. More generally there was evident inefficiency in production. Thus in 1957 a fundamental reform to reorganise the administrative basis of the economy was initiated, with the object of reducing waste and generating greater efficiency in production. But there was a crucial political dimension. Khrushchev attacked the ministerial structure of the economy and ministerial power, and thereby threatened entrenched state interests. In 1956, in an apparent attempt to consolidate state control over the economy the State Economic Commission had been set up. At this time, it must be remembered, Khrushchev did not enjoy individual power in the Council of Ministers, and he sought to resist this extension of ministerial power in the economy by launching an attack on the ministerial structure of control. Industrial ministeries were entrenched interests, discouraging cross-ministerial links, behaving with too high a degree of autonomy. It was, for instance, far easier and more convenient for supplies of raw materials and semi-manufactures to be obtained, as far as possible, from within the same ministry as the productive enterprise concerned. There was thus much duplication and waste. Goods were sent great distances from one enterprise to another in order to avoid going to an alternative supplier within the orbit of a different ministry, which may have been nearer at hand. Among the many examples of such waste that Khrushchev referred to was the case of a ministry bringing prefabrica-ted houses into Krasnoyarsk, from great distances. At the same time other ministeries were making prefabricated houses in Krasnoyarsk and sending them out great distances. Such administrative shortcomings were dealt with by administrative reform, when more rational pricing might have been more appropriate. However, clipping ministerial wings could also give more power to Khrushchev, indirectly.

The solution, introduced in 1957, was virtually to abolish the ministries and replace them with a regional organisation. In effect this meant that the industrial enterprise would no longer be responsible to the appropriate ministry but to the appropriate regional economic council or *sovnarkhoz*, a name familiar from the 1920s. The expecta-tion was that a greater degree of enterprise specialisation and co-operation would develop between enterprises producing widely different products but within the same unit of control. A total of 104 regional economic councils was set up, following administrative boun-daries (there were several in the RSFSR, Ukraine and other large republics, and one for each of the smaller republics). The State Economic Commission was phased out, and Gosplan lost much of its powers to the regional economic councils. Twenty-five ministries were abolished. There was, of course, considerable opposition to the reform, which weakened ministerial power and sent the large personnel away from Moscow to the drabness of the provinces.

More seriously, the reform did not tackle economic difficulties at the micro-level. In essence all that the reform achieved was to alter the system of disaggregating the plan. The allocation and supply system was shifted from the ministry to the regional economic councils. Fundamental economic questions remained unanswered, though they were raised and discussed in later years. However, the implementation of a wholesale reorganisation would have done little to aid the smooth running of the plan. The ambitious sixth five-year plan was abandoned, and replaced by a slightly more modest seven-year plan, scheduled to run from 1959 to 1965.

This plan aimed for a growth rate of 8.6 per cent per annum; overall industrial growth of 80 per cent (85-8 per cent for producer goods, 62-5 per cent for consumer goods) over 1958 levels. National income was to rise by 62-5 per cent and all real incomes by 40 per cent. This demanded high levels of investment; capital formation to reach 25 per cent of GNP at factor cost, and labour productivity to rise by 40-50 per cent (*Kontrol'nye tsifri . . . na 1959-65 gg.*, 1958). There was more emphasis on new products; in particular, chemicals (to grow by 300 per cent), artificial fertilisers (by 300 per cent), synthetic fibres, non-ferrous metals, oil and gas. Consumption was to be improved by increasing agricultural production and by further expansion of the housing programme.

Not surprisingly, the plan proved to be unduly optimistic. An index of gross industrial production reached 184 in 1965 (1958 = 100), thus exceeding plan, and national income grew by 59 per cent, little short of the planned figure. But the shortcomings were evident for consumption. The great advances in agricultural production and housing construction made before 1958 could not be bettered, though such levels formed the basis of wildly optimistic forecasts. Khrushchev confidently (and publicly) predicted that the USSR would overtake capitalist countries in output per head, the UK and West Germany by 1965, the USA by 1970! And this was to be achieved with a reduction in the average working week. Such ambitions could not be achieved and were quietly forgotten. Agriculture provided the major disappointment. Against a forecast increase of 70 per cent in gross production from 1958 to 1965 the real increase was only 15 per cent (*SSSR v novoi pyatiletke*, 1966, p. 5).

Economics is about scarcities, yet the constraints imposed by scarcity were apparently neglected. Deteriorating international relations after the Cuban blockade and the building of the Berlin wall, as well as the ideological rift with China, brought greater military demands and an increased burden on the economy. Military expenditure averaged 12 per cent of GNP, 1953 to 1965, or three times the West European level. The space exploration programme, which brought the first 'sputnik' and great international prestige, was enormously costly and a greater real burden than in the USA, which had a GNP about double that of the USSR. The high hopes for consumption could not be met fully. Resources were stretched too thinly. After 1958 agricultural production met with setbacks; clothing output fell below target, though output of consumer-durables increased more in line with plan, from very low levels. Producer-goods industries were persistently able to meet targets not simply because of a high priority but because of accumulated capital and expertise which had resulted from high priority in the past. Productivity improvements were easier to fulfil in heavy industry. The economy was so vast, the industrial structure so complex that adjustments to priorities within the structure could at best be marginal. Heavy capital equipment could not be shifted to consumer-goods production at the stroke of a pen. The technical expertise and talents employed to put a man in space or build a hydro-electric dam could not be used to make shoes.

Retail trade turnover continued to grow after 1958, but at a rate slower than in preceding years (Table 6.2). Income tax, a small enough burden on the average Soviet citizen anyway, could not be abolished as had been the announced intention, but compulsory bond purchases (a disguised form of direct taxation) were phased out after 1958. This was a popular move even though repayment of interest was indefinitely 'postponed'. Personal consumption did increase, though the rate of increase fell below expectations. The currency reform of 1961 which introduced the 'new ruble' at a ratio of 1 to 10, had no effect on purchasing power and no cash balances were lost. Price reductions and wage increases extended purchasing power (the problem was to increase production to match it), and private savings grew. Savings banks provided credit for state and co-operative enterprises, and from 1959 there was limited personal credit made available for the purchase of consumer-durables. A fall in the effective tax burden on the population, including the peasantry, also resulted from the cuts in turnover tax, used to reduce retail prices. Turnover tax continued to provide the major source of state revenue but industrial profits were becoming increasingly important (Table 6.3). The economic advances made should not be underestimated. Khrushchev had overestimated them and mistakenly supposed that early promise, before 1958, could be maintained and improved.

The slackening in growth came just at the time when Khrushchev was expressing his highest expectations for both industry and agriculture. After 1958 the overall growth rate declined to a level nearer that of other industrial economies. From 1958 to 1965 the annual average growth rate was 5.2 per cent compared with 5.1 per cent for France and Italy, 4.8 per cent for West Germany, 4.5 per cent for USA and 9.6 per cent for Japan (Cohn, 1970, p. 45). The USSR was among the European leaders, but the small deceleration suggests that the economy was much nearer to a stage of maturity with a tendency for growth to come much nearer to West European levels after the rapid 'recovery miracles' of the 1950s.

Table 6.2: Retail Trade Turnover 1958-64 (at 1958 prices) (state and co-operative trade only)

1958	=	100		1962	131
1959		108		1963	137
1960		119		1964	145
1961		124			

Source: *Razvitie sots. ekon.* (M. 1965), p. 444.

Table 6.3: State Budget Revenue (per cent)

	From turnover tax	Profits
1950	55.8	9.5
1955	43.0	18.2
1958	45.3	20.1
1960	40.7	24.2
1962	39.0	28.2
1964	37.5	31.4

Source: *Razvitie sots. ekon.* (M. 1965), p. 475.

However, the substantial diversion of income to consumption and services, evident in Western Europe, was not so apparent in the Soviet Union. The supposed superiority of the Soviet system in achieving limitless growth had become seriously at question. This was not for the want of overall investment; Western estimates put the rate of capital formation between 1953 and 1965 at 23 to 24 per cent of GNP at factor cost (Maddison, 1965, p. 119) (equivalent to nearer 30 per cent at Western market price levels), a rate well above West European levels and comparable with absolute levels in the much richer USA. The underlying problem in this sense was the waste and inefficiency in the Soviet economy. The growth of earlier decades had been achieved by huge infusions of capital and labour. Growth in the 1950s and 1960s was much more the result of improvements in labour productivity, but there was a tendency for the capital-labour ratio to rise. The incremental capital-labour ratio increased from 6.9 per cent per annum, 1950 to 1958, to 15.7 per cent between 1958 and 1964. The capital-output ratio was also tending to rise. Thus the increases in labour productivity were expensive, and the USSR was being 'out-performed' by a number of capitalist countries (Table 6.4). The Soviet figure for output per man-hour is higher than per employed person because of the reduction in average working hours in this period.

Table 6.4: Growth Rates of Real GNP (annual average) 1953-65

	Per employed person (%)	Per man-hour
USSR	3.8	5.2
France	4.6	4.6
West Germany	4.6	5.4
Italy	4.3	4.5
USA	2.3	2.2
UK	2.4	2.7
Japan	7.7	7.8

Source: A. Maddison, *Economic Growth in Japan and the USSR* (1969), p. 109.

Soviet indices of labour productivity show increases for all workers in state industry of 136 per cent from 1950 to 1963 (*Promyshlennost' SSSR*, 1964, p. 56). Even so, in 1963 productivity remained only about 40-50 per cent of American levels so that output was considerably behind the USA, though there were more workers in the USSR (*Promyshlennost' SSSR*, 1964, p. 478). On the eve of Khrushchev's fall from power the anticipated relative progress of the USSR had clearly not fulfilled expectations, as real as the improvements had been in themselves. The furnace of growth could not burn simply on constant stoking with capital, and the dynamic of the mass consumer market, which came to be important in generating further expansion in the post-recovery period in Western Europe, was lacking in the Soviet Union.

It was clear that there was much capital wastage. This was nothing new, but efforts to tackle the problem were to become so. The problem of capital inefficiency had been evident from the 1930s, but under Stalin few had dared to point it out. In any case, the high rate of investment had been successful in achieving substantial rates of growth. This indeed was one of the problems: high rates of capital formation had become established within the political doctrine.

The concern over returns on capital investment was one of the main subjects of the active debate on economics and planning that developed in the early 1960s. The best-known contributor to the debate was Professor Liberman of Kharkov, and his name has been associated with reformist ideas that emerged, though there were many other contributors. The significance of most of the ideas floated (by Liberman, Trapeznikov and such notables as Kantorovich and Nemchinov) was their primary concern with micro-economic levels, i.e. the enterprise. It was thought that alleviation of plan anomalies at this level would have favourable consequences throughout the economy through greater efficiency and reduction in waste. The second major significance was that the solutions suggested to the various anomalies were essentially economic rather than administrative. The whole planning system hitherto had depended on administrative measures to deal with local planning problems and indeed the effective implementation of economic management. Khrushchev was no different, in this respect, from Stalin. His 'remedies' amounted to tinkering with administration. His partial recentralisation of economic control in 1962 can be seen as a response to the beginnings of public debate about long-run economic problems. The number of regional economic councils was reduced to forty-seven, an economic council for the whole of the USSR, with responsibility for current planning, was established and, from March 1963, the supreme economic council (*VSNKh*) reappeared, with responsibility for long-range planning. These reforms were to misfire, because they were misdirected; Khrushchev's major contribution was to create the environment wherein public debate on economic matters could take place.

It would be a mistake to gain the impression that the 'reformers' spoke with one voice. Some advocated increased centralisation of control using computers to balance input and output for enterprises in physical terms (i.e. making the established system of 'material balances' work better); some advocated computerisation without centralisation; others wanted planning in value terms. Liberman's ideas were first put forward in articles in *Kommunist*, the leading ideological journal, in 1956 and 1959, but the main and best-known thesis was published in *Pravda* in September 1962. Appearing in such publications the flotation of these ideas can only have had support at the highest level.

Liberman's major suggestion was that the enterprise manager should be given an easier task in plan fulfilment by a reduction in the number of plan indicators. It was often impossible to reconcile different plan indicators at the micro-level, finance plans being inconsistent with physical output or inadequate material supplies being made available. Rewards for overfulfilment naturally led managers to underestimate their capacity and go for an easy output plan. The result was often excess production and waste. Further, there was no charge for the time capital was tied up in production, which encouraged inefficiency in its utilisation. Thus Liberman suggested that the enterprise plan be expressed in one criterion only, the rate of profit, and that maximum rewards be given for fulfilling and not overfulfilling the plan. There would thus be more incentive for the manager to aim for optimum production levels and greater efficiency. Implicitly the need for a rate of interest was raised, and this was made explicit by Academician Nemchinov. Coming from such a prestigious person the suggestion caused a stir, especially as it was contrary to the dogmatic notion of the labour theory of value. But Nemchinov was moderate in advocating decentralisation. In his view central control should be maintained but the central plan should do less, confining itself to setting major targets and the most important prices. If profitability was to be crucial (and it was to be in Nemchinov's scheme) then clearly rational pricing was necessary. Prices had always been arbitrarily fixed at the centre. Kantorovich now advocated rational pricing to reflect relative scarcities, measure true production costs and opportunity costs.

Such radical suggestions did not go by without opposition, the 'debate' had many sides. And no action to implement reform was taken until after Khrushchev's removal from office, and then only on a limited scale. There was no suggestion that planning should cease, rather it should be made more efficient by concentrating on long-term and macro-economic objectives. The productive unit should operate more within a quasi-market place, subject to economic controls such as taxation, interest charges and prices. Khrushchev had not created the planning system. It had evolved in an environment quite different from that obtaining in the late 1950s and early 1960s, by which time the economy had become infinitely more complex than a generation earlier. No amount of administrative tinkering could remove the rigidities of the system as it was.

The extended, and officially sponsored, debate about the future of planning and control in a socialist economy was not confined to the USSR. Indeed earlier ideas had developed in Poland, Czechoslovakia and Hungary, and later reforms in those countries were to take on a more extreme tinge. The wide range of ideas had a common element of emphasising costs against physical measures of output and once again acknowledging a law of value. Thus the debate has been likened in historical significance to the great debates of the 1920s. In the Soviet Union the debate was timely. As growth began to level off more attention was being paid to optimising returns to scarce economic resources.

Industrial objectives under Khrushchev, however, did not represent a radical departure from established doctrine. Investment in consumer goods industry increased but remained at modest levels: from 9.7 per cent of the total between 1951 and 1955 to 12.9 per cent from 1955 to 1960 (*Istoriya*, VI, 1980, p. 315). More significantly, the long-run intention of concentrating new industrial development in regions east of the Urals was maintained and achieved with more effect than in earlier years. This policy of industrial location has shown long-run continuity (see p. 86). It may be argued that Khrushchev's regional basis of planning was, in part, designed to such an end. Production of construction materials, such as cement, was more evenly distributed regionally and new construction of heavy industry was concentrated in eastern regions, near to sources of raw materials. This was particularly evident in ferrous metallurgy and in chemicals. The oil and natural gas deposits of the Volga basin had been developed first during the war, 1941-5, when the Caspian oil-fields were under threat, but their full exploitation came about after the war. Taking eastern areas as a whole (i.e. east of the Urals, but excluding the Urals industrial region itself) they contributed 21.1 per cent of total industrial production in 1960 compared with 17.5 per cent in 1950 (*Istoriya*, VI, 1980, p. 455).

Such developments in turn required improved transport facilities, to overcome bottlenecks which had been so evident in the first decade of planning. In the 1950s, 7,300 km of new railways were built, as well as over 33,000 km of trunk roads. Between 1960 and 1970 over 9,000 km of railways were added and a massive 240,000 km of hard surfaced road, nearly all of which was improved rather than newly built roadways. The greater part of railway construction was in Siberia, Kazakhstan and the Urals region. In addition, there were extensions of oil and gas pipelines (of nearly 15,000 km in the 1950s, 20,000 km in the 1960s). Oil and gas are easier and cheaper than coal to transport, and provide a more varied raw material. Under Stalin, oil had been relatively neglected with coal taken as the major prime source of energy. In 1950 coal provided two-thirds of total energy production. In subsequent years oil was more fully exploited, so that by 1970 it provided a larger share of energy supply (38 per cent) than coal (34 per cent).

Industrial growth was by no means confined to eastern areas. The main concentration of population, and therefore of markets and labour supply, remained in European Russia. Light and consumer goods industries were much more dependent on local resources and markets. More notably the greater part of engineering and machine-making was oriented more towards markets and labour skills than raw materials. Thus specialised and technologically advanced industry was more likely to grow in areas of well-developed labour skills. This is the major reason why there was such a rapid rate of industrial growth in western areas such as Estonia, Latvia and Moldavia (newly incorporated into the Soviet state after the war), Belorussia and the Ukraine. New automobile works, making buses, were built in the Ukraine and Belorussia, agricultural and electrical engineering developed in Estonia and Latvia, food-processing in Moldavia.

Agriculture

When Stalin died there was no political dispute over the need for urgent measures to improve the lot of the peasantry. Procurement prices had changed hardly at all since 1933; between 1949 and 1953 grain output was only 12 per cent above the 1909-13 level (when there had been substantial exports) and per capita production was obviously very much lower. A special plenum of the Central Committee, called in September 1953, agreed higher prices, especially for meat, milk and vegetables. Outstanding debts were cancelled and taxes on income from private plots were reduced. None of these measures resulted in any increase in state retail food prices. Khrushchev set out both to increase peasant income and to increase production. His policies met with both great success and abject failure, and were probably instrumental in his eventual removal from office in 1964.

Increases in total production and food supply were spectacular in the early years – to 1958 – but the momentum could not be maintained. Most of this increase was attributable to bringing new areas into cultivation for food crops and extending fodder production elsewhere to improve animal-product output. The best-known project was the 'virgin lands' scheme, which involved ploughing up previously unexploited land or land which had been left fallow for thirty years or more (*zalezh*).[1] These areas were in Kazakhstan and the eastern region of the RSFSR (Siberia, the Urals). The original intention in putting these areas under the plough was to achieve a short-term boost to production while freeing some western areas to produce more fodder, and to allow time for intensification and productivity increases in the traditional wheat-growing regions of the Ukraine. The extension of sown area was therefore something of a stopgap measure and can only have had a once-and-for-all effect. This expectation also accounted, in the short run, for the continuous cropping monoculture that was adopted, which was to produce diminishing returns and later more serious consequences.

The programme was initiated in 1954 and by August of that year 3.6 million hectares of land had been newly sown. Opening new areas brought out a pioneering spirit. New farm-centres were established literally in the middle of nowhere and workers (many of whom were quite genuine volunteers, it seems) lived in tents or other makeshift accommodation. Logistically, the creation of a farming system in these remote areas in such a short time was a major achievement in itself. In terms of production also the achievements were spectacular. By 1958 the virgin lands had 41.3 per cent the total area sown to grains (80.7 million out of 195.6 million hectares) or 65.3 per cent of the area under wheat (Kulikov, 1979, p. 7). The virgin lands accounted for all the increase in grain production from 1954 to 1958 (Table 6.5). Indeed, grain production in the traditional areas declined in these years. The adventurous scheme certainly seemed to be paying dividends. Farms in the virgin lands regions had high average delivery ratios (*tovarnost'*). In 1958, 72 per cent of their production was delivered to the state compared with 45.9 per cent for all state farms and 28.8 per cent for collective farms (Kulikov, 1979, p. 10). Great hopes and expectations were therefore placed on future production. This proved to be mistaken.

Table 6.5: Virgin Lands: Production and Procurement of Grain (all grains)

	Sown area (million hectares)	Gross harvest (million tonnes)	as percentage USSR total	As percentage total state procurements
1950	32.4	25.6	31.5	35
1960	60.3	58.7	46.8	62
1961	60.5	50.6	38.8	45
1962	65.9	55.8	39.8	48
1963	65.0	37.9	35.3	37
1964	65.8	66.4	43.6	55
1970	59.7	74.2	39.7	52

Source: *Sel'skoe khozyaistvo SSSR* (M. 1971), pp. 158-60.

The year 1958 marked a peak, not a breakthrough – a tragic miscalculation which caused unrealistic optimism about future food production to be expressed in the seven-year plan from 1959. Diminishing returns had already started to set in before 1958, yields in the new areas declining after 1956. In fact, average yields were relatively low, at 7.9 centners per hectare, 1954 to 1960 (Kulikov, 1979, p. 7) against more than 10 centners national average for the same years. The natural fertility of the soil was quickly being exhausted by continuous cropping, yet the programme was maintained, not through ignorance but rather through determination to maintain the overall expansionary effort in the face of disappointments in raising productivity. The virgin lands had become an essential food-producing area, and their exploitation had to be continued. Thus declining yields actually demanded further expansion of sown area to maintain production. There were crop losses because of weeds and, more seriously, wind erosion. The new lands are particularly dry – one reason why they had remained uncultivated – and, like much of the country, subject to periodic strong winds. These dangers were well known but warnings were apparently ignored. Deep ploughing was used, which only loosened the top soil, and continuous cropping maintained by order in the face of expert advice. Strong winds struck in 1960, creating vast dust-storms. Again in 1962 and 1963 local dust-bowls were created in Kazakhstan. In Pavlodar *oblast* in 1962, 1½ million hectares of land were stripped of top-soil, all of which added to the calamitous results of 1963, after which grain imports from the West were required.

The virgin lands scheme did not solve the problem of food supply despite the great advances made, and it proved extremely expensive. The cost of opening the new areas involved heavy capital expenditure, above-average labour costs (though there were huge numbers of student 'volunteers' to help with harvests), vast infrastructure investment and the opportunity cost of diverted resources from traditional grain regions. A recent and detailed study of the virgin lands programme has calculated that losses on the investment set in after 1962 (McCauley, 1976, pp. 147-52), and a Soviet analysis points out that untapped sources of land were exhausted so that further production increases would depend on improving yields (Kulikov, 1979, p. 16). Nonetheless the programme cannot be regarded as a failure. There was a substantial increase in overall production, which has remained. In many ways the policy was mishandled, being introduced too hurriedly and with too little consideration for natural obstacles. For ignoring good counsel and the resultant waste Khrushchev must take the ultimate responsibility.

Almost as ambitious as the virgin lands programme was the maize campaign. The maize area was expanded to increase fodder supply, a reasonable policy and common practice in Western Europe and North America, but the programme was overdone and spoiled by ineptness. Increasing peaks of sowings were reached in 1955, 1960 and 1962. Maize became almost a mystical crop to be grown everywhere, including the Baltic and far north, where it was quite unsuitable. By 1962, 37 million hectares had been sown of which 7 million were to produce ripe maize, 7 million unripe and 23 million maize for silage. The main success of the policy was in improving on the 'grasslands' scheme adopted under Stalin, with conspicuous lack of success, to increase fodder supply. Between 1953 and 1959 meat production increased by 53 per cent and milk by 69 per cent, mostly because of the increase in silage feed, of which maize constituted 90 per cent (UN, 1961, 4, p. 9).

After the peak of 1962 the maize area contracted to reasonable levels. In principle, the maize campaign was sound and in effect largely successful. But the manner of its implementation illustrated ill-directed administration and clumsy intervention which inhibited best use of resources. Neither did it provide the hoped-for breakthrough, since fodder shortages, although alleviated, persisted.

The State and Co-operative Sectors

The division of agriculture into the state (*sovkhoz*) sector and the co-operative collective farms (*kolkhozy*) presented an economic and ideological dichotomy. Collective farms have never been part of the state socialist sector, collective farmers never state employees. Thus various moves to bring collective farmers more within the state orbit were tried under Khrushchev, both to 'proletarianise' the peasantry and for more rational economic reasons. The number of collective farms was reduced by converting some to state farms and through a process of amalgamation, with the object of bringing their size to an optimum 2,500 to 3,000 hectares, and so exploit economies of scale. State farms had grown slowly in number largely because of their costs — a result of inelastic wage costs and higher capital input. Nonetheless, in the 1950s and 1960s their numbers were increased, through conversion and because many of the new farms on the virgin lands were state farms. By 1960 they had an aggregate sown area equivalent to more than half the total for collective farms. By 1970 the figures were almost level (Table 6.6). State farms had, on average, higher levels of productivity than collective farms but higher fixed costs. As late as 1960 it

Table 6.6: Collective and State Farms

	Collective farms[a]				State farms			
	Number (thousands)	Average sown area (thousand hectares)	Average No. households	Tractors[b] (15 hp)	Number	Average sown area (thousand hectares)	Total No. workers[c] (millions)	Average[b] tractors (15 hp)
1927-8	14.8	0.04	13	0.2	1.4	0.8	0.3	2
1940	235.5	0.5	81	2.4	4.2	2.8	1.8	24
1950	121.4	1.0	165	6	5.0	2.6	2.6	26
1960	44.0	2.7	383	24	7.4	9.0	6.7	103
1965		2.9	421	38		7.6		114
1970	33.0	3.0	431	60	15.0	6.2	9.8	123

Notes: a. Agricultural collectives only — excludes the small number of fishing collectives. b. Tractors are converted to 15-hp units. The real numbers are much smaller because of increasing power output, e.g. in 1960 there were 4.7 tractors per collective, 5.5 per state farm. For collective farms tractors numbers, before 1960, include those in MTS. c. Includes all state agricultural enterprises.

Source: *Sel'skoe khozyaistvo* (M. 1971), pp. 10, 11, 13.

was reported that two-thirds of state firms were operating with sub-stantial losses (Zoerb, 1967, p. 102). The process of conversion tailed off thereafter, presumably because marginal returns had been exhaus-ted. Thus state farms were important in some specialised production, such as urban milk supplies, while mixed farming remained the pro-vince of the collectives.

Capital investment increased substantially under Khrushchev. The amount of machinery in use doubled between 1950 and 1958. Combine-harvesters numbered 180,000 in 1958 against 30,000 in 1950 (Khlusov, 1977, p. 258). The lion's share of this investment went to state farms. Under the seven-year plan state farms were to receive more investment than any industry save chemicals. This latter industry was itself to serve agriculture with the provision of artificial fertiliser, the application of which was planned to increase from 10.3 million tonnes in 1958 to 31 million in 1965 (*Kontrol'nye tsify na 1959-65*, 1958, p. 54). The optimistic expectations on productivity increases were not met, however. As co-operative enterprises, collective farms were largely responsible for funding their own investment, and the effective finan-cial burden this involved was aggravated with the abolition of the MTS in 1958.

The MTS had been the main agent for providing collective farms with machinery, but increasingly after the war their running costs had outstripped revenue, and were funded from the budget. Thus, in part to save this drain on expenditure, the MTS were scrapped and their machinery sold to collectives. This put poorer collectives under finan-cial strain, further aggravated by having to employ some of the MTS technical personnel. Subsequent demand for new machinery tailed off so that, ironically, the provision of equipment in many cases deteriora-ted. General standards of technical maintenance fell, at least in the short term, as the scheme was pushed ahead too quickly — only thirty-four MTS remaining by the end of 1959. The Repair and Technical Stations (RTS), established in their stead, were a flop and were soon replaced by a state-sponsored servicing unit. This was yet another example of a misdirected policy. Though the immediate objective of saving state costs was evidently achieved, the collective farm peasants were little nearer to the status of state employees.

Attempts to lure peasants away from a private property mentality were nowhere more evident than in the policy towards the private holdings, though this was in itself inconsistent. Between 1953 and 1955 reductions in taxation and compulsory deliveries indicated a conciliatory attitude. In 1958 compulsory deliveries from the private plot were dropped altogether and incentive prices paid to attract voluntary sales. Local pressure, however, persisted to maintain some minimum delivery to the state from private holdings after this date (Wadekin, 1973, p. 275). However, at the same time there were attempts to limit the extent of private holdings of land and livestock. The size of the permitted private plot was linked to the amount of work done in the collective fields. Permitted livestock holdings were reduced and, in 1959, private holdings by urban workers were prohibited altogether. It was consistent with the optimism of the time that the socialised sector was expected to provide the increases in food supply, and that the disincentive to work on private holdings would be as good as an incentive to work harder in the collective holdings. But it was not to be. The successful production of more fodder helped to increase meat and milk, but there was little net increase in livestock numbers on collective farms, the privately owned numbers going down as collective herds increased (Table 6.7). In effect, a margin of private livestock was transferred from the collective farmers to their respective collective farms. State farms showed an increase though there was an all-round fall in the number of pigs because of the widespread slaughter after the poor harvest of 1963.

Table 6.7: State, Collective and Private Livestock (millions)

		Cattle	of which cows	Pigs	Sheep
State farms	1959	8.2	2.8	8.1	26.2
	1961	16.5	5.7	15.9	33.6
	1964	24.1	8.6	11.7	46.8
Collective farms	1959	32.1	11.5	23.1	73.8
	1961	36.2	12.8	27.4	71.3
	1964	37.3	13.8	16.0	60.6
Privately owned	1959	20.3	12.7	11.1	22.1
by collective	1961	15.0	10.4	10.3	19.5
farmers	1964	14.7	9.5	8.7	17.5

Sources: *Narodnoe khozyaistvo SSSR v 1958 g.* (M. 1959), pp. 447-8: *Sel'skoe khozyaistvo* (M. 1971), pp. 246-9.

The policy of discriminating against private holdings underestimated the importance of personal ownership to the collective farmer and, more particularly, the importance of private holdings in peasant consumption. Thus, reducing private holdings simply increased demand for vegetables, meat and milk through the state and co-operative network without there being a comparable increase in productive resources.

Despite the negative policies the private holdings account for 90 per cent of the potatoes, vegetables, fruit, meat, eggs and milk consumed by collective farmers themselves between 1959 and 1964 (Wadekin, 1973, p. 56). Khrushchev's attack on the private sector was arguably the most serious error in his agricultural policy.

After 1960 criticisms of the private holdings from the centre were relaxed, though at a local level they continued. The contribution of the private collective farm market to total retail supplies fell absolutely as well as relatively after 1958, so that when disaster struck in 1963 there was only a reduced private sector to help meet the shortages. It is significant that after Khrushchev's removal there were renewed and rapid concessions to the private sector.

Despite the strong and genuine concern with agricultural affairs Khrushchev failed to meet his own high expectations, and because he took such a personal interest in agriculture he must bear a deal of personal responsibility. Yet his policies were far from failures. Production increased substantially (Table 6.8) and the new areas brought into cultivation in the virgin lands and the great increase in fodder supply from the maize campaign were prime contributors to this. But these essentially sound ideas were disturbed by administrative interference. An apparent obsession with reorganisation of control systems served to disorganise. His policies failed to meet the expectations put upon them so that there was no great breakthrough in consumption levels to match those in the West. Khrushchev's mistakes and vagaries of climate conspired to unseat him when the country was forced to import large quantities of food after the disastrous harvest of 1963. But the gains made by Khrushchev indicate a totally changed priority to agriculture which has continued.

Khrushchev's Achievement

Khrushchev is remembered with affection in the West. After years of darkness he presented an open and often smiling face. At various times he was benign, bombastic, gregarious and entertaining, qualities not readily associated with Russian political figures. In his home country, on the other hand, his memory is more one of embarrassment, and one all but expunged from official history.

The performance of the economy in his years in office was far from negligible; nonetheless it fell short of the high expectations Khrushchev

Table 6.8: Agricultural Production 1950-64

	Gross harvest all grains (million tonnes)	Average yield (centner per hectare)	State procurement (million tonnes)	Meat[a] (carcass weight million tonnes)			
				Total production	State farms	Collective farms	Private holdings
1950	81.2	7.9	32.3	4.9	0.25	1.1	3.3
1953	82.5	7.8	31.1	5.8	0.4	2.1	3.0[b]
1958	134.7	11.1	56.6	7.7	0.9	2.4	4.1[b]
1960	125.5	10.9	46.7	8.7	1.4	3.2	3.6
1961	130.8	10.7	52.1	8.7	1.6	2.6	3.9
1962	140.2	10.9	56.6	9.5	1.8	2.9	4.2
1963	107.5	8.3	44.8	10.2	2.1	3.1	4.4
1964	152.1	11.4	68.3	8.3	1.7	2.5	3.4

Notes: a. Figures are rounded. State farms (*sovkhozy*) proper do not account for all state enterprise production; therefore the three smaller figures do not sum exactly to the total. b. Residual figures, including private holdings within collective farms and by other citizens.

Sources: *Narodnoe khozyaistvo SSSR v 1958 g.* (M. 1959): *Sel'skoe khozyaistvo* (M. 1971), pp. 152, 289.

himself expressed. There were two clear achievements, both of them intertwined with widely acknowledged failures. First, the consumer got a much better deal. Real incomes increased, even though consumer-goods production did not match expectations and came nowhere near the wild claims of the seven-year plan. Per capita private consumption increased by 5.5 per cent per annum, 1950-65. More consumer-durables were made available, many for the first time. The second main achievement was in agriculture — paradoxically, for this was also the area of considerable failure. Khrushchev's policies did not solve agricultural problems absolutely but they did mark a change from using the agricultural sector as a source of supply pure and simple to a position whereby agriculture and the agriculturalist received substantial increases in capital and income. Peasant incomes increased substantially and agriculture took a far higher priority in the economy than under Stalin. Its position has not been eroded since Khrushchev's fall.

Thus Khrushchev's years signalled an adjustment in priority; corrective measures, overdue yet previously impossible under the strictures of Stalin. The basis of the system, established by Stalin, remained unchanged, however. Extensive tinkering did little to alter the basic structure and at times inhibited its operation. Perhaps Khrushchev's most important legacy was the liberal environment he allowed to develop which fostered debate about the nature and organisation of the planning system. This provided the basis for experimental reforms adopted after Khrushchev's demise.

Note

1. For convenience the term 'virgin lands' is used throughout.

7 AFTER KHRUSHCHEV

After being forced to resign in 1964 Khruschev retired with grace and a pension, to lead an untroubled and untroublesome life. The post of Prime Minister was taken by Alexei Kosygin; Leonid Brezhnev became Party Secretary and, in 1977, President. It was Brezhnev who held the greater power to the extent that there were suggestions of neo-Stalinism emerging. The invasion of Czechoslovakia in 1968 and of Afghanistan in 1979, with consequent reversals of international attempts at 'detente', lent credence to this view, though in economic terms there was little to support it.

In the realm of the economy Khrushchev's successors set out to achieve essentially similar objectives but by different means. The prime task was to make the economy function more effectively at reduced cost — produce more for less and thereby increase real incomes. Costs were becoming much more of a constraint. In the past, under Stalin, it had been possible to overcome them by coercion or forced labour. Khrushchev had established a degree of liberalism which made such methods no longer possible, if indeed they had been desirable. It was now increasingly necessary to go for cheaper, more effective productive options. To do so, the new leaders moved away from Khrushchev's pattern, quickly correcting some of his policies, especially in agriculture. The regional economic councils (*sovnarkhozy*) were abolished and the ministerial structure of control re-established.

Reforms in 1965

Premier Kosygin announced substantial reforms in September 1965 which affected above all the industrial enterprise. As an implementation of the 'Liberman' proposals of earlier years they were somewhat modest, though they moved in the direction of increased managerial autonomy. In summary the reforms contained a reduction in the number of plan indices passed to enterprises: the volume of goods to be sold; the main range of goods to be produced; the size of the wages fund; the planned rate of profit and level of cost accounting (*khozraschet*); payments to and from the budget. Enterprises were further directed as to the volume of centralised capital investments, the introduction of new technology, material and technical supplies. The objects were to simplify the tasks of industrial management, to allow an increased degree of autonomy, to ease the supply and distribution system and eventually to move to wholesale trade. Enterprises would be encouraged to retain more profits (for bonuses and welfare expenditure) and would be required to sell their product. In other words, the profit motive was being implemented and plan fulfilment would depend on the product having an end-use — no more piles of useless goods which in the past had nonetheless met planned output targets. Fixed capital was to be funded through long-term credit, no longer a free grant. Similarly, working capital was provided on credit, not from the budget. Capital therefore bore a charge.

The reform 'system' was introduced experimentally in two textile factories before September 1965 and thereafter steadily extended, though still on an experimental basis. By mid-1966, 430 factories were affected. At first there was a particular emphasis on light industry and consumer-goods, with apparent success in achieving above-average labour productivity and profits. From 1967 the reform was extended to all branches of industry, so that by the beginning of 1970, 41,000 industrial enterprises were affected, accounting for 93 per cent of factory production. The reform was least-developed in the less industrialised republics — Azerbaidzhan, Kirgizia, Turkmenistan and Armenia (Beilina, 1976, p. 108). Even state farms were included (Lavrent'ev, 1970, p. 38).

Although reform was most significant for the factory they were not confined to this level. A new 'all-union' or national body was set up, the state committee for material supply or *Gossnab*, to administer the supply plan drawn up by *Gosplan*. This did not seem to square with moves towards wholesale trade. One of the problems was that there was no real wholesale market, there usually only being a single specified supplier of any requisite goods. Thus another bureaucratic element was built in.

The extent of administrative complexity has long been recognised and, as an extension of the reform, measures have been taken to alleviate it. Put very simply, economic control (through the plan elements) was implemented through the appropriate ministry (at 'all-union' or republican level) to the enterprise or productive unit, via an appropriate ministerial department of *glavk*. Through the 1960s amalgamation of enterprises producing similar goods to 'firms' (*firmy*) was encouraged. By 1969 there were 500 such 'firms'. From 1973 these amalgamations — now renamed productive associations (*ob''edineniya*) — were to become the lowest effective unit of plan control, thus reducing the number from the thousands of enterprises. At the same time it was intended to replace the *glavki* with industrial associations. This process of reform and simplification of administration was incomplete during the course of the tenth five-year plan. Using such means some manpower had earlier been saved reported in the administration of the coal industry (*Ekon. Gaz.*, 1970, 13,p. 15). Similar savings may be applied throughout the economy. Alternatively there is the danger of minor dislocation through yet more administrative measures.

Western commentators have tended to see the reforms as having only a modest effect, either missing the target by being concerned with the enterprise when the real problems lay higher up (Abouchar, 1973) or failing to function properly by continuing to restrict managerial initiative (Schroeder, 1972). There is no doubt that the reforms came at a time of relative crisis. The growth of production from 1963 to 1964 was the lowest of the plan period; real inefficiencies and increasing costs were strongly evident. However, the introduction of the reforms has had no great impact on the economy as a whole, so that many of the entrenched problems have remained. Certainly the reforms were less far-reaching than those adopted in East European countries, Hungary in particular. With such an entrenched and extensive administrative machinery as that obtaining in the USSR, and which was in itself far more deeply rooted for half a century, it was little wonder that the bureaucracy was unwilling to relinquish power or pass responsibility to a mass of smaller units. The Russian state has been highly centralised since the days of Peter the Great. Decentralisation, even if confined to the economic sphere, would not easily be introduced.

In considering the macro-economic developments that took place in the first decade of reform it is not merely the reform that is at issue. Reforms sought to improve the implementation of the plan; they had nothing to do with the priorities expressed therein. Brezhnev has put more emphasis on agriculture (see below, p. 160) to improve consumption and counteract some of the misguided enthusiasm of his predecessor. There was also a continued priority to the 'new' industries, chemicals and petro-chemicals in particular, and to the introduction of new technology. The eighth five-year plan, 1966-70, was in general achieved and it has been claimed that the reform aided the intensification of production which was evident (Beilina, 1976, p. 111). However, similar success cannot be claimed for the ninth five-year plan which failed, by a long way, to achieve its targets. For the first time a higher priority was given to consumer-goods than producer-goods, but the outcome was disappointing (Table 7.1). National income increased by less than 5 per cent per annum, a respectable figure by British or American standards, but well below target, being weighted down by the poor performance of agriculture. Productivity improvements, although substantial, were also below plan. The economy remained extensive, dogged by inefficiencies and diminishing returns. The graph of growth levelled off in the 1960s and no solution was found.

Table 7.1: Economic Indicators 1965-75 (index numbers)

	1970 (1965=100)		1975 (1970=100)	
	Plan	Real	Plan	Real
National income	140	141	138.6	127.5
Industrial production	147-50	150	147	143.2
group A	149-52	151	146.3	145.4
group B	143-6	149	148.6	137.4
Agricultural Production	125	121.4	121.7	101.8
Labour productivity:				
Industry	130	132	138.8	133.8
Construction	125	122	137	128.5
Collective farms		136)	138	107
State farms		138)		102
Real income				
per capita	130	133	130.8	123.9

Sources: *SSSR v. novoi pyatiletke* (M. 1966), pp. 11, 17, 18, 19, 20, 78: *Gos. pyat. plan na 1971-75* (M. 1972), pp. 193, 195: *Nar.khoz. v 1975 g.* (M. 1976). pp. 113, 115: *Raz. ekon. SSSR V des. pyat.* (M. 1977), p. 9.

Economic Performance

The five-year plan directives since 1965 have consistently emphasised improvements in quality and technical specification, with the introduction of labour-saving technology to boost productivity. Engineering was one of the few success stories of the ninth five-year plan, growing significantly faster than industry in general. Instrument-making increased output by more than 200 per cent between 1965 and 1970 (*Gos. pyat. plan.*, 1972, p. 69). In order to improve quality further and extend technological innovation, imported technology was built into the plan for 1971 to 1975 in large measure. Technological innovation has nonetheless been slower in the USSR than in the West. This is not simply that the state of knowledge is lacking in the USSR, for that is far from the case. Rather, relatively simple technology is

..tcomings in quality control are frequently reported. Up to a
..f new tractors are returned to the factory for maintenance
..re being used; a similar proportion of lorries coming off the assem-
..ly line in the Kama river plant are rejected and returned before leaving
the factory. Long delays in breakdown and shortages of spare parts are
frequently reported in the Soviet press. Such shortcomings reflect a
lack of commercial penalty in the planned economy.

Despite reform and the appeals made in the debate preceding them,
prices remain arbitrary and long delays in fulfilling production or, more
particularly, in new developments do not bear an effective cost penalty.
This has been evident in the exploitation of natural resources, on which
the Soviet foreign trading position so strongly depends. Even in the
early 1970s, when concern with despoilation of the environment in the
West was becoming strong, there were naive claims in Soviet publications that such problems would not apply under socialism, where
exploitation of resources was planned. Such views no longer have
serious credence and there has been growing concern with the environment, with protective measures being built into the tenth five-year plan.

Particular stress was laid on the conservation of water resources with
'recycling' of water used in industrial processes and reduction in pollu-
tion levels. It appears that Soviet authorities have come late in the day to
matters of environmental concern and it is too early to judge the effec-
tiveness of recent policies. There is evidence of growing anxiety over despoilation of the environment in non-government circles, even to the point
of a dissident group being organised about the subject. There is, however,
no room for concerted public opposition to nuclear power programmes
as there has been in the West (though with conspicuous lack of success).
Indeed, atomic engineering was one of the highest priority industries in
in the tenth five-year plan. One serious nuclear accident has been unofficially reported, but development of this most potent pollutant force
presses on.

Natural resources lie at the basis of the Soviet economy. Through the
1970s the USSR was the largest producer of coal, oil, iron ore, manganese, chrome ore, potash and phosphates and a major supplier of
natural gas, lead, zinc, copper-nickel, molybdenum, tin and asbestos.
One of the few major industrial raw materials it lacks in quantity is
bauxite. The export of primary products, oil in particular, is the major
source of convertible currency. The dependence on primary products
for export presents major problems as, increasingly, extraction of these
resources is undertaken in remote and inhospitable regions of the country. The Siberian share of total oil production increased from 10 per
cent in 1970 to 30 per cent in 1975. The tenth five-year plan figures

saw bigger increases. Supplies of coal, natural gas and electric power from Siberia have also increased, though by smaller amounts. Siberia was made a priority area under the tenth five-year plan and this was largely because of its abundant wealth in energy and mineral resources, the demands for which are increasing both as absolute demand grows and as earlier developed resources are meeting diminishing returns. Early in 1980 it was reported that average reserves per oil-well were falling (*Ekonomika*, 1980, pp. 66-71); total oil production fell short of target between 1970 and 1975. Only 10 per cent of coal reserves lie west of the Urals, where there is greatest demand, and in 1979 coal output actually declined to 719 million tonnes from 724 million tonnes in 1978.

The response to these difficulties has been to put more capital into exploiting new resources (as in Siberia), transportation systems and alternative sources of energy. Despite consistent measures to develop manufacturing industry near to energy sources in the east, the major area of demand for raw materials and energy has continued to be in the developed European part of the country. Thus a major and growing problem has been the logistical one of transport and distribution of these resources. Underground storage areas for natural gas were enlarged in the tenth five-year plan period and pipelines for oil and gas extended. Further, through the 1970s, oil- and coal-burning power stations have been built in number near to the wells and mines so that electricity can then be supplied through the national grid. As oil prices have shot up there has been more priority to coal-burning, even to the extent of converting existing power stations. Potential in HEP is uncertain. These stations are expensive to build but cheap to operate, the great disadvantage being in the limits on their location. In the 1960s there was some slowdown in HEP station construction, but in the 1970s major new projects were intiated on the Angara and Enisei rivers in Siberia and the Syr Darya in Kazakhstan, the latter to be the world's largest such station with a capacity of 6.4 million kilowatts (*Raz. ekon. v des. pyat.*, 1977, p. 12). Nuclear power stations are also in use, with more planned, ironically perhaps in the country with the greatest reserves of hydrocarbon fuels, but their siting in areas of high demand obviates the need to transport coal or gas over long distances. Even so, under the tenth five-year plan, nuclear power and HEP together were to provide less than 20 per cent of total electricity demand.

Naturally, transport has played a vital part in the extension of economic activity into remote areas. Substantial improvements in railways have been incorporated into recent plans, particularly in the form of electrification and containerisation of goods haulage. The USSR is one of the few major countries where new railway track is still being laid. Between 1971 and 1975, 3,600 km of new lines were brought into use with a further 3,000 km planned in the subsequent quinquennium. Most spectacular is the Baikal-Amur railway (BAM), initiated during the ninth five-year plan, though originally conceived before the war. The BAM will run north of the Trans-Siberian railway to link west of Lake Baikal to the Pacific. It will provide the basis for a new industrial area and provide export facilities for oil and other minerals to Japan. A single track of 3,163 km over difficult terrain is due for completion in 1983. In general, railways are used extensively for freight traffic. The Trans-Siberian line has a container service for trade from the East (principally Japan) to Western Europe. The goods are carried on to Western markets by heavy lorry, thus earning hard currency. Even short-haul goods carriage is largely transported by rail, even though it is more expensive than road haulage. Within the country road transport has been developed slowly, with roads relatively neglected until recent years. In the plan period 1971-5, 117,000 km of roads were built or resurfaced. This exceeded both plan targets and the total figure for the whole of the 1950s. Even so, as late as 1975 only 16 per cent of roads had a hard surface suitable for heavy traffic, the rest being little more than country tracks. Apart from the major highways, the best roads are in the western regions, so that the areas of most recent development are particularly poorly served. Even the new Kama river truck plant was built without adequate road links being established, which is something of a paradox in view of its purpose. From the mid-1960s there has been a far higher priority to road-building and a virtual revolution in road transport. Whereas Khrushchev all but dismissed private transport, concentrating on the provision of public services, since 1966, and the building of the plant at Togliattigrad by Fiat, private car production has multiplied, from 230,251 to 1.3 million in 1978. The production of lorries has been boosted by the Kama river plant.

Construction of this plant began in 1973, being undertaken by the Swindells branch of the American Pullman corporation, and other Western companies. However, Western designers and engineers building the plant were held up for two years before they actually got to the construction site. The whole complex is easily the largest in Europe. In 1976, 5,000 finished units were produced, in 1977 22,000 (*Ekon. Gaz.*, 1978, 8, p. 2). By October 1979 daily output was 240 units with a planned maximum daily output of 500 units. There has, however, been a high rate of rejection of finished lorries. Many more engines than finished trucks are produced and this may be to ensure a supply of spares, given the problems of quality and reliability. On the other hand, it has been suggested that these extra engines might have a military use, though this remains speculative.

Engineering, in its many diverse forms, is the largest single industry in the Soviet Union. The country can also boast the world's largest steel industry. But the foundation industries of steel, coal and heavy engineering have diminished in relative importance as industrial structure has become more complex. In the 1950s and 1960s the fastest-growing industry was chemicals, and chemical engineering, in the 1970s one of the leaders. Total production of the chemical industry grew by almost three and a half times from 1960 to 1970, and doubled from 1970 to 1979. Plastics, artificial fertilisers and synthetic fibres are among the most important sectors of the chemical industry.

The development of resources in eastern regions has, as we have seen, been a long-term policy and one followed with increasing evident success in the years since Stalin's death. This development is likely to become more important to meet the demands of the economy. One aspect of this policy has been the use of regional wage differentials as an incentive to encourage workers to settle in remote areas. Yet, despite these efforts, regional imbalances in income and production levels have continued to be in favour of western regions. The high standards of consumption are to be found in Estonia, Latvia, Lithuania, the western RSFSR and the Ukraine. This reflects relative levels of industrialisation, but that is not the only factor. Estonia is the most industrialised republic of the Union, and most of this development occurred in the 1960s, during which time national income doubled, and subsequently. The Baltic republics were little industrialised before the war, when they were independent. Thus, after the blood-letting associated with their incorporation into the Soviet state, the Baltic republics have, in economic terms, prospered within the USSR. As we have seen, industrial relocation has been marginal in effect so that main industrial centres remain in the west. The Ukraine, with less than 20 per cent of the population in 1970, produced over 40 per cent of the nation's steel, nearly half the coal and a large share of all machinery. Industry is not the only cause of regional differentials; agricultural incomes in the Baltic are above the national average and the Ukraine is also an important agricultural area. In Georgia agricultural incomes (from relatively expensive fruits and vegetables) are significantly higher than those from industry. The poorest republics are, however, those which are the least urbanised and industrialised: Tadzhikstan the poorest in 1970, followed by Azerbaidzhan and Uzbekistan.

Agriculture

After hurriedly correcting some of the eccentricities of Khrushchev's later years Brezhnev saw to it that there was more consistency in agricultural policy. The Ministry of Agriculture was reorganised early in 1965, once again bringing ultimate control of agriculture under a single umbrella. Procurement plans were stabilised and prices increased, without the increase being passed on to the state shops. Thus effective price subsidies, which had been introduced under Khrushchev, were markedly increased, especially on meat, dairy and vegetable products. They reached 4 milliard rubles in 1966, 9.3 milliard in 1971 and 19 milliard in 1977. This is a radical change from earlier years, when food sales constituted the largest source of turnover tax revenue. From July 1966 monthly pay was introduced for collective farmers, so that their pay became first call on resources. This did not represent a fixed monthly wage but rather an advance, though the income was guaranteed. Nonetheless it was an important step in the relative social and economic standing of the collective farm population symptomatic of a conciliatory political attitude. This was further indicated by the provision of pensions and internal passports as a matter of right.

Such policies have had beneficial consequences for total production, though fluctuations, largely for climatic reasons, persist (Table 7.3). There have been both substantial investments in the socialised sector and encouragement for the private sector — the reverse of Khrushchev's policies — as well as extending material incentives. Farms have had more freedom to decide what to grow, with one result in the reduction of the sown area of maize. Livestock production remained important, however. Indeed, in recent pronouncements Brezhnev stated that increasing meat production was to be the top priority (*Pravda*, 4 July 1978). One way of achieving this objective was to allow more private livestock production. After 1964 there were immediate concessions to the private sector, though it took some time for private livestock holdings to recover the damage done to them by Khrushchev. Despite the higher prices for state purchases from the private sector its share in total state procurement declined, because of the growing output from the socialised sector.

The private sector continued and continues to provide a vital share of consumption, especially of perishables (Table 7.2). Even by 1978 most potatoes and a substantial share of vegetables, meat and dairy products were privately produced. Much of this production did not enter the market, of course, being grown for direct consumption, but

Table 7.2: The Private Sector in Agriculture 1950-78

| | Share of total production in private holdings of all kinds (%)[a] | | | | | |
	1950	1960	1965	1970	1975	1978
Grain	7	2	2	1	1	1
Potatoes	73	63	63	65	59	61
Vegetables	44	44	41	48	34	29
Meat	67	41	40	35	31	29
Milk	75	47	39	36	31	29
Eggs	89	80	67	53	39	34
Wool	21	21	20	19	20	19

Note: a. This is a residual figure taking in all non-socialised production, including collective and state farm private plots and urban allotments.
Sources: *Sel. khoz. SSSR* (M. 1971), p. 27: *Nar. khoz. v 1978 g.*, p. 196.

the private sector contributed a vital marginal share of state procurements as well as total consumption through the free market. Measurements of the share of collective farm market sales in total sales of foodstuffs are complicated by there being different price levels and, to a large extent, state shops and free markets selling different commodities. Corrections for these differences to comparable prices and commodities, in Soviet statistical handbooks, suggest that collective farm markets accounted for about 28 per cent of sales in 1950, less than 5 per cent in 1978. Such figures (which would anyway be put higher by some Western estimates) make no allowance for quality and availability. Anyone in the Soviet Union who has tried to buy decent fruit and vegetables, for instance, would know the value of the collective farm market.

The private and socialised sectors have, to a point, been complementary. They tend to produce (or concentrate on) different items. The state procurement and distribution mechanism still calls on the private producer, and the collective farmer can receive certain inputs, such as fodder, from the farm for his privately owned livestock. While the position of the private market has clearly declined, its importance has been officially reaffirmed. The 1969 New Model Charter for collective farms consolidated increases in the size of private plot and linked it to family size. Buildings for markets in main urban centres have been opened or extended, accommodation is provided for market traders in hostels in Moscow, and presumably elsewhere. Investment in agriculture has increased substantially. The following figures of the percentage share of total investment allotted to agriculture were announced by President Brezhnev: during the seventh five-year plan (1961-5), 20 per cent; the eighth (1966-70), 23 per cent; the ninth (1971-5), 26 per cent and the tenth (1976-80), 27 per cent planned (*Pravda*, 4 July 1978). These figures include some non-productive investment such as housing. The figures for productive investment proper (machinery, fertiliser, farm buildings, etc.) were 14.3 per cent in 1961, 17.7 per cent in 1967 (Lemeshev, 1970, p. 111) and 20.7 per cent in 1976-7 (UN, 1979, p. 98). Even these lower figures are extremely high — much more so than in Western economies. Yet even these produce relatively poor results. In 1970 one expert reckoned that the provision of machinery available was one-third of the optimum required (Buzdalov, 1970, p. 76). There is still considerable ground to make up for the years of neglect under Stalin, even a quarter of a century after his death. A considerable proportion of the investment has gone on buildings, for storage and livestock husbandry. The bumper crop of 1973 was too great for the existing storage and transport network. Inadequate lorries and poor roads have often led to high wastage in the past. Brezhnev's 1978 speech emphasised the need to design special heavy-duty lorries for agricultural purposes and improved maintenance standards. The latter point is most important. Buzdalov noted in 1970 that tractors were lasting only 5 to 6 years with up to 300,000 per year falling out of use (1970, p. 76). This compared with a total production in 1970 of 458,000 tractors (*Nar. khoz. 1970 g.*, p. 218). A considerable proportion of new production was, and has remained, for replacement. There have been further complaints of poor design. A recent article pointed out the deficiency in small tractors for use on the private plot (Ivashchenko, *Izvestiya*, 15 August 1979, p. 2). Problems of waste and inefficiency cannot be solved simply by putting in more material resources. Artificial fertilisers have increased yields, yet here again there have been complaints. An article in *Pravda* in May 1979 pointed out the inadequacy of mineral fertiliser. Appearing in such publications, these comments amount to official exhortations to do better.

Despite the great increases in investment, Soviet agriculture remains labour-intensive. The provision of capital per worker is lower than in the USA or Western Europe. Although the share of the labour force in agriculture has fallen, it has done so only slowly by world standards, from 27 per cent in 1970 to 22 per cent in 1977 (agriculture and forestry). The problems are familiar, as the migrants tend to be young, leaving the relatively old on the land. Yet there are seasonal labour shortages when students and soldiers are drafted in to help with the harvest. Ironically, there appears to be labour wastage with numerous specialist employees — tractor drivers, combine operators, etc. In the late 1970s about one and a half million agricultural workers were 'specialists' of some kind, and 20 per cent of the total was classified as machine operators. Specified tasks like these imply a curious degree of demarcation in rural labour, in contrast to Western agricultural employment.

Low labour productivity and an increasing capital-output ratio indicate persisent problems of inefficiency in agriculture. A major problem is the weather. A dry climate leaves a small margin in time of drought. Nonetheless, Soviet wheat-yields fell behind those of the Canadian prairies in the 1970s and were also below yields in neighbouring Poland. Bad weather brought a poor harvest in 1972 and a severe shortfall in 1975, each of which required substantial imports from the West. After cleverly playing the market in 1972, the Soviet authorities were obliged to be more orderly after 1975 and undertake regular, if small, purchases from the USA. It is significant, however, that such purchases can be made with no political consequences at home, though they illustrate that Soviet agriculture is a long way from producing plenty for its population.

Table 7.3 shows a clear upward trend in total production, but one marked by great fluctuations in gross harvest of grain. Western esti-

Table 7.3: Agricultural Production 1965-78

	Grain harvest[a] (million tonnes)	State grain procurement (million tonnes)	Average yield (centner per hectare)	Meat and fat production (million tonnes)
1965	121.1	36.3	9.5	10.0
1970	186.8	73.3	15.6	12.3
1966-70 average	167.6	66.0	13.7	
1972	168.2	60.0	14.0	13.6
1973	222.5	90.5	17.6	13.5
1975	140.1	50.5	10.9	15.0
1971-5	181.6	67.6	14.7	
1976	223.8	92.1	17.5	13.6
1977	195.7	68.0	15.0	14.7
1978	237.2	95.9	18.5	15.3

Note: a. All grains, for human and animal consumption
Sources: *Sel. khoz. SSSR*, (1971), pp. 152, 287: *Nar. khoz v 1973 g.* (1979), pp. 343, 351, 356, 438: *Nar. khoz v 1978 g.* (1979), pp. 194-5, 202.

mates suggest that these gross figures should be reduced by 15 per cent or more to bring them into line with American definitions. Nonetheless, the trend is clear. The main problem has been feed-grains. There is no shortage of bread, but frequent shortages of meat. Meat production has been steadier than grain output, but has grown more slowly. Ironically, after a bad harvest meat supplies can increase as more animals are slaughtered because of feed-shortages. This happened in 1975. It then takes time to build up the herds again. The livestock plans for 1976 to 1980 were much more modest than the previous five-year plan period.

Despite the many shortcomings — climatic, structural and historical — agriculture, the 'problem child' of the Soviet economy, has made substantial progress since Khrushchev's demise. In large measure this can be attributed to extension of a more liberal economic regime and material incentives to the agriculturalists. It is evident that the profound change in political attitude initiated by Khrushchev has been matched by his successors, with stability of policy and improved provision of resources. From being a major source of revenue, agriculture is now a major recipient of subsidy — in the form of investments, cheap credits and grants, as well as price subsidies which are more directly to the benefit of the consumer. Further, there has been much less political interference and more effective autonomy for collective farms and, since 1967, state farms.

The continued need to import remained a problem into the 1980s. Although imports help to overcome domestic shortages, of meat especially, there are, no doubt, higher priorities on the foreign trade list.

Material incentives in production, rather than 'administrative measures', have clearly paid dividends but, given the proven success of the private sector within the USSR and beyond its frontiers, the in-transmutable and ideologically symbolic collectivised structure of Soviet agriculture does little to offset the natural disadvantages of the country.

Summary

Western observers frequently refer to the crisis in the Soviet economy in the late 1970s, partly because of the underfulfilment in the ninth five-year plan to 1975. Output forecasts in the plan quinquennium to 1980 were accordingly more modest. But the main problems evident before 1975 were no less so after that date. The growth of the economy, although faster than in the West, is slow by the standard of Soviet history and current expectation. Severe inelasticities in labour supply put great reliance on improvements in labour productivity, which have been disappointing in the outcome. This may be because too much improvement has been expected in the planned growth figures. There is the further problem of shortages of consumer-goods. Material incentives in the form of higher money incomes have met with a degree of success, but this has been necessarily limited by non-availability of certain goods. Early in 1980 shortages of children's clothes, bed-linen, toothbrushes, light bulbs, etc. were reported in the press. Real unreported shortages may be more severe. The problems are more acute in remote regions, which is where the labour-deficit is at its most extreme. Despite high wages, labour turnover and outward migration from the far north and east are substantial. Yet it is precisely on the production of such areas that future development depends. The exploitation of the natural resources of Siberia and the far east (with 80 per cent of fuel reserves) is necessary to meet the energy needs of the economy and provide vital foreign exchange. Ironically, in order to develop these resources quickly imported technology (particularly Japanese) is required – there being a direct oil-for-technology exchange. No doubt, exploitation and development could proceed without knowledge and equipment imported from capitalist countries, but it would be slower.

Technological innovation has gone ahead at a faster rate in the capitalist world than within the USSR. In particular, the USA has been the fountain of technology and the capitalist market, and the international companies in particular, have enabled new technology to be spread about the world. Some technological shortcomings may be one reason for the continued relative inefficiency of Soviet production.

To secure Western technology the USSR in the 1970s became increasingly indebted to the Western banks and governments. While its credit has remained sound, the need to service such debts has in turn imposed further demands on the economy and in particular on the extraction of oil and other resources. In 1976, 22 per cent of hard currency earnings were required for interest and amortisation payments, and this at a time when, because of rising oil prices, the terms of trade had never been more favourable.

One of the problems long evident in the Soviet economy has been its chronic inefficiency; reforms have not yet overcome the lags and transformed extensive productive techniques into intensive ones. Low maintenance standards and long-neglected infrastructure investment in the past have meant that much investment has been needed for replacement rather than a net addition to capital stock. The scarcity of productive capital has been further exacerbated by the conflicting demands between the high costs of armaments, the huge costs of opening up new areas and resources and the increasing production of consumer-goods. The 'problems' of the modern economy have not been absolute: growth has continued, consumption has improved. Rather, the economy has failed to meet the expectations of the country and of the political leadership, both in the particular — the plan forecasts (the ninth five-year plan being particularly disappointing) — and in the general. In November 1979 President Brezhnev made public criticisms at the failure to meet plan figures. In a speech to the Central Committee of the Communist Party he even went so far as to name the ministers responsible for railways and electric power in criticising the inefficiency of their ministries; not only were consumer-goods in short supply but even coal and oil and, as ever, meat. Plan targets for 1980 were reduced because of the very poor overall showing of industry in 1979. The output of many basic industries showed an absolute fall. As well as coal, steel production fell, 1978-9, from 151 million tonnes to 149 million tonnes, and iron from 111 million tonnes to 109 million tonnes. In 1976 the Prime Minister, the late Mr Kosygin, had looked forward to a period of efficiency and quality, with particular emphasis on improving technical standards and labour productivity. The results have clearly been disappointing. The superiority of the Soviet system in providing plenty, which had been the expectation since the inception of central planning, remained unproven at the end of the 1970s.

8 POPULATION, LABOUR AND INCOMES

Historically, Russia has had a rapidly growing population and an abundant supply of unskilled labour. Under planning, a general labour shortage developed which has not been eased. However, even before the resolution there were cases of local or periodic shortages, particularly of skilled labour. In the 1920s urban unemployment resulted from the continued increase in population and slack demand for labour. The position was changed radically in the 1930s, when unemployment disappeared, millions of peasants entered the industrial labour force for the first time and women took an increasing share of industrial employment. Labour became scarce; the birth-rate declined a little, though it remained the highest in Europe. Welfare facilities for families and children were greatly extended.

The Great Patriotic War caused a severe loss of life, disturbing the birth-rate and balance of the sexes. Although the population recovered, since the war the birth-rate has declined, causing some concern to policy-makers. In the 1960s and 1970s there remained a labour shortage, signs of an ageing population and a diminishing proportion of the population engaged in 'productive' work. The labour shortage has been aggravated by low productivity, particularly in the agricultural sector, where an unusually high proportion of the workforce is still engaged.

Population: General Trends

Table 8.1 shows the main trends in popuation since 1913. Absolute figures have been much affected by boundary changes after 1917 and the Great Patriotic War of 1941-5. Post-war USSR has the largest population of any state after China and India. Nonetheless there is some political concern at the slow growth of population.

Before the revolution the Russian Empire had by far the fastest-growing population in Europe, because of the very high birth-rate. Although the rate of growth slowed after the revolution it continued to exceed that of other European countries, until 1941, again because of a relatively high birth-rate. In 1926 the net reproduction rate was 1.72, and even in 1939 it was as high as 1.54, by far the highest in Europe (Kirk, 1946, p. 56). Population growth was checked in these

167

Table 8.1: Soviet Population

Year	Total population (millions)		Urban (%)	Female (%)
	I	I I		
1913	159.2	139.3	18	50.3
1917	163.0		18	
1926		147.0	18	51.7
1939		170.5	33	52.1
1940	194.1		33	52.1
1951	181.6		40	56.0
1961	216.3		50	54.7
1971	243.9		57	53.9
1980	265.5		63	53.3

Note: Figures are for 1 January in each year, except for 1980, which is mid-year. I refers to present (post-war) boundaries of USSR. II refers to pre-1939 boundaries of USSR.
Sources: D. Kirk, *Europe's Population between the Wars* (1946), p. 63: F. Lorimer, *The Population of the Soviet Union* (1946), pp. 66, 147: *Narodnoe khozyaistvo SSSR v 1979 g.* (M. 1980), pp. 7-8.

years by a relatively high infant-mortality rate (at 187 per 1,000 live births in 1926) but more particularly by the effects of the collectivisation campaign, and the subsequent famine of 1932-4. Estimates of the excess deaths resulting directly or indirectly from collectivisation range from one million to 10 million, most being at about 5 million (Dalrymple, 1964, p. 259). The matter is still obscure; Nove suggests that there were 4 million 'kulaks' whose fate remains unclear (1969, p. 180). Recent figures published in a Soviet journal are 115,231 kulak families deported in 1930 and 265,795 in 1931, with a new wave of deportations beginning in autumn 1931 (*Voprosy istorii*, 1975, p. 140). The social and physical upheavals involved in the changed living and working circumstances resulting from the industrialisation drive led to a decline in birth-rate from 45 per thousand in 1926 to 38 per thousand in 1938 (Lorimer, 1946, pp. 87, 131). Total population growth between the census years 1926 and 1939 was 15 per cent, about the same as the shorter period 1950 to 1959, when the birth-rate was lower. Notwithstanding the decline in the very high birth-rate in the 1920s and 1930s the main check on population was the mortality-rate to which, it may be assumed, collectivisation and the purges of the later 1930s, contributed. Because of its very nature it is impossible to be precise about the effect of the great purge. That the losses were severe is suggested by the suppression of census data in the late 1930s. The census of 1939 was reconducted after initial results.

The Great Patriotic War caused almost unimaginable loss of life. Writing immediately at the end of the war Lorimer estimated a 'demographic loss' (the deficit of births plus the excess deaths compared with 'normal' rates) of 20 million (1946, p. 181). Later census figures have revealed greater real losses. Newth's estimates show an absolute decline of 20 million, 1941-50, for pre-war boundaries (from 198.2 million to 178 million) against an expected increase of 20 million; thus a demographic loss of 40 million (Newth, 1964, p. 347. Table 8.1 shows an absolute decline of 12 million for post-war boundaries.) Other estimates are even higher. Eason reckons that there was a demographic loss of 45 million: 25 million excess deaths, and a deficit of 20 million births. (Eason, in Moller (ed.), 1964, pp. 110-11.)

A large proportion of those who died were civilian, which reflects both the cruel occupation and the general deprivation endured by the population in the war years. The losses had a severe sexual imbalance, with male deaths exceeding female by a substantial margin: about one-third of men of working age were killed. The disturbance to the balance of the sexes was such that in 1951, 56 per cent of the population was female, compared with 52 per cent in 1940 and 50.3 per cent in 1913. Even in the late 1970s the ratio of females to males exceeded the pre-war level (Table 8.1). A preponderance of females is a normal part of the natural ageing process of populations, but the differences cannot be explained in this way. A proportion of the excess male deaths may have been accounted for by deaths in camps within the Soviet Union, particularly those who would otherwise have been in the age-cohorts 55-9 and 60-9 in the 1959 census. The male population of these age groups (20 years younger in 1939) were of prime age for arrest during the purges (Conquest, 1973, p. 712).

There was no 'baby boom' in the USSR at the end of the war. Population continued to grow but largely because of declining mortality rates and increased life-expectancy. Increasing urbanisation, rising consumer-expectations and improved contraception appear to have been critical factors in reducing the birth-rate, just as they have in Western societies. The birth-rate fell from 26 per thousand in 1950 to 19 in 1964 to 18 in 1975. Severe housing shortages also appear to have contributed to the trend for family limitation. From having the fastest-growing population in Europe before the war, the USSR has now been overtaken. Total population growth from 1913 to 1965 has been greater in USA, Germany and Japan (Maddison, 1969, p. 157). In the inter-war years countries of high immigration such as USA and Australia had higher rates of population-growth.

Because of the 'overfull' demand for labour in the economy there is virtually a constant shortage of labour. There are various means used to encourage families to have children, ranging from propaganda to material incentives such as a discriminatory 'bachelor tax', family allowances for the fourth child and family-income supplement for larger families. Abortion was legalised in 1918 for health reasons and made readily available in the 1920s as a factor in the liberation of women, but was severely curtailed in 1936 because of concern with the birth-rate. Easy abortion was legalised again in 1955, though there appears to have been no link with changing birth-rates in the latter case. It was more a move to prevent dangerous illegal abortion, and to reassert the freedom of women from unplanned childbirth. Concern with the birth-rate persists, however, and in the 1960s there were even serious suggestions in academic circles that mothers be paid a salary to stay at home and bring up children.

The problems of an ageing population are by no means peculiar to the USSR. More and more pensioners put a greater burden on the working 'productive' population. Soviet pensions have never been generous but were recently increased. In addition, in 1966, collective farm peasants became eligible for pensions, as a result of which total demands have increased. In 1970, 11.8 per cent of the population was aged over 60 (6.8 per cent in 1939) (*Nar. khoz.*, 1970, p. 13) but the proportion of children under 15 had fallen (from 37.3 per cent in 1959 to 30.9 per cent in 1970). The proportion of the total population in the labour force of the national economy and collective farms increased between 1959 and 1970, probably because more pensioners have remained in part-time work, which would be particularly evident in agriculture.

The birth-rate is, and has generally been, higher amongst non-Slav populations than Slav. In 1926 Russians proper (Great Russians) made up about 70 per cent of the total population. In 1959 all Slavs (Russians, Ukrainians, Belorussians, etc.) made up 75 per cent and Russians alone 55 per cent of the total. In 1970 Russians constituted 53.4 per cent of the total. The lowest birth-rates are recorded in the Baltic republics (Latvia and Estonia) and Lithuania, Moscow and Leningrad; the highest in Tadzhikstan, Uzbekistan and Kazakhstan, republics which are relatively little urbanised. There may be a fear that the Russians will be a minority in a multilingual country they dominate (Russians make up a substantial minority of most republics outside the RSFSR and are even in the majority in Kazakhstan). This is another dimension to political concern over the birth-rate.

The Labour Market

Although constituting a tiny proportion of the whole, the industrial proletariat provided the basis of Bolshevik party support before the revolution. The revolution was quickly followed by the 'dictatorship of the proletariat' even though the size and structure of that proletariat was somewhat changed from the pre-war (1913) position. The industrial labour force had fallen in size in the early 1920s because of the drift back to the land and the slack demand for labour. There was in addition a sizeable temporary migration of peasants to industrial and construction work. This seasonal or short-term migration (*otkhodnichestvo*) continued through the NEP period despite the persistence of urban unemployment (see p. 59). There was no clear-cut dividing line between peasant and proletarian. There was an overall excess supply of labour in the economy, with local shortages caused by seasonal factors or demand for skills. As industrial production recovered so employment increased.

The introduction of central planning changed the equation radically. Excess demand for labour developed quickly. Official (urban) unemployment figures are shown in Table 8.2:

Table 8.2: Registered Unemployed (in thousands)

1 October 1928	1,365
1 October 1929	1,242
1 October 1930	240

Source: *Narodnoe khozyaistvo za 60 let* (M. 1977), p. 462.

Since 1930 there has been no recorded unemployment, though there may have been some real unemployment. The figures in Table 8.2 probably underestimated the real position and there is some evidence to suggest occasional frictional unemployment (see p. 178).

Large numbers of new workers were needed to meet the demands of the plan and the principal source of this labour was the peasantry. In 1928 71 per cent of coal-miners in the Donbas were from peasant families, in 1930-1 the figure was 79 per cent. The process of collectivisation accelerated a process of rural-urban migration. This produced not only enormous strains on urban services, particularly housing, but also great economic costs. The problems of adjustment to factory discipline for the first time coupled with the unplanned growth in labour demand resulted in rapid labour turnover (at over 100 per cent per annum on average until 1935) and some inflationary wage payments. Many of the newly recruited workers were simply unused to machinery and inadvertently damaged equipment. Labour productivity fell well below expectations in the years of the first five-year plan, which in turn led to extra demands for labour to maintain planned output. Labour productivity increased significantly in later years, however. The increase in the number of industrial workers from 1928 may be seen in Table 8.3.

Table 8.3: Numbers Employed in the USSR 1928-78 (in thousands)

| | Manual and clerical workers | | | Scientific and technical (ITR) | |
	Industry	*(including clerical)*	*Construction*	*Industry*	*Construction*
1929	3,124	236	646	119	
1932	6,007	700	1,923	420	
1937	7,924	649	1,340	722	
1940	8,290		1,281		
1945	7,189	570	1,300	806	93
1950	11,308	710	2,263	1,197	156
1955	14,281		2,794	1,545	221
1960	18,574	897	4,544	2,018	385
1965	22,206	1,080	4,892	2,860	549
1970	25,631	1,275	5,824	3,687	819
1975	27,507	1,280	6,478	4,287	1,041
1978	28,981	1,270		4,816	

Sources: Senyavskii, 'Rabochii klass . . . ', *Istoricheskie zapiski*, 100 (M. 1977), pp. 46-8: *Promyshlennost' SSSR* (M. 1964), p. 84: *Narodnoe khozyaistvo v 1978 g.* (M. 1979), p. 125.

In the second and subsequent plan periods labour productivity was set at more realistic norms and increased more in accordance with the plan.

In addition to the permanent movement of workers, temporary or seasonal migration continued; indeed it was systematised. The casual movement of labour was organised under *orgnabor* (meaning 'organised recruitment') from 1931. Thus despite restriction on mobility introduced in 1932, temporary migration continued (informally as well as formally under *orgnabor*), there being as many as 4 million migrant peasant workers in 1937, at the end of the second five-year plan.

Forced Labour

Quite how important forced labour has been is impossible to say. It is unlikely that it has played any major part in production since 1956, if not since the war. In the crucial decade of the 1930s, however, forced labour was used to provide some labour for projects in remote areas. The White Sea Canal is the best-known example. However, there is evidence that much of the construction work in Magnitogorsk was undertaken by labour under duress – not imprisoned in the camps but rather under exile, including, especially, many dispossessed kulaks (Wheatcroft, 1981, 291n). It is not known how many exiled workers, not in camps, were employed, nor how extensively. Similar uncertainty applies to the numbers in labour camps. The nature of such camps has been documented by Solzhenitsyn in *Gulag Archipelago* and in other such sources, but numbers of prisoners, and how they were employed, are less certain. One authoritative source has estimated a total of 6.9 million in mid-1941 (Swaniewicz, 1965, p. 39), equivalent to about 8 per cent of the total labour force. Other estimates vary about this figure for other years, ranging from 2 million to more than 10 million (Conquest, 1973, p. 706). More recent research, however, suggests a maximum number in the camps of 4 to 5 million in 1939 (Wheatcroft, 1981, p. 286). This was a peak year, following the purges, but with the annexation of the Baltic states and invasion of eastern Poland after the 1939 treaty with Germany, an unknown number of foreign citizens were deported, which may have increased numbers in the camps. There was some renewal of imprisonment after the war, but from 1956 the camp population was reduced substantially.

According to Swaniewicz most of this labour was used in construction and mining. Such labour was not totally without cost – there were minimal subsistence and substantial security costs. Productivity was low, one supposes, and no doubt the labour would have been more productively employed elsewhere. But there were two advantages to forced labour. First, it made a marginal contribution to production without an increase in purchasing power; it was anti-inflationary. Second, the work was in remote regions where it was difficult to attract free labour. Although the NKVD made a contribution to the 1941 plan (to mine coal in the Arctic, cut timber and manufacture furniture, among others things) which can only have been with forced labour, it seems unlikely that labour was imprisoned, on any scale, specifically for productive purposes. It was simply too inefficient. The trials and purges of the 1930s were an elaborate, costly and bloody exercise – more than a mere charade to secure labour. It seems more likely that prisoners were found a job to do, as they still are. On the other hand, the NKVD (renamed MVD after the war) developed extensive economic enterprises and thus had an interest in maintaining a supply of labour.

Under Stalin, the number of prisoners or forced labourers increased because it became so much easier to transgress the law. Absenteeism became a punishable offence from 1933. In 1938 this offence was defined as arriving late for work twice and was punishable by forced labour at the place of work, simply working for no wage or for a substantially reduced one.

The potential supply of imprisoned labour was reduced when many were released from the camps in 1956. Further, the economic enterprises under the control of the security service had been disbanded after Stalin's death in 1953. However, since Khrushchev's time there are renewed suggestions of prison labour being used in a variety of productive enterprises. Former inmates have reported that suspension units and other components for motor cars (including export models) are made in labour camps.

Women in the Economy

There is a common view that women engage in unusually heavy manual labour in the USSR. There is some truth in this: there are women builders and bricklayers and other manual labourers — tasks not normally undertaken by women in industrial societies. However, there is nothing unusual about women engaging in heavy manual labour in Russia, nor indeed in much of the world. It is the common lot of women in peasant societies. What is distinctive about the Soviet case is that women have entered the industrial labour force in great numbers. With the ever-growing demand for labour generated by the plans and the exhaustion of ready supplies of (male) workers from the countryside women provided a new marginal source of labour. About half of the increase in industrial workers, 1928-37, were women. Of course, many of the peasant workers entering industry in the 1930s were women so that two categories were not distinct. Thus there was a significant increase in the share of women in the total labour force after 1928 (Table 8.4). The trend was accelerated in the war, when, as in other combatant nations, women replaced conscripted men in a number of occupations, even in 1945 making up 56 per cent of the total labour force. With the re-employment of demobilised soldiers the proportion declined a little thereafter, though increased in the 1960s to over 50 per cent of the total by 1970. Women's employment has increased similarly in Western economies but not to the same extent. A higher proportion of women of working age are employed in the Soviet Union than in Western Europe.

The pattern of employment differs less from Western economies

Table 8.4: Women in the Soviet Labour Force (percentage of total manual and clerical workers)

	Total	Industry	Agriculture	Construction	Public health	Education
1929	27	28	28[a]	7		
1933	30	31	24[a]	16	71	56
1940	39	38	30	24	76	59
1950	47	46	42	32	84	69
1960	47	45	41	30	85	70
1965	49	46	44	30	86	72
1970	51	48	44	29	85	72
1975	51	49	44	28	84	73

Note: a. These figures appear to exclude non-collectivised agriculture.
Sources: Rashin, *Iz istorii rabochego klassa* (M. 1958), p. 535: *Narodnoe khozyaistvo v 1970 g.* (M. 1971), p. 516: *Narodnoe khozyaistvo v 1975 g.* (M. 1976), p. 543.

than might be supposed. Women dominate the Soviet labour market in areas similar to those in the West: light industry, services and education. That most school-teachers are women is no surprise in a comparison with any European economy. However, there are probably more female engineers and economists than one would find in Britain, for instance. The medical profession in the Soviet Union is dominated by women — but junior doctors are not particularly well paid. Women occupy few senior posts in education and medicine. Few academicians, factory directors or similar senior personnel are women. Soviet women, in other words, have tended to occupy relatively low-paid jobs, so that although equal pay for women has obtained since the 1920s the average earnings of women are probably lower than men as the distribution of employment is skewed towards the lower end of the scale in any occupation.

One occupational area where women have taken an increasing share of total employment since the war is agriculture. This is a pattern not universally reflected in the West but evident in some of the poorer agricultural regions of Europe (the *mezzogiorno* of southern Italy for example). This pattern is a function not of women entering the labour force but rather of men leaving it at a faster rate. Indeed, a high proportion of agricultural labour is relatively old— the young, particularly the young men, having left to work in the towns.

The rapid entry of women into the urban industrial labour force in the 1930s brought necessary welfare provisions. Crêches for children below school age were gradually provided and are now more plentiful than in most Western countries. Maternity leave with security of employment was introduced as early as 1918, with up to 16 weeks' paid leave being provided depending on the nature of the work (Dodge, 1966, p. 57). Nursing mothers were allowed half-hourly breaks to feed babies every three hours.

The high level of employment of women suggests that further supplies are inelastic. The 'pool' of readily available labour in the countryside was exhausted before the war; since then the employment of women has probably reached a peak. Most wives and mothers available for work in the Soviet Union are already working. This may, in turn, have inhibited the birth-rate, thus aggravating future labour supplies. Certainly Soviet women appear to have a difficult time; for the cultural changes associated with their political and economic emancipation have, according to all reports, been slow in coming. Few men it seems, help in domestic chores. Household shopping can be a slow procedure, with few supermarkets or 'self-service' shops to speed the process; and the task is usually left to women who rush to the shops on leaving work. More particularly, labour-saving devices in the home are few, expensive and of a design obsolete in the West. All this adds to the general burden on Soviet women.

Labour supply in the post-war Soviet economy is relatively inelastic. In the early years of planning (to the outbreak of war), on the other hand, the non-agricultural labour force increased at a rate faster than any comparable period in the history of industrial nations, at 3.7 per cent per annum 1928-37, 3 per cent per annum 1937-40 (Kuznets, 1961, p. 34). In a closely similar period, 1926-39, the total population of working age (16-59 years) increased by an annual average of 1.3 per cent (Eason, in Bergson and Kuznets,1963, p. 45). Thus the increase in industrial labour supply was a result of the elimination of unemployment, the transfer of agricultural labour to industry and the employment of hitherto non-working women, rather than an overall increase in population. There was thus a rapid jump in the labour participation ratio (Table 8.5) to a level of around 70 per cent. There was a further increase in the early 1960s. This level appears to be a peak; it is much higher than other major industrial economies. Indeed, the ratio has tended to fall elsewhere partly because of the extension of higher education (Cohn, 1970, p. 66). A Soviet estimate for 1970 shows that 92.4 per cent of the appropriate age group are either in work or education (Beilina, 1976, p. 116). 'Overfull' employment in the Soviet Union and the very tight labour market which results suggest that increases in production since the war, and especially since the end of the 1950s, have been associated with improvements in productivity. Certainly, future increases will depend on productivity improvements. There appears to be scope for greater efficiency in employment. The absence of commercial cost criteria might encourage the maintenance of superfluous labour in some sectors.

Table 8.5: Soviet Labour Participation Ratio

Employed population as percentage total population of working age (state and co-operative sectors)

Year	Ratio
1928	56.8
1937	70.1
1950	71.7
1958	70.8
1964	76.1
1975	85

Sources: S. Cohn, *Economic Development in the Soviet Union* (1970), p. 66: W. Berner, *The Soviet Union 1975-76* (1977), p. 110.

Relative underemployment is a phenomenon readily apparent to Western visitors. Any administrative work (of which there is plenty) seems to demand enormous numbers of workers, and security at its various levels employs thousands. The use of labour-saving technology in clerical work has been slow to develop. In manufacturing there is frequent overmanning as a result of managers hoarding labour. Such problems which have been considered critically in the Soviet press have been acknowledged by policy-makers. The advent of economic reform in the 1960s reduced the interest in hoarding labour at the enterprise level and from 1967 a limited experiment was introduced, allowing some enterprises to make workers redundant and use the consequent savings for incentive payments. Since its initial introduction at the Shchekino chemical plant near Tula, this experimental system has been applied to about 1,000 factories. In 1980 renewed suggestions were made to extend such a system to the country as a whole, allowing an end to industrial overmanning and renewed incentives for increased productivity. The floating of such ideas in *Pravda*, albeit from an academic economist, can only have had some official sponsorship, for it was through such means that preliminary debate to the 1965 reforms began. As far as it has progressed, the 'Shchekino experiment' is a long way short of similar developments in Hungary, yet it is a radical departure from implicit security of employment. It can presumably operate because of abundant employment opportunities elsewhere. Under

Khrushchev personal labour mobility was greatly eased, following the strictures of Stalin, yet a parallel law against 'social parasitism' was introduced to discourage voluntary unemployment. The work ethic is imposed by law. Even so, labour turnover was high in the 1970s, with workers readily moving jobs for better pay, conditions or housing, a phenomenon which yields quite high, if unrecorded, frictional unemployment.

Wages and Material Incentives

Under planning, labour cannot be allocated in the same way as other resources. The labour market has remained essentially a market and material and non-material incentives have been employed to overcome supply bottlenecks and to increase production. Wage differentials have therefore become an essential element in the plan. Thus the notions of equality or at least greater relative equality in wages and incomes which developed in the years after the revolution were abandoned after 1930. In 1926 there was a move to reduce income differentials which by that time had become roughly comparable with their 1913 levels, but a short time later, with the construction of socialism, wage differentials were increased, wage egalitarianism was dismissed as 'bourgeois'. Increasing differentials became evident from 1931 to reward skills, act as an incentive and reduce labour turnover. (Significantly also senior party personnel who, under NEP, had their incomes restricted to the levels of manual workers were now able to gain substantial increases.) Payment according to work done; work according to ability became the essence of socialism – and established as doctrine. Thus according to a Soviet economics textbook (wage) payment is made for the quantity and quality of labour and individual material self-interest is recognised (*Politicheskaya ekonomiya*, 1971, p. 139).

There are three main occupational groups in the state economy (collective farm peasants are co-operative workers and are not therefore part of the state socialist sector): workers proper (*rabochie*), which include state-farm members; clerical or 'white collar' workers (*sluzhashchie*); and scientific and technical workers (*inzhenerno-tekhnicheskie rabochie* or *ITR*). These groups are sometimes combined for statistical purposes. Wages or salaries for all state employees are fixed, according to the job, at the centre as part of the finance plan. The system of centralised wage-fixing was established in the first five-year plan and has, in principle, remained in operation, though the details have changed over time to meet varying demands in the economy.

Originally there was a range of eight wage tariffs, but bonuses were paid to manual and clerical workers for exceeding (or helping their enterprise to exceed) production norms. Through the 1930s these bonuses made up an increasing proportion of total wages. In the first five-year plan there was a tendency towards wage inflation as the level of employment exceeded expectations (labour productivity fell below expectations) and generous bonus payments were made.The effect was added to by 'disguised promotions'. The wage scales published in 1931 increased official differentials between unskilled and skilled manual workers from a 1928 ratio of 1:2 to 1:3.7 ('technical' workers could receive greater differentials and enterprise managers and senior administrators could earn substantially above-'average' incomes). The high rate of labour turnover experienced in these years led many enterprise managers to pay unskilled workers as 'semi'-skilled, and to contrive at easy output norms to boost bonus earnings. Thus managers at the micro-level were exercising a degree of tolerated discretion to influence their labour-supply position, even though this was without the strict parameters of the plan. The consequent inflationary wage pressure compounded the need for rationing, which obtained until 1935. Thus differential rations for food, clothing and housing entered into the system of differential payment. As piece-rates were paid progressively actual payments came to depend on output, the region of employment (workers in remote regions such as the far north or Siberia received higher pay) and the nature of the job. Yet basic wage *rates* remained unchanged between 1931 and 1957. The real changes were substantial and owed more to the labour market than the plan *per se*. Groups of high-priority workers emerged. The overall ranking of workers in the coal industry jumped from fourteenth in 1928 to fourth in 1935, to first in 1940. Coal miners have been the highest paid workers ever since. Other highly paid industries in the 1930s and subsequently were oil- and iron-ore extraction, electric power generation, steel and machinery production.

Propaganda played some part in increasing output also. In 1935 a new hero of labour emerged to become the centre of a nationwide propaganda exercise. Alexei Stakhanov, a miner at the Irmino mine in the Ukraine, was able to increase his and his three workmates' shift output substantially by organising the work along simple division of labour lines. The Stakhanovite movement was born. Gradually a similar system to boost output and productivity was extended to other mines and other occupations. Successful participants received effective pay increases, while for others output norms were increased, thereby limiting their bonus earnings. The Stakhanovite movement did not survive the war. During the war years there was substantial labour-dilution and heavy priority to the war effort, so that output norms were reduced and incentive bonuses increased, thus, in effect, changing earnings. By 1944 average wages were 53 per cent above their 1940 level yet basic wage-rates had remained unchanged.

With the readjustment of the economy to peacetime conditions it became evident that wage payments owed less to central planning *per se* than to accident and 'market' forces. Real differentials in payment had increased from the pre-war position. As a partial corrective low wages were raised in 1947, but there was no fundamental adjustment until after Stalin's death. In 1956 a minimum wage was established – at 27 rubles per month in rural areas and 30 in urban areas, when average wages were 72 rubles per month. At the same time a general review of wage-rates was instituted which continued to 1962. The number of wage-tariffs was reduced, low wages were increased and there were some reductions in higher administrative salaries.

Payment according to work done remains the governing principle; piece-rates are still a major form of payment, but in the late 1950s and 1960s (and probably since, but data are scarce on this latter period) there has been a reduction in wage-differentials. This has come about largely by increasing minimum wages: to 40-5 rubles per month in 1965, 60 in 1968, 70 in 1975. Differentials between manual and clerical workers have narrowed (the official ratio was reduced to 1:2.6 in the 1960s) as manual workers' money incomes have increased at a faster rate than salaries for clerical workers or technical personnel (ITR). Technical personnel remain more highly paid on average but clerical workers have been overtaken as the required clerical skills, even literacy, scarce in the 1930s, have become commonplace. Clerical employees, workers in health and education, have fallen behind manual workers in post-war years (Table 8.6).

Such a move reflects the market but it is evident also that welfare considerations have been operating since the mid-1950s in the adjustment of incomes and their distribution. Under Stalin, income-differentials were used as reward and incentive. Since his death the principle has remained unchanged, but there appears to have been a deliberate attempt to moderate differentials for what are not strictly 'economic' reasons. Official data on income differentials are, however, very scarce indeed. Recent research by Western scholars (Wiles, 1974; McAuley, 1979) sometimes reaches slightly different figures, but in general shows

Table 8.6: Relative Earnings of Major Occupational Groups (state employees: average monthly wage in rubles)

	All employees	Industry			State agriculture		
		A	B	C	A	B	C
1940	33.1	32.4	69.6	36.0	20.7	50.4	31.1
1950	64.2	69.0	122.9	39.5	36.2	84.6	51.4
1960	80.6	89.6	135.7	73.5	51.9	114.9	66.2
1970	122.0	130.6	178.0	111.6	98.5	164.3	95.6
1978	159.9	176.1	208.4	142.7	141.9	185.8	121.9

Notes: A = manual workers (*rabochie*). B = technical workers (*ITR*). C = clerical workers (*sluzhashchie*). Figures for agriculture exclude collective farm incomes.
Sources: *Narodnoe khozyaistvo v 1922-72 gg*, pp. 350-1; *Narodnoe khozyaistvo v 1978 g.* (M. 1979). p. 372.

that income-differentials are slightly less than in Western market economies, and that inequality declined in post-war years to 1967-8, the most recent date for which data are available. McAuley deduces a decile ratio[1] of 3.00 for the non-agricultural population in 1968, and 3.55 for collective-farm members (1979, p. 65). With the substantial increase in farm prices in the 1950s collective-farm incomes increased, and the introduction of guaranteed wages in 1966 improved their relative position. Average payments per labour day increased from 2.68 rubles in 1965 to 4.11 rubles in 1972. Higher payments to collective farmers appear to be both a catching-up exercise, for the extremely unfavourable position they enjoyed in the past, and an extension of material incentives to increase production. Further, since 1968, peasant mobility has been eased and increased wages have possibly been designed, at least in part, to help keep workers on the land. However, collective farm incomes remained behind state-farm incomes and further behind non-agricultural state incomes. The steady increase in the minimum wage of industrial workers has also offset some of the relative gains made by the collective farm peasantry. Collective farmers remain amongst the poor by Soviet standards, but poverty is by no means universal in the countryside nor confined to rural incomes. In 1967-8, 35-40 per cent of the total population had per capita incomes below the official poverty line (McAuley, 1979, p. 70), most of them being urban dwellers. Welfare provisions, although extensive, are far from perfect.[2]

The relative position of workers in various industries at the top (Table 8.7) with an excess over the average for all industry is greater than that in Western capitalist economies. They received further increases in 1979. As well as higher wages, coal miners can have better housing and more comfortable holidays than many of their fellow-workers. The providers of fuel and metals remain a labour aristocracy in the USSR.

Table 8.7: Distribution of Industrial Wages (selected industries). (Average for all industry = 100)

Industry	1950	1955	1959	1965
Coal	155	148	167	189
Non-ferrous metals		137		147
Ferrous metals	130	123	123	123
Petroleum	118	111	104	110
Chemicals	102	102	94	101
Machinery	103	101	97	100
Electric power	99	96		
Woodworking	88	90	92	89
Light industry		82		80[b]
Food industry	67	69	68	75[c]
Construction[a]	(85)	(92)		105

Notes: a. The bracketed figures refer to construction materials. b. 1965 figure refers to textiles only. c. 1965 figure excludes fish industry.
Sources: G. Schroeder, 'Industrial Wage Differentials in the USSR', *Soviet Studies* (1966), p. 316; P. Wiles, in NATO (1975), p. 117.

It is clear that differentials in income, both in money and non-monetary terms, have been used as an incentive and reward for labour and acquired skills (i.e. as transfer payment). Thus some of the revolutionary ideology was diluted in order to meet demands of the economy. In the more mature economy under Khrushchev and Brezhnev there is some evidence of compensation and correction for welfare purposes; witness the family-income supplement from 1974, for instance. However, there is strong evidence to suggest that high incomes are used to reward a privileged elite and that this reward has no necessary link with economic criteria. The existence of an elite has long been recognised. Privileges accorded to senior party members, under Stalin, do not appear to have diminished. Matthews calculates that *c.* 1970 the elite, which he defines as in receipt of an income above 400 rubles per month (compared with an industrial average of 130, minimum of 60-70 rubles per month), numbered approximately 227,000, or 0.2 per cent of the labour force. Clearly, this group does include some with particular economic responsibility, such as senior industrial management, or great political responsibility, such as diplomats, but there is also an element of privilege. The list includes, as well as those mentioned, a small number of writers and artists, senior academic personnel, top doctors, legal officials and some journalists (Matthews, 1978, pp. 23-7). There is no single occupational group, rather the higher echelons of a number of occupations. As well as salary there is a variety of 'payments' the elite might receive — depending in turn on their status. These include the 'Kremlin ration', or access to goods otherwise not available to the general public, sometimes even from 'secret' shops (four such shops have been identified in Moscow); part-payment in hard currency which can be used to purchase imported consumer-goods; above-average housing (allocated by employers); access to private transport, ranging from a chauffeur-driven limousine to jumping the queue to buy a car; special medical services; educational and cultural benefits (using influence or *blat* to gain access to higher education, obtaining scarce tickets to the Bolshoi theatre, etc.); privileged holidays in reserved areas on the Black Sea or relatively luxurious country *dachas*; and, in some cases, foreign travel.

In 1722 Peter the Great established his famous Table of Ranks, whereby status became determined by occupation, in the Civil Service, Church or armed forces. The higher the rank in employment, the higher the social status. The upper levels in the table carried heritable title and further privileges. Historical parallels are of limited value, but it is a nice irony that in the contemporary USSR there is a secret list (*nomenklatura*) of established privileges which accord with given status in employment. The privileged elite in the Soviet Union is small and some of their privileges may seem trivial compared with those available in capitalist countries. Certainly their relative incomes are insignificant in comparison with the fabulously rich in the West and it is uncertain how far privileges may be hereditary. However, the continued maintenance of such an elite seems to be consistent neither with ideology nor some crucial economic compromise.

Consumption

To increase consumption and create plenty is one of the prime objectives of Communism, yet one of the anomalies of Soviet history is that the development of the economy has necessitated consumer-deprivation and postponed gratification. Holding down consumption has been an important means of achieving rapid development. It is, however, particularly difficult to measure consumption, for even where data are readily available much depends on subjective criteria. In the Soviet case there are further difficulties with the paucity of data, and the wholly artificial exchange-rate between the ruble and Western currencies hinders any comparison of purchasing power. Further, while private consumption has been adversely affected the consumption of communal services has moved ahead more steadily in the USSR. Despite such difficulties of measurement it is evident that standards of consumption in the Soviet Union have improved enormously since its inception. Hanson estimates that personal consumption levels doubled between 1913 and 1965 (1969, p. 39). This improvement has accelerated in the 1960s and 1970s. Thus although living standards are in most respects inferior to Western industrial economies, the gap has probably narrowed.

As production recovered after the civil war so too did consumption, though the average was weighted down by the persistence of unemployment and occasional urban food shortages. Relative incomes had changed markedly. The small luxury-consuming class of Imperial Russia had disappeared, and although some private producers and traders (*Nepmen*) were able to enrich themselves their consumption never matched such levels.

The advent of planning and collectivisation severely reduced peasant incomes and brought about an increase in wage-differentials. However, there seems to have been no average improvement in consumption. The great increases in production in the 1930s were primarily to serve the state, for future industrial and military needs. Consumption lagged because consumer-goods output fell below plan, consumer-goods prices bore the burden of inflation (thus wiping out many of the gains in money wages); the severe famine of 1932-4 affected everybody. Although the hunger, suffering and loss of life was far worse in the rural areas there was a general and substantial decline in consumption in these years, and rationing was retained until 1935. Consumption was conditioned not simply by price but also by availability (and this has obtained to a lesser degree ever since). The deficit in supply was reflected in the peasant free-market prices greatly exceeding regulated state prices (Table 8.8).

There was recovery of agricultural production after the main collectivisation campaign, and private-market prices declined somewhat. Nevertheless there was a general inflationary trend, 1928-40, which was far greater in consumer-goods than producer-goods prices (Table 8.8). As a result of such forces, real non-agricultural wages declined by 40 per cent 1928-37, at 1928 prices (Jasny, 1961, p. 447).

Hanson, allowing for the provision of communal services as well as personal incomes, estimates that consumption was about the same

Table 8.8: Price Indices 1928-40 (1928 = 100)

| | Basic industrial goods[a] | Consumer-goods | |
		State[b]	Private[c]
1930	96		
1932	97	200	3,000 (max.)
1933	100	400	1,500-2,000
1935	103	700[d]	900-1,470
1937	175	700	700
1940	231	1,000	1,780

Notes: a. Producer-goods, excluding oil. b. State = state and co-operative trade.
c. Private = collective-farm market. d. 1936.
Malafeev (1964, p. 402) shows a similar but less complete index,
1927-8 = 100, the figures for 1930 109 for state,   231 private
                                            1931 137   409
The collective-farm market was not fully legalised until 1932, before which time
sales were less ordered and less well recorded; some were illegal.
Source: F.D. Holzman, 'Soviet Inflationary Pressures 1928-57', *Quarterly Journal of Economics*, 74, May 1960, p. 168.

in 1937 as in 1928, though it fell thereafter (Hanson, 1969, p. 31). The dictatorship of the proletariat was not evidently accompanied by significant material gain.

Preparation for war after 1937, and the war itself, brought marked reductions in consumption which were hardly alleviated at the ending of hostilities with another major famine in 1946-7. Although war-rationing was ended in 1948 the supply position was not eased, and it was not until the following year that consumption reached the levels of 1928 (Hanson, 1969, p. 31). After Stalin's death greater priority to personal consumption in the plans resulted in marked improvements but shortages persisted. It was a case of control by the queue, where supply and demand were in disequilibrium and prices arbitrary. Usually demand far exceeded supply, so that all consumer-goods found a market, despite poor quality and relatively high prices. Goods were bought when available rather than when necessary. The system of distribution has changed little in the last twenty years but availability has improved substantially. As a result the Soviet consumer has become far more discriminating, so that poor-quality goods (shoes are a well-known example) have remained unsold. Shops sometimes even require state subsidies to cover unsold inventories. One Western estimate shows an average per capita increase in consumption of 58 per cent from 1960 to 1973 (including food, clothing, services and durables), consumption of durables alone increasing by two and a half times in the same years;

sales of radio sets increased from 4.2 million in 1960 to 6.1 million in 1973 and refrigerators from 518,000 to 4.9 million in the same years (Schroeder, in NATO, 1975, pp. 44-5). Private cars have become widely owned, though there remains a two- to three-year waiting list. In foodstuffs consumption of meat and dairy produce has increased, that of bread has declined a little.

The Soviet economy is much more consumer-oriented than in the past but is still far from being dependent on a large consumer market. In the ninth five-year plan, running to 1975, consumer-goods (group B) output was underfulfilled (increasing by 37 per cent over 1970 against a plan figure of 48 per cent). Producer-goods nearly matched the plan, with 45 per cent increase against a planned 46.3 per cent. Targets for the tenth plan to 1980 were more modest and, significantly, gave higher priority to producer-goods. This suggests that the Soviet economy is much more geared towards production of producer-goods than consumer-goods, so that more consumer-goods are imported. The increase in real incomes recorded in the ninth plan to 1975 from 100 to 124 (against a target of 130.8) includes imported consumer-goods — mostly from CMEA partners. However, even imports from Western countries are used to alleviate consumer-demand. Shoes and other clothing were imported under Khrushchev and since, and in 1980 an Italian company was contracted to build a factory to make denim jeans.

Physical shortages have resulted in a 'parallel' market developing, whereby private services — from a plumber, mechanic or even dentist — can be obtained, at a price. Similarly there is a good second-hand market in motor-cars with prices exceeding new car prices. Any Western tourist will know that some items of fashionable Western clothing evidently command a high ruble-price. Limited private enterprise is permitted — the best-known example being the collective-farm market. Expenditure in such 'grey' or parallel markets may figure highly in the household budget, but is not recorded in official price statistics.

It is particularly difficult to make cross-cultural comparisons with societies where allocation is made through the market. Prices for consumer-goods are high in the USSR but housing is cheap. In 1973 the average work-time required to earn enough to buy most foodstuffs in Moscow was considerably greater than in Western capitals; but it took the Soviet worker only eight hours work per month to pay his rent (including heating and lighting) compared with 67 hours in London and 102 in Paris (NATO, 1975, p. 56). But quality and availability are poor — the average living space being only about one-third of West European standards. Overcrowding and often shared bathroom and kitchen facilities persist. Cheap housing means, however, that the Soviet consumer enjoys a high discretionary income compared with his Western counterpart. There is, on the other hand, less choice of goods available. Further, the Soviet citizen has long enjoyed high consumption of communal services (which increased in the 1930s while private consumption did not): cheap travel, free medical treatment, education, etc. There is no doubt that personal consumption improved substantially after the war and post-war austerity, but this is a phenomenon evident throughout Europe. Indeed, in the 1960s the rate of growth of personal income in the USSR was not impressive by international comparison (Table 8.9).

Table 8.9: Growth in Per Capita Personal Private Consumption 1958-70 (annual average rates, %)

Japan	6.4
West Germany	4.8
Italy	4.5
France	3.7
USA	3.2
USSR	2.8
UK	2.6

Source: Cohn, *Economic Development in the Soviet Union* (1970), p. 45.

Inflation has much less cruelly eroded incomes in the Soviet Union than in the West. Until very recently it did not exist officially, not being recorded in the retail price index, but in fact there has been much disguised and repressed inflation. New models of motor cars bear substantial price increases — though this is not a 'real' price increase as the product has changed. Similarly, ladies' tights were more than twice the price of the stockings they were replacing. Similar changes occur in the West. The great increases in world coffee prices (1976-8) were eventually reflected by increases in the Soviet shops (before the increase coffee had disappeared altogether); and in 1979 petrol prices were increased substantially from what were hitherto very low levels. Late in 1979 retail-price inflation was officially acknowledged — though attributed to imported inflation from the West. Some inflationary pressure is repressed by subsidy; meat and dairy products are sold below cost for intance, the increase in procurement price not having been passed on to the consumer. It is not clear how long such subsidies can be maintained. Attempts to raise meat prices in Poland to reduce the level of subsidy had profound political consequences.

Overall purchasing power has tended to run ahead of supply. Much of the excess liquidity — resulting from improved money incomes — has been soaked up by the parallel market and the free-farm markets. However, large unspent balances have persisted. In 1960 state savings bank deposits were equivalent to less than 45 per cent of the total value of stock in retail shops. By 1970 the figure had reached 120 per cent. If prices cannot be increased substantially, and the economy is unable to produce consumer-goods to plan, there are alternatives of a currency reform as in 1948, which would no doubt prove extremely unpopular, or importing more consumer-goods, which is expensive and governed much by Soviet terms of trade (see Chapter 9).

The Soviet Union is still some way from full consumer-orientation. It is evident also that the country is not totally insulated from world inflationary pressures. Nonetheless, although the ideological objectives of abundance for all are still far away, there has been a clear, if unsteady, move towards the gratification of consumer-demands.

Notes

1. The methodology of the decile ratio is discussed fully by P. Wiles in *Income Distribution East and West* (1974), Ch. 1.

2. Poverty and welfare is extensively examined by A. McAuley, *Economic Welfare in the Soviet Union* (1979).

9 THE USSR IN THE WORLD ECONOMY

Through most of her history the Soviet Union has had a small involvement in foreign trade, and has been characterised by a policy of economic self-sufficiency or autarky. This has effectively withered away as a policy since the end of the Great Patriotic War. Before the First World War the Russian Empire's share of world trade had been increasing, with major exports of food, timber and other primary proucts which paid for substantial imports of machinery and investment capital (see Chapter 1). During the First World War and civil war trade dwindled, to a minimum in 1919. After the Treaty of Rapallo in 1922 there was a substantial recovery in trade but it was never to reach the 1913 volume until after the Great Patriotic War. In the 1920s trade was inhibited by the movement in terms of trade against primary producers and by the difficulty in producing an export volume within the USSR. The policy of 'Socialism in One Country' might be seen as reinforcing a trend towards relative autarky in the late 1920s. However, the eventual policy was as much the product of economic forces as deliberate political decision.

In 1926 Stalin declared that Soviet industry would grow not on the basis of an export market (as Britain had done in the nineteenth century) but on the basis of the home market. Stalin's implication in this speech was that the Soviet Union would pursue total economic independence. It was never wholly possible, but in the later 1930s the country reduced foreign trade turnover to negligible levels. Lend-lease deliveries during the war 1941-5 changed the volume but not the character of foreign trade under planning. It was only after 1949, with the establishment of CMEA and a so-called socialist market and, more particularly, since Stalin's death, that foreign trade increased significantly. Over the same years through the huge growth of the merchant marine, membership of shipping and airline cartels and other international organisations the Soviet Union has entered more fully into the international economy. Most of this change has resulted from a shift in economic circumstance, though it indicates, also, a changed political attitude. 'Peaceful co-existence' is good for business. However, the Soviet share of world trade is still small in relation to the volume of production and the Soviet economy still remains relatively isolated from the rest of the world.

Foreign Trade in the 1920s

The Soviet government established a monopoly over foreign trade in April 1918 and has never relinquished it. Even during the most liberal years of NEP foreign trade remained firmly in state hands. Currency-instability in the early 1920s and low production for export made for payment difficulties. In 1926 the newly stabilised ruble was removed from the foreign exchanges and has remained so. Accordingly exchange-rates have been, since that time, notional rather than real and payments have been made in other currencies. There were thus problems with raising foreign currency to pay for essential imports. There were some attempts to secure foreign loans immediately after the civil war, though these met with political blocking from former investors in the Tsarist empire – most important amongst which was France.

Lenin put much emphasis on the need to secure trade relations, particularly with Britain, then the major trading nation in the world. Thus after emerging from civil war and a war of intervention the new Soviet state was pursuing active economic contact with erstwhile enemies. As early as March 1921 a temporary trade agreement with Britain was made (this followed peace treaties in 1920 with newly separated Baltic neighbours, Estonia, Lithuania, Latvia and Finland, which contained some trading elements). The Treaty of Rapallo with Germany in 1922 was perhaps a more significant turning-point. Under the treaty Germany renounced war losses and was offered concessions to exploit resources within Soviet Russia. By 1924-5 the USSR, as it had now become, was exporting to thirty-three and importing from thirty-eight countries (Chuntulov, 1969, p. 237). The first years of Soviet power saw an energetic pursuit of trade links with industrial economies under the patronage of Krasin, who was foreign trade commissar to 1926. A confirmed trade treaty with Britain in August 1924 allowed a trade representative to be resident in London and a state trading company – 'Arcos' – was registered. Similarly, the 'Amtorg' company represented the state trade monopoly in New York, even though the USA did not yet recognise the Soviet regime.

As well as 'wholly owned' trading companies abroad the Soviet authorities also took part in 'mixed' companies with foreign capital, usually specialising in a particular product (timber being most prominent). There were twenty-four mixed companies in 1923 (Gladkov, 1960, p. 514), e.g. the Russo-German Trade Co., Russgolondoles (forest-products trade with Holland), Russo-Persian Co., etc. Such companies handled only a small proportion of trade. Less important still were a few foreign companies operating on a concession basis. Another layer of trade was co-operatives, of which the long-established *Centrosoyuz* was the most important (it dated from 1898). However, co-operatives were also directly subordinate to the state. Thus although foreign trade was conducted at different levels by a variety of organisations the Soviet state was in ultimate control (Table 9.1).

Table 9.1: Control of Soviet Foreign Trade 1924-5

Agency	Export (%)	Import
State institutions and enterprises (including trusts)	47.3	86.6
State companies (e.g. *Exporthhleb, exportles*, etc.)	31.6	6.4
Co-operatives (*Centrosoyuz, sel'skosoyuz*)	12.5	3.8
Mixed companies with foreign capital	5.5	1.3
Foreign companies	1.1	1.3
Private enterprises	0.7	0.3
Other	1.3	0.3

Source: I. Gladkov, *Sov. nar. khoz. 1921-25*, (1960), p. 515.

The limited decentralisation allowed by the commissariat for foreign trade (*Narkomvneshtorg*) was reduced later in the 1920s, and by the end of the decade foreign trade was confined solely to state monopoly corporations.

Political control enabled clear concentration on import priorities, though less perfectly than in later decades. Capital imports to aid recovery were encouraged; from 1924 superphosphates, machinery, tannin and similar items were admitted free of duty. Agricultural machinery, a major import before the revolution, reached 55 per cent of the pre-war level by 1924-5 (excluding tractors). Imports of tractors — to be used mostly on a few collective and state farms — increased more quickly still. Imports of agricultural machinery grew from 11.9 million rubles in 1921-2 to 74.4 million in 1924-5, that of tractors and tractor parts from 0.4 million to 30.5 million rubles in the same years (Gladkov, 1960, p. 521). Fords sold, in 1923, 402 tractors and 3,108 units in 1924, 10,515 in 1925, 5,432 in 1926 (Wilkins and Hill, 1964, pp. 209-10). The priority given to imports aiding the growth of agriculture in the early 1920s reflected the priority to agriculture within the economy in these years. In the 'post-recovery' years, after 1926, with the advent of ambitious investment plans more priority was given to imports of industrial machinery and energy-generating equipment. At the same time there was a deliberate policy-shift towards the creation of a self-sufficient industrial economy and Socialism in One Country, which in turn required more emphasis on industrial production. Throughout, however, the major problem was how to pay for necessary imports. Grain had been the major export before the war but now the trade had all but collapsed, largely because of the drastic fall in production in the civil war. The recovery years of 1925-6 saw the USSR providing 3.9 per cent and 16.9 per cent of world exports of wheat and rye respectively compared with 25 per cent and 33.4 per cent before the war (Carr and Davies, 1974, pp. 747-8). Oil was taking a larger share of total exports. Oil products accounted for 10.3 per cent of exports in 1925-6 compared with 3.3 per cent in 1913 (*Vnesh, torg. 1918-1966*, 1967, pp. 16-17). By 1926-7 agricultural exports accounted for about half the total (80 per cent pre-war) and in the same year foreign trade turnover represented 4.7 per cent of national income (13.2 per cent pre-war) (Carr and Davies 1974, p. 748). Even so, the need to find export surpluses put some strain on domestic consumption (though little compared with the first five-year plan) and made relations with the peasantry all the more acute. The USSR was fortunate in having large known oil deposits at a time of growing world demand for oil and exports reached 14.4 per cent of the total in 1930, thus limiting some of the burden on the agricultural sector. However, the country continued to be a primary exporter, importing the means to effect industrialisation.

Concessions

The Soviet Union was able to obtain foreign expertise and equipment, without trading, by granting concessions to foreign concerns, predominantly in the exploitation of natural resources. They had the advantage, in theory at least, of giving the Soviet state access to new technology and equipment without direct payment in world currencies. The real effect of such concessions is less clear, however. For one thing they tended to be shortlived, even though they were originally conceived as likely to be operative for over twenty years. In fact, 1926 was the peak year and all were abolished in 1930. Preobrazhensky calculated that by 1926 concessions had brought in only 50 million rubles of investment, or 2½ per cent of the level of foreign joint stock companies in 1913 (McKay, 1974, pp. 351-2). Sutton, on the other hand, maintains that such concessions were the major source of advanced technology and expertise in the period of NEP, and were thus a major factor in enabling recovery and growth. Although they were quantitatively minor in significance, qualitatively they were essential. Far from being discontinued because they were unsuccessful, they were curtailed, according to Sutton, when they began to be profitable for the Western companies involved (Sutton, 1971, p. 18).

In all there were 127 pure concessions (entirely using foreign capital) and 94 mixed concessions (with equal Soviet participation) in operation at some time during the 1920s. There was clearly a change about 1926, after which date there was an increasing reluctance to allow foreign capital under concession. The international political position worsened in 1927 when the UK broke off diplomatic relations and the Arcos company temporarily ceased trading. The flow of technology and expertise, however, did not diminish. Concessions began to be supplanted by technical agreements which persisted into the planning era. Under such agreements technical and managerial expertise was provided in exchange for a fixed payment. No foreign investment was involved. Already before 1930, 118 such agreements were in operation including such firms as Thyssens A.G. of Germany, BSA of UK and Fords of USA.

To Sutton the maintenance of this dependence on capitalism, if not on foreign capital, illustrates the technological lag in the Soviet economy and the vital part played by foreign expertise in the growth of the Soviet economy before the era of central planning. A particular case may illustrate the point. In 1923 the famous Putilov works in Leningrad was reopened and began producing tractors – known as the Krasnyi Putilovets – modelled on an American Fordson.

Few of the tractors produced actually worked, however. In 1926 a Ford delegation visited Russia and expressed horror at the low standards of construction, repair and maintenance they found (Wilkins and Hill, 1964, p. 214). The Putilov works was completely re-equipped with Ford machinery, with a number of Ford personnel employed. Soviet engineers went to Ford's US plant to gain expertise. Similar stories apply to other companies. It remains disputed how far such transfers were essential to the recovery of Soviet industry.

Foreign Trade under Planning

Strictly speaking, all foreign trade has been subordinate to planning in the USSR. Even in the years of NEP Gosplan prepared export and import plans for the foreign trade commissariat. The buying and selling was conducted by trading corporations (*Khleboexport* for grain exports, *Stankoimport* for machinery imports, for example) which had very little initiative of their own. Under planning the structure remained essentially the same. The plans for the economy threw up demands for goods unobtainable in the Soviet Union; these became imports. Exports were 'surplus' goods or whatever could be spared to pay for the imports. Thus exports were a 'loss' to the economy, diverted from domestic demand. What was imported or exported was determined by 'material balances' of the plan, rather than by cost or price. Price was of secondary significance, because the Soviet price level was insulated from world prices. However, Soviet export prices were seriously affected by the world recession, coincident with the first five-year plan. In subsequent years the total volume of foreign trade fell quickly and there was *de facto* a move towards autarky.

There were several reasons for this development, some more apparent than real. It is easy to see a political motivation associated with the doctrine of Socialism in One Country and the objective, for strategic reasons, of limiting dependence on capitalist powers. Further, there was the economic consideration that it was far easier to make planning decisions without the intrusion of the independent variable of the world market. Against both these points, however, is the evidence that the first plan assumed an expansion in foreign trade and staunch efforts to extend foreign trading outlets had been made throughout the 1920s. Dohan has argued that, far from being deliberately pursued, autarky was forced by economic circumstances (1976, pp. 603-35). The overwhelming difficulty which faced the Soviet economy was in finding exports during the grain crises which preceded the advent of planning. The total volume of exports was well below the pre-war (1913) level. Forced procurement which accompanied collectivisation enabled an increase in exports, but at the cost of domestic consumption. Thus foreign trade increased to a peak in 1930 as substantial imports of capital equipment were made. The international terms of trade moved severely against Soviet exports, further restricting her importing capacity. The gap between average export prices and import prices was greatest in 1932-3. The trading position was made the worse by the difficulty of raising credits abroad. Such difficulties affected all primary producers in the depression and protective trade barriers further reduced export opportunities. Even Britain, the major food importer, took measures to protect her agriculture and, from 1932, gave preferential access to Commonwealth producers. Other West European economies took more extreme protective measures.

The Soviet economy was thus not inherently autarkic; rather it became so because of adverse economic circumstances which coincided with its drive for industrialisation (Dohan, 1976, p. 635). However, as the terms of trade improved, from 1934, and as world trade grew in total (though it always remained below 1928 levels) the USSR became more autarkic. And this was despite the easing of credits by Britain, Germany and Czechoslovakia after 1935. Political factors appear to have had some influence over the course of foreign trade in the later 1930s. Trade fell to a minimum in 1939, though grew thereafter with the signing of the trade treaty and non-aggression pact with Nazi Germany, as a result of which the USSR supplied Germany with vital supplies, particularly of oil products, minerals and some foodstuffs in return for industrial equipment. It may be argued that, until June 1941, Soviet deliveries aided the German war effort. Because of the treaty the German share of Soviet trade jumped from 7.4 per cent in 1939 to 40.4 per cent in 1940. In the latter year the Soviet exports totalled 125.1 million rubles, imports 71.2 million rubles (*Vnesh, torg, 1918-1966*, 1967, pp. 8-9, 14).

With the German invasion in 1941 virtually all 'normal' trade ceased. As an ally of the Western powers the USSR received lend-lease deliveries which effected a substantial increase in trade turnover. Such deliveries are not included in the wartime trade figures shown in Table 9.2. Allowing for these, the real trade imbalance would be something nearer to the 1:15 ratio suggested by Hutchings (1971, p. 228).

In the immediate post-war years reparations payments from former enemies (e.g. oil from Rumania, steel, timber and ships from Finland) alleviated the international position of the USSR by overcoming some supply bottlenecks. In addition, the Soviet zone of Germany was stripped of industrial capacity and Poland, liberated by the Red Army, was required to deliver underpriced coal. The significance of such deliveries lies more with their saving foreign currency than with their absolute size. It is contradictory that the Soviet Union was extracting productive capital from her newly allied east European neighbours[1] yet at the same supplying them with much-needed foodstuffs and raw materials thereby aiding their recovery (Dewar, 1951, p. 2). More formal commercial relations were established with the formation of the Council for Mutual Economic Aid (CMEA or Comecon) in January 1949. For the first time there was a socialist market of politically allied states.[2] Ironically, the USSR had not been an important trading partner with the neighbouring countries of east Europe before the war, so that

Table 9.2: Foreign Trade Turnover (selected years). (Figures in million rubles at current values converted to rubles at 1961 exchange rate)

Year	Export	Import
1913 (Empire)	1,192	1,078.2
1918	6.4	82.5
1920	1.1	22.5
1925-6	555.5	589.1
1930	812.7	830.3
1933	388.7	273.1
1939	103.9	167.5
1940	239.7	245.5
1942	65.7	173.1
1944	114.9	198.8
1941-5 average	145.5	218.2
1949	1,302.5	1,340.3
1955	3,084	2,754
1965	7,357.2	7,252.5
1975	24,034	26,670
1978	35,667.8	34,556.6

Note: Figures for the war years exclude lend-lease and other Allied deliveries. The real import levels would therefore be substantially higher.
Sources: *Vneshnyaya torgovlya SSSR 1918-1966 gg.* (M. 1967), pp. 8, 9, 60, 62, 63, 233: *Vnesh. torg. 1978 g.* (M. 1979), p. 9. *Nar. khoz. v 1970 g.* (M. 1971), p. 615: *Nar. khoz. v 1977 g.* (M. 1978), p. 573.

the effect of CMEA membership for east European countries was to divert trade links away from former markets. For the USSR the advantage was substantial. Products of relatively advanced industry could be obtained from established industrial producers like Czechoslovakia and Poland without recourse to 'hard' currency. However, the advantages of trade were slow to develop. East European members of CMEA were bound to accept the Stalinist dogma of industrial development along the Soviet pattern and with a relatively low reliance on foreign trade. Experiment and historical experience in the peculiar circumstance of th 1930s in the USSR were now moulded into an 'economic ideology' and superimposed on a number of economies, some of which were far in advance of their Soviet master. Thus centralised planning by material balances and even collectivisation were arbitrarily introduced from the Baltic to the Balkans. Comparative advantage had no place in this scheme. The system was also adopted while reparations deliveries were being made by most members. Accordingly foreign trade grew slowly in comparison with Western Europe.

After Stalin's death, reparations demands were dropped and a period of relative liberalism initiated. Khrushchev advocated moves towards joint planning and the exploitation of comparative advantage. Although these ideas offended the sensitivities of some — particularly Rumania, who had no desire to remain the kitchen-garden of Comecon — there was a sound economic rationale for their advocacy. Although trade has mushroomed since, per capita trade within CMEA remains low, being weighted down by the Soviet Union. Trade is also inhibited by some organisational characteristics.

Economies planned on the Soviet model do not have a rational pricing system in Western terms. Prices are determined ultimately at the centre and do not necessarily reflect equilibrium between demand and supply. Thus foreign trade between planned economies has presented some problems in the absence of a socialist international price level to follow. Therefore world capitalist prices are used as the basis for pricing between CMEA members. This has led to a number of jokes about the march of Soviet socialism leaving at least one capitalist economy intact so that the planners will know what prices to charge for exports and imports. Adjustments to world prices are made to allow for transport costs, fluctuations and removal of 'monopolistic elements'. Thus CMEA prices are more stable than world prices; they also tend to lag. Prices for the 1966-70 period were, for instance, based on the 1960-4 average world prices. There is, however, always room for adjustment; prices for Soviet oil exports to East Europe have increased substantially since 1973, though they have been lower than OPEC prices. Despite this apparent concession to her East European partners and the fact that she is a staple supplier of raw materials and basic foodstuffs at stable prices, the Soviet Union has been accused of exploiting her strength in negotiations with her neighbours. Indeed the author has heard complaints that shoes were being sold from Czechoslovakia to the Soviet Union at 3 rubles a pair (in 1972 — about £1.50 at those prices). The anonymous informant simply asked 'Is three rubles a world price for shoes?'

Despite such suggestions, more objective evidence seems to suggest that the USSR has not 'exploited' Eastern Europe in this sense. It is only since the substantial increase in oil prices that the terms of trade have moved in the Soviet Union's favour, and then far less than if full world prices had been imposed. There is no doubt that the main advantage to the USSR of trade within CMEA is the ability to trade without using foreign exchange. The currency used is the credit ruble. As far as possible, trade is conducted on a bilateral basis with an attempt to keep trade in balance with each partner. This principle applies to the West as well, so that trade can be balanced almost on a barter basis, only the outstanding balance being settled in world currencies. There are some exceptions. The USSR for most years (pre-war and post-war) has enjoyed a trade surplus with Britain, which has helped to pay for a deficit with West Germany and other states. The proportion of trade with CMEA and other socialist countries is shown in Table 9.3. Consistently it has accounted for the majority of Soviet trade, but there has been a small swing to trade with capitalist economies. This reflects both the fact that CMEA is far from being a complete trading area and, more particularly, a continued need to import Western technology (see below), as well as marginal food supplies.

Table 9.3: Distribution of Soviet Trade (percentage total turnover)

	1963	1968	1973	1975	1978
Socialist countries[a]	70.4	67.4	58.5	56.3	59.8
including CMEA members[b]	59.2	57.5	54.0	51.8	55.7
Developed industrial economies	18.7	21.3	26.6	31.3	28.0
Developing economies	10.9	11.3	14.9	12.4	12.2

Notes: a. All CMEA members plus China, (North) Vietnam, North Korea, Cuba, Albania, Yugoslavia. b. Albania left in 1961, Mongolia joined in 1961, Cuba in 1972.
Sources: *Vneshnyaya torgovlya za 1964 g.* (M. 1965) p. 16: *Vneshnyaya torgovlya za 1968 g.* (M. 1969) p. 16: *Vneshnyaya torgovlya za 1974 g.* (M. 1975) p. 16: *Vneshnyaya torgovlya za 1978 g.* (M. 1979) p. 8.

Although commercial activity within CMEA is confined largely to trade there are other areas of co-operation, such as a joint pipeline project to transport Soviet natural gas to East Europe. In 1964 Hungary, Poland and Czechoslovakia signed the *Intermetal* agreement on co-operation in iron and steel production. The USSR, GDR and Bulgaria have also joined the agreement which now helps co-ordinate national production plans for iron and steel.

There appears to be no great political reason for trade to be concentrated with CMEA members. The overwhelming reason is the advantage of saving foreign currency. It is significant that Finland is amongst the major non-CMEA trading partners of the USSR because their trade is settled in credit rubles and not in hard currency. Of course, politics does influence Soviet trade but probably little more than in other powers.[3] During the Vietnam war the Soviet Union traded much with North Vietnam; Greater Vietnam is now a full member of CMEA. Similarly, trade with North Korea may be politically influenced; trade with China was reduced after the political rift in 1961 and that with Israel ceased in 1956. The USSR did not trade with Rhodesia but has with South Africa. There is also evidence of effective aid through trade with some developing nations in return for political or strategic advantage — for example, the Somalia naval base or former purchases of Egyptian cotton. Soviet arms sales are something of a mystery but it seems that sales to the Middle East have earned a cash surplus which has helped pay for imports elsewhere. In general, Soviet foreign trade is conducted with great commercial acumen and is determined by wholly economic considerations. The glowing exception is Cuba. Cuba relies heavily on the Soviet market for her staple exports. In return she imports almost everything from the USSR and, as is well known, receives substantial and vital subsidies in the process.

Trade with Western Capitalist Economies

The USSR has moved a long way from being a European granary; indeed it regularly imports foodstuffs. Major exports are machinery and industrial equipment, but to Western countries oil is the major single item. Thus the bulk of trade is of primary products in exchange for industrial producer goods. Imports of consumer goods were increased during Khrushchev's office, and since, but for the most part they came from CMEA partners. There has been an evident and deliberate expansion of trade with Western countries, supporting the notion that autarky has not been a long-term strategy, rather a short-term expedient. In 1973 Foreign Trade Minister Potolichev expressed the wish that trade with the West should grow on the basis of the international division of labour (*Pravda*, 27 December 1973, p. 4) — an oblique reference to the US Congress holding up a trade treaty because of the question of Jewish migrants from the USSR. And in 1977 the hope and expectation that the Helsinki agreement had made for an international climate favourable to the expansion of trade with Western Europe was voiced (Simakov, 1977, p. 21).

Soviet trade with capitalist economies is conditioned by problems of hard currency, the lag of technology and the deficit in food supplies. In order to find the earning power internationally to pay for necessary imports the price of exports is fixed at maximum earning power but low enough to find a market — a procedure which leads to undercutting Western producers and to occasional accusations of dumping. Soviet export prices bear no relation to domestic prices and often include subsidies. In the 1970s West European car manufacturers were particularly concerned at Soviet and other East European motor exports which enjoyed an effective subsidy for the sake of earning hard currency. No Soviet industry needs to export to survive — the home market could absorb all the volume — but exports must be diverted to pay for imports, demand for which is generated by the plan. There are also occasional needs to import foodstuffs in large quantities (1963, 1972, 1975) and there are regular imports of small quantities of food (EEC butter, Australian and New Zealand dairy products, Irish beef). Despite its development, the Soviet economy can still be thrown out of gear by a bad harvest. Following the disastrous harvest of 1975 substantial imports of grain (especially of feed-grains) were necessary. The USA was the main source of supply. In order to avoid disturbance of the world market and prices which followed Soviet grain purchases in 1972, the USSR agreed to purchase 6 to 8 million tons of grain per annum from the USA until 1981. Basic food imports thus not only make up a significant proportion of the total but they appear to have become staple imports. Trade has often depended on credits from Western banks and governments and the country has been heavily indebted in the 1960s, 1970s and into the 1980s, though she also grants credits to developing economies. To meet the credits (and the USSR is regarded as a safe risk in this respect) she must strive for a surplus on visible account. In turn this demands a maintenance of the state monopoly to keep a tight rein on domestic demand for imported commodities.

Internationally, Soviet industry has tended to be poor in quality competing largely on price. Her great strength, to date, lies in her natural resources. She is a major producer of gold, platinum and nickel as well as oil. In the mid-1970s it was estimated that one-third of all known oil reserves were in the USSR, and the OPEC price increases have automatically and fortuitously (USSR has no connection with OPEC) increased her foreign earning power. More recent discoveries of oil in Mexico and elsewhere have changed the balance a little, and there have even been estimates by the CIA that the USSR will cease exporting oil to the West in the 1980s, perhaps even becoming a net importer, though such suggestions are not widely taken seriously. For the time being, oil and oil products provide a staple export in particular to Western economies. In 1978 over one-third of all exports was fuel (mostly oil and natural gas) and electric power (Table 9.4) and oil exports produce 51 per cent of her convertible currency earnings. The structure of Soviet foreign trade has changed in accordance with the structure of the economy. Machinery and industrial equipment has

Table 9.4: Structure of Foreign Trade: Exports 1913-78 (percentage share by value). (Soviet categories are used, excluding those consistently below 10 per cent value)

Category	1913	1925/6	1930	1940	1950	1960	1970	1978
Machinery[a]	0.3	0.2	0.2	2.0	11.8	20.5	21.5	19.6
Fuel[b]	3.5	11.6	16.9	13.2	3.9	16.2	15.6	35.6
Ore and concentrates	2.8	7.9	2.8	4.1	11.3	20.4	19.8	10.3
Forest products[c]	10.9	8.3	16.5	6.4	3.1	5.5	6.5	4.5
Raw textiles[d]	8.9	7.9	5.4	18.1	11.2	6.4	3.4	2.5
Furs and leather	0.4	9.9	7.4	7.7	2.3	0.8	0.4	–
Food products[e]	54.7	41.0	32.1	27.7	20.6	13.1	8.4	2.2

Imports 1913-78 (percentage share by value) (excluding categories consistently below 10 per cent)

Category	1913	1925/6	1930	1940	1950	1960	1970	1978
Machinery	16.6	20.6	46.8	32.4	21.5	29.8	35.1	42.0
Fuels	7.1	0.7	0.1	6.5	11.8	4.2	2.0	3.7
Ores and concentrates	6.9	7.8	15.8	26.6	15.0	16.8	10.5	9.7
Chemicals and rubber	7.9	10.0	5.5	4.3	6.9	6.0	5.6	4.1
Raw textiles[d]	18.3	26.3	1.6	6.7	7.7	6.5	4.8	2.0
Food products[e]	21.2	9.9	11.1	14.9	17.5	12.1	5.0	19.2
Industrial consumer-goods	10.3	9.2	1.4	1.4	7.4	17.2	18.3	11.8

Notes: a. Includes equipment. b. Includes electrical energy from 1950 on.
c. Includes paper cellulose. d. Includes semi-manufactures. e. Includes unprocessed foodstuffs.
Sources: *Vneshnyaya torgovlya 1918-1966 gg.* (M. 1967), pp. 15, 72-3, *Vneshnyaya torgovlya stat. sbornik*, annual editions for 1970, 1975, 1978.

become a major export in the post-war period, though it remains the largest import category. Foodstuffs, historically a major export, have fallen steeply as a proportion of exports since the war, particularly since 1960, and have taken a correspondingly larger share of imports. Industrial consumer goods fell to an insignificant ratio of imports in the 1930s but have taken a much larger share in the 1960s and 1970s, indicating the growing role of imports in popular consumption.

The Flow of Technology

It has been argued that all Soviet economic development has been ultimately dependent upon imported technology (Sutton, 1968, 1971, 1973). There is no doubt that imports of advanced technology have played, and continue to play, an important part in the Soviet economy. The concept of a bridgeable technology gap has been shown to be unreal, for technological innovation continues in the West. Catching-up is not a once-and-for-all process. A matter of dispute would be just what role technology has played in the development of the Soviet economy. Learned authorities disagree on its significance in this case, as they do in a general theoretical sense.

With the advent of planning at the end of the 1920s concessions to Western companies were wound up and replaced by technical assistance contracts (see above, p. 193). Under such agreements equipment and know-how was bought. Thousands of enigeers went to work in the USSR — usually as their company's employees, sometimes freelance. (The recession in the West had put many engineers out of work at a time that coincided with the first five-year plan.) In 1932 there were 6,800 foreign specialists employed in the USSR, including 1,700 American engineers (Sutton, 1971, p. 11). From 1937 these foreign contracts were formally ended, when a Soviet-trained technical elite had emerged. Sutton maintains, however, that even after that date there was a number of unpublicised agreements with American companies.

The (early) agreements covered everything, from bicycles (BSA of Birmingham) to bearings (RIU of Italy and SKF of Sweden). Altogether Sutton lists 217 foreign companies operating between 1930 and 1945 (including some under wartime Allied terms aid and lend-lease). In addition to this a number of Soviet nationals were trained abroad, 1,039 arriving in the USA between June 1929 and June 1930 alone (Sutton, 1971, p. 277). The value of knowledge so gained is immeasurable, although it remains a matter of debate as to how important the flow of technology was alone.

In the first five-year plan 14-18 per cent of industrial investment was imported machinery. In the second plan it fell to 2 per cent, but this is very far from being a measure of technological dependence. Stalin is said to have admitted (in 1944) that two-thirds of large-scale industry had been built with the help of technical assistance of American companies (Sutton, 1971, p. 8). In post-war (and more particularly post-Stalin) USSR the import of technology has been maintained, indeed increased as the economy has become more complex and consequently more demanding. Soviet use of computers, for instance, is relatively undeveloped and Western computer companies have found outlets. There are hardly any photocopying machines in use — except a small number from Rank-Xerox. Technical assistance has persisted. The best-known example is the giant automobile works in Togliattigrad built by Fiat while Japanese concerns are co-operating in the exploitation of Siberian resources. Ironically for such a large oil-producer, oil-drilling equipment is imported from the UK.

Such technology is obtained in a number of ways, not dissimilar to the international technology transfer in the rest of the world. In the immediate post-war years there was evidence of plunder: the first MIG jet was a disguised Messerschmidt built from plans taken from the German factory; the first post-war Moskvich car was a transformed Opel; the good-quality Soviet cameras were produced after Zeiss of Jena had been taken over. Nowadays the Soviet Union operates in the international market, buying licences and setting up joint ventures with Western companies. These require sufficient exports to pay back the hard currency costs. As well as importing equipment the USSR has bought patents, as in artificial fibres, and whole productive plants, such as the Fiat motor plant or the Kama river lorry plant, which has a complex of six factories built with the aid of Western expertise (*Ekon. Gaz.*, 1978, No. 8, p. 2). In mid-1979 it was reported that approaches had been made to Volkswagen to build the Passat model under licence in the USSR. There has been an increasing trend to negotiating barter agreements under which imported technology is repaid with exports of finished goods; Japanese aid in Siberian oil-extraction is being repaid with oil exports for instance. But where manufactured goods are produced their export can disturb Western markets. Such barter agreements may therefore not long be attractive to Western concerns, though they are valuable to the Soviet Union in avoiding further Western debt or sales of gold to cover trade deficits with capitalist countries.

How important is such imported technology? There can be no question that in certain areas and at crucial periods it has been of immense value. The first five-year plan was dependent upon imported equipment and expertise. Thereafter, apart from the special circumstances of the war, it is highly debatable how essential such imports were. More recently it has become clear that Western technology plays a very large part in certain sectors — notably automobile production, shipping, timber and paper pulp, computers, chemicals, oil drilling and refining (Hanson, NATO, 1976, p. 37). In 1974, one third of sugar-beet was processed in factories using predominantly imported equipment, one third of beer was produced in breweries built by foreign contractors, one third of cement was produced in plants using some foreign equipment (Kroncher, NATO, 1976, p. 95). Altogether about 15 per cent of equipment in operation in 1976 was imported.

These figures are probably quite low by international standards. The share of imported productive equipment in the whole stock of capital is higher in a good many Western countries. The Soviet Union has no monopoly of technological imports. The international flow of technology and knowledge is widespread and even the most advanced of economies is a beneficiary — the USA imports specialised computers, even though it is the largest producer. The USSR has joined the apparatus of international technological transfer but has contributed little to it. The Soviet Union has a very large net import of technology and, in exchange, remains highly dependent upon exploiting natural resources.

Shipping and Merchant Marine

The extension of international economic activities has not been confined to trade; Western banks have opened offices in Moscow and Soviet banking operations overseas have been extended. The USSR remains outside IMF, however, as well as GATT and OECD. Of greater significance has been the great expansion of the Soviet merchant marine.

Shipbuilding had a low priority until the second five-year plan. Traditionally, Russia was land-oriented with an internal Empire. There was no history of overseas exploration in any way comparable with the maritime nations of Western Europe, and this inhibited a merchant marine. In the pre-war years the Soviet Union lacked the capacity to build and operate ships on any scale. Growing trade after the war increased the demand for merchant shipping. Captured German ships and some left over from lend-lease provided a flimsy basis, and most new post-war ships (military and merchant) were bought from Poland or Eastern Germany. The very large growth in merchant tonnage came after 1956, when gross tonnage reached 2.5 million tons (Hanson, 1970, p. 45). In 1970 the gross figure was over 12 million tons (*Morskoi flot*, 1970, 1, p. 3) and in 1972 over 16 million.

The fast growth in shipping capacity has obviously accompanied the rapid increase in foreign trade turnover. As trade expanded it became much more significant that foreign-based shipping lines were carrying this trade so involving the Soviet economy in real or opportunity costs in world currencies. By 1970, 60 per cent of Soviet foreign trade was carried in Soviet ships (*Morskoi flot*, 1970, 1, p. 3). It is impossible for all trade to be carried in national ships without a great deal of wasted capacity. The existence of spare capacity on certain lines led Soviet companies to enter the international carrying market. Soviet exports are often more bulky than imports so that ships were frequently travelling in ballast on the homeward leg. Thus Soviet ships have entered the cross-carrying trade, whereby they might pick up wool or lamb from Australia or New Zealand, carry it to Britain before picking up a cargo in Western Europe for a Soviet port. In order to enter these markets Soviet companies undercut the shipping conference (cartel) prices, though later, having secured a share of the market, they joined the conference and respected its rules. This was certainly the pattern on the Pacific routes, though on other routes continued undercutting has caused great anxiety to Western shipping companies. Thus as well as saving overseas expenditure the merchant marine has become a small foreign currency-earner. And this is not confined to cargo. Soviet passenger lines operate in various parts of the world, even offering luxury cruises.

The fishing fleet has shown a similar growth to become the world's largest. This has given rise to international anxiety about disguised military vessels patrolling the oceans of the world. Indeed, there are some who see the merchant marine, fishing fleet and Red Navy as one — an impression confirmed by the sight of so-called trawlers bristling with detection-equipment trailing NATO ships in the North Sea. Nonetheless there can be no doubt that Soviet fishing vessels are designed to catch fish. In pursuit of fish and, sadly, whales, the Soviet fleet ranges far and wide, plundering traditional fishing grounds of other nations. The danger of overfishing is real and immediate and the reason for this plunder is linked to the growing demand for protein in the USSR. Although, as we have seen, agricultural production has increased enormously, fish remains a prime source of protein. The total fish and whale catch in 1975 exceeded total meat production in weight. So, to an extent, the shortcomings of domestic agriculture have generated the growing demand for fish.

Summary

Soviet involvement in the world economy remains small both in per capita terms and in relation to her productive capacity. Foreign trade played only a small part in the great industrialisation drive of the 1930s, though imported technology was crucial in the major growth sectors of industry. This period saw import-dependent growth rather than export-led growth. Since the end of the war Soviet foreign trade has grown at a pace comparable with the overall growth in world trade. This expansion has in large measure, but by no means exclusively, been associated with the development of a 'socialist market' of politically allied states, in particular in CMEA. In the 1970s the USSR has extended economic as well as political influence beyond her borders. Her sheer size makes her a large market. In 1970 exports accounted for about 6 per cent of national product; by 1975 they reached 8 per cent. The Soviet economy is, thus, far from being foreign trade-oriented. In 1975 imports and exports were lower than those of the Netherlands, which had a population of 14 million (UN, *Yearbook*, 1976, pp. 27, 686, 983). In an international league table of foreign trade the USSR would, in the late 1970s, have figured in eighth position – no higher than the Russian Empire at the end of the nineteenth century.

The pattern of its foreign trade has reflected rather than determined its economic development. Foodstuffs no longer constitute major exports. Marginal food supplies and consumer-goods are imported. The Ministry of Retail Trade has even been importing some goods directly (from CMEA members), bypassing the Ministry of Foreign Trade. This suggests some liberalisatiom of trade, though there is no possibility of the state abandoning its monopoly in this area of the economy or allowing free exchange of currency. Import demands have been growing and may well continue to do so. The restraint on a further expansion in trade will be export capacity. Natural resources, particularly oil, provide the lions' share of exports to the West. If oil supplies diminish sharply, as has been forecast, this is likely to reduce the Soviet Union's import capabilities unless some alternative export staple can be found. This in turn will require an increase in agricultural production (already underway) to offset food imports. Large imports of foodstuffs after 1975 plunged the Soviet Union further into debt at a time when the recession in the West led to slack demand for her oil exports. The USSR is part of the world economy more fully than ever before; autarky has been abandoned. International trade was planned to grow at twice the rate of production in the tenth five-year plan, but in entering more fully the international market the Soviet Union has thus become increasingly sensitive to its fluctuations.

Notes

1. Austria and Finland, both subject to partial Soviet occupation until 1955, became neutral.

2. Poland, Czechoslovakia, Hungary, Bulgaria, Rumania and Albania joined in 1949; the GDR in 1950, Mongolia in 1962, Cuba and Vietnam in the 1970s. Albania left in 1961. Yugoslavia has observer status.

3. A. Boltho, 1971, p. 55, suggests that Soviet trade with developing countries is politically inspired.

CONCLUSION

Western historiography in recent years has tended to stress the negative aspects of the Soviet economy — the failure to meet plan targets, shortcomings in the supply and availability of consumer-goods, shortfalls in labour productivity and occasional agricultural crises. This is supported by much evidence but, nonetheless, the story is far from altogether negative. The Soviet economy has achieved rapid growth to become the second largest in the world, providing the basis on which political influence and military strength has been built. Thus the relative position of the Soviet economy has changed markedly from the days of Empire. If the extent of backwardness of Russia before the revolution is sometimes overstated so, too, is the crisis affecting the economy at the beginning of the 1980s. The rapid growth of industrial output in pre-war years was characterised by very high levels of saving, and therefore restraint on private consumption; a similarly high rate of increase of labour input into industry; relatively inefficient utilisation of labour and capital; and highly centralised control of resources, expenditure and production through the planning mechanism. In more recent years there has been some moderation of these features. Growth-rates have levelled off and more reliance has been placed on improvements in productivity and efficiency; personal consumption has improved, especially from the 1960s; and there has been some, albeit modest, decentralisation of the planning mechanism. The basic structure remains, and there is no suggestion of 'consumer sovereignty'.

Although the mechanism of economic planning established under Stalin has changed, and certainly become more sophisticated, there have been, and are, strong undercurrents of continuity. A consciousness of relative weakness, anxiety over vulnerability to invasion, proven over centuries, has conditioned all aspects of Soviet policy and has, accordingly, provided a strong dynamic in economic control and decision-making. Thus defence has always been a major consideration if not consistently a major economic priority. Another consistent aspect of policy might be termed ideological, an objective of improvements in consumption. It is hard to substantiate this statement for consumption has often been sacrificed to finance investment or, more likely, fund defence expenditure. There has thus been a trade-off between consumption by the state on defence and by the citizen. The two elements of continuity have, therefore, been in conflict but both have rested on the growing productive base. However, whereas defence has tended to have the best, the consumer has tended to get the worst. Despite adjustments in policies since Stalin's death, the economy has consistently failed to match the expectations for consumption expressed in the plans, to say nothing of the expectation of the citizens. The economic system seems far better able to make producer-goods and has proved relatively inflexible. Similarly, collectivised agriculture has remained a weak sector, despite massive infusions of capital in the last twenty years. The share of agriculture in total employment, and new investment, is high by the standards of other industrial economies. Yet the substantial productivity improvements and tendency to overproduction characteristic of agriculture in Western industrial economies are embarrassingly absent in the USSR. For all this, the USSR has achieved great power status, politically and militarily, built on the foundations of a planned economy and distinctive ideology.

It is often said that it was anomalous that the doctrine of Marxian socialism took root in a society and economy some way from mature capitalism. Marxism was taken up as a revolutionary doctrine and became an ideology of economic development. However distorted, Marx's concept of future society provided the ideological impetus for growth, in contrast to the ethic of individualism more readily associated with developments in Western Europe. Marxian notions became inextricably intertwined with Russian tradition. Anti-individualism appealed to deep-rooted philosophy in Russian society. The mistrust of dissent, the concept of centralised ideological leadership, the heavy-handed totalitarian controls that developed in the early years of the USSR were more developments of Russian tradition than 'socialist' ideology. When the Soviet state was faced with economic problems, and international weakness and insecurity, in the 1920s those in power used the tools which were at hand. And the tools had been fashioned long before 1917; well-tried instruments of central control backed up with ideological dogmatism. Moscow continued to be the third Rome; only the faith has changed.

The elements of continuity are well known; but it is important, also, to stress the new. The concept of planning, directing a national economy without the market, was new, untried and necessarily experimental when introduced in the USSR. This was a clear break in continuity. In the outcome, planning involved a highly centralised bureaucracy, with coercion and punishment employed in the execution of economic aims, all of which might be termed as much 'Russian' as

'Soviet'.

As successful as the Soviet planned economy has been, it is not without reserve. Growth-rates have levelled off, improvements in labour productivity have been disappointing, social problems such as delinquency and alcoholism have become more evident (or more widely acknowledged) and the economy is subject to fluctuations in world capitalist demand. These points might apply to almost any Western market economy. The peculiar experiment of Soviet economic history has not rendered the country immune from worldwide economic movements.

GLOSSARY

ARTEL'	Gang or co-operative group; used specifically as type of collective farm. See KOLKHOZ
BATRAK	Rural labourer
BEDNYAK	Poor peasant
CHEKA	Political police force established in civil war (renamed GPU, OGPU in 1920s; see also KGB)
CHERVONETS	New currency introduced in the 1920s
FIRMA	'Firm', organisation of factories producing similar goods
GLAVK	Chief department of a commissariat or ministry
GOELRO	State committee for electrification of Russia, founded 1920
GOSPLAN	State planning committee
KGB	Committee of State Security, embracing political police
KHOZRASCHET	Commercial profit and loss accounting
KHUTOR and OTRUB	Types of individual farm, encouraged by Stolypin reforms
KOLKHOZ	Collective farm
KOMBEDY	Committees of poor peasants formed in civil war
KOMMUNA	Commune; an early form of co-operative farm
KULAK	Rich peasant; one who exploited others
KUSTAR	Peasant domestic handicraft industry
MIR	Traditional village commune (= OBSHCHINA)
NARKOMFIN	Commissariat for finance; also NARKOMPROD for food supply; NARKOMTORG for trade; NARKOMZEM for agriculture. They were superseded by ministries in 1946
NEPMAN	Private trader operating in the years of NEP

211

OB' 'EDINENIE	Association of factories in same ministry
OBSHCHINA	Traditional village commune (= MIR)
POLITOTDEL'	Political department of KOLKHOZ
PRODRAZVERSTKA	Compulsory procurement of foodstuffs
PROMYSLY	Crafts and trades; peasant side-employment
SEREDNYAK	Middle peasant
SKHOD	Peasant village gathering
SMYCHKA	Alliance or link
SNKh or SOVNARKHOZ	Regional economic council
SOSLOVIE	Legal class or 'estate' in Imperial Russia
SOVKHOZ	State farm
SOVNARKOM	Council of Peoples' Commissars
SOVZNAK	The name given to the paper ruble in the early 1920s
STO	Council of Labour and Defence
TOLKACH'	'Pusher' or 'fixer' operating illegally to secure supplies for enterprises
TOZ	An early form of co-operative farm
TRUDODEN'	Labour day; work and pay unit in the KOLKHOZ
VSNKh or VESENKHA	Supreme economic council
ZEMEL'NOE OBSHCHESTVO	Land society; the name given to the local body of peasant government in the 1920s
ZEMSTVO	Rural local government in Imperial Russia

REFERENCES

Abouchar, A. 'Inefficiency and Reform in the Soviet Economy', *Soviet Studies*, 25, 1973

Antonova, S.I. *Vliyanie Stolypinskoi agrarnoi reformy na izmeneniya v sostav rabochego klassa*, Moscow, 1951

Arskii, R. *10 let bor'by na khozyaistvennom fronte*, Leningrad, 1927

Barsov, A.A. *Balans stoimostnykh obmenov mezhdu gorodom i derevne*, Moscow, 1969

—— 'Sel'skoe khozyaistvo i istochniki sotsialisticheskogo nakopleniya v gody pervoi pyatiletke', *Istoriya SSSR*, no. 3, 1968

Beilina, E.E. 'Razrabotka novykh printsipov khozyaistvovaniya i ikh osushchestvlenie v promyshlennosti SSSR' in *Sotsial'no-ekonomicheskie problemy istorii razvitogo sotsializma v SSSR*, Moscow, 1976

Bergson, A. *The Real National Income of the Soviet Russia since 1928*, Harvard University Press, Cambridge, Mass., 1961

—— and Kuznets, S. *Economic Trends in the Soviet Union*, Harvard University Press, Cambridge, Mass., 1963

Berner, W. (ed.) *The Soviet Union 1975-6*, Hurst, London, 1977

Boltho, A. *Foreign Trade Criteria in Socialist Economies*, Cambridge University Press, Cambridge, 1971

Brown, A.J. and Kaser, M. (eds.) *The Soviet Union since the Fall of Khrushchev*, Macmillan, London, 1978

Buzdalov, I. 'Fakty i stimuly uskoreniya nauchno-tekhnicheskogo progressa v sel'skom khozyaistve', *Voprosy ekonomiki*, 2, 1970

Carr, E.H. *The Bolshevik Revolution*, Penguin, Harmondsworth, 1966

—— *The Interregnum*, Penguin, Harmondsworth, 1969

—— *Socialism in One Country*, Penguin, Harmondsworth, 1970

—— and Davies, R.W. *Foundations of a Planned Economy*, Penguin, Harmondsworth, 1974

Chayanov, A.V. *The Theory of Peasant Economy*, Irwin, Illinois, 1966

Chuntulov, V.T. *Ekonomischeskaya istoriya SSSR*, Moscow, 1969

Cohn, S. *Economic Development in the Soviet Union*, Heath, Lexington, 1970

Concessions in the Far East, USSR, 2 vols, Khabarovsk, 1925

Conjuncture, Institute of, *Economic Conditions in the USSR after War and Revolution*, Moscow, 1928

Conquest, R. *The Great Terror*, Macmillan, London, 1973

Cooper, J. 'Defence Production and the Soviet Economy', *CREES Discussions Papers* SIPS, 3, Birmingham, 1976

Crisp, O. *Studies in the Russian Economy before 1914*, Macmillan, London, 1976

Dalrymple, D. 'The Soviet Famine of 1932-34', *Soviet Studies*, 15, 1964

Danilov, V.P. 'Zemel'nye otnosheniya v sovetskoi dokolkhoznoi derevne', *Istoriya SSSR*, 3, 1958

—— *Sovetskaya dokolkhoznaya derevnya*, Moscow, 1977

Davies, R.W. *The Development of the Soviet Budgetary System*, Cambridge University Press, Cambridge, 1958

—— 'Planning for Rapid Growth in the USSR', Economics of Planning, 5, 1965

—— and Wheatcroft, S.G. 'Further Thoughts on the First Five Year Plan', *Slavic Review*, 34, 1975

Dewar, M. *Soviet Trade with East Europe 1945-49*, I.E.A., London, 1951

Dobb, M. *The Development of the Soviet Economy since 1917*, Routledge, London, 1966a

—— 'The Discussion of the Twenties on Soviet Economic Growth', *Soviet Studies*, 17, 1966b

Dodge, N.T. *Women in the Soviet Economy*, Greenwood, Westport, 1977

Dohan, M.R. 'The Economic Origins of Soviet Autarky 1927/8-34', *Slavic Review*, 35, 1976

Dunmore, T. *The Stalinist Command Economy. The Soviet State Apparatus and Economic Policy 1945-53*, Macmillan, London, 1980

Ekonomika i organizatsiya promyshlennogo proizvodstva, January 1980

Ekonomicheskaya Gazeta, published weekly, Moscow

Ellman, M. 'Did the Agricultural Surplus Provide the Resources for the Increase in Investment in the USSR in the First Five Year Plan?' *Economic Journal*, 85, 1975

Erlich, A. *The Soviet Industrialization Debate 1924-28*, Harvard University Press, Cambridge, Mass., 1967

Falkus, M.E. 'Russia's National Income in 1913: A Revaluation', *Economica*, 35, 1968

Fainsod, M. *Smolensk under Soviet Rule*, Macmillan, London, 1958

Fallenbuchl, Z.M. 'Collectivisation and Economic Development', *Canadian Journal of Economics and Political Science*, 33, 1967

Gerschenkron, A. 'The Rate of Growth in Russia since 1885', *Journal of Economic History*, 7, supplement 1947
—— 'Russia's Trade in the Post-War Years', *The Annals of the American Academy*, 1, 1949
Gladkov, I.A. *Sovetskoe narodnoe khozyaistvo (1921-25)*, Moscow, 1960
—— *Sotsialisticheskoe narodnoe khozyaistvo SSSR v 1933-40 gg.*, Moscow, 1963
Goldsmith, R. 'The Economic Growth of Tsarist Russia 1860-1913', *Economic Development and Cultural Change*, 9, 1961
Gosudarstvennyi pyatiletnyi plan razvitiya narodnogo khozyaistva SSSR na 1971-75 gg., Moscow, 1972
Greenwood, R.H. 'The Soviet Merchant Marine' in Symons, L. and White, C. (eds.), *Russian Transport*, Bell, London, 1975
Hanson, P. *The Consumer in the Soviet Economy*, Macmillan, London, 1969
—— 'The Soviet Union and World Shipping', *Soviet Studies*, 22, 1970
Hart, Sir B. Liddell, *A History of the Second World War*, Cassell, London, 1970
Holzman, F.D. 'Soviet Inflationary Pressures', *Quarterly Journal of Economics*, 64, 1960
Hunter, H. 'The Overambitious First Soviet Five Year Plan', *Slavic Review*, 32, 1973
Hutchings, R. *Soviet Economic Development*, Blackwells, Oxford, 1971
Industrilizatsiya SSSR, Dokumenty i Materialy, 4 vols. Moscow, 1969-72
Istoriya sotsialisticheskoi ekonomiki SSSR, 7 vols, Moscow, 1976-80
Itogi vypolneniya narodnokhozyaistvennogo plana SSSR i soyuznykh respublik v 1964 g., Moscow, 1965
Izvestiya, published daily
Iz istorii rabochego klassa i revolyutsionnogo dvizheniya, sbornik statei, Moscow, 1958
Jasny, N. *Soviet Industrialization, 1928-1952*, Chicago University Press, Chicago, 1961
—— *Soviet Economists of the Twenties: Names to be Remembered*, Cambridge University Press, Cambridge, 1972
Kaser, M. *Comecon*, Oxford University Press, London, 1967
Katkov, G., Oberlander, E., Poppe, N. and von Rauch, G. *Russia Enters the Twentieth Century 1894-1917*, Methuen, London, 1973
Karcz, J. 'Thoughts on the Grain Crisis', *Soviet Studies*, 18, 1967
Kirk, D. *Europe's Population Between the Wars*, UN, Geneva, 1946

Khlusov, M.I. *Razvitie sovetskoi industrii 1946-1958*, Moscow, 1977
Khromov, P.I. *Ekonomicheskoe razvitie Rossii v xix-xx vv.*, Moscow, 1950
Khrushchev, N.S. *Khrushchev Remembers*, ed. and translated by S. Talbot, 2 vols, Penguin, Harmondsworth, 1977
Kontrol'nye tsifry razvitiya narodnogo khozyaistva SSSR na 1959-65 gg., Moscow, 1958
Koval'chenko, I.D. 'Sootnoshenie krest'yanskogo i pomeshchich'ego khozyaistva v zemledel'cheskom proizvodstve kapitalisticheskoi Rossii' in *Problemy sotsial'no-ekonomicheskoi istorii Rossii, Sbornik statei*, Moscow, 1971
Krasin, L.B. *Vneshnyaya torgovlya SSSR*, Moscow, 1924
Kravchenko, G.S. *Ekonomika SSSR v gody velikoi otechestvennoi voiny 1941-1945 gg.*, Moscow, 1970
Krzhizhanovskii, G.M. *Desyat' let khozyaistvennogo stroitel'stva SSSR 1917-1927 gg.*, Moscow, 1927
Kulikov, V.I. 'Mesto i rol' osvoeniya tselinnykh zemel' v uvelechenii proizvodstva zerna v SSSR', *Voprosy istorii*, 3, 1979
Kuznets, S. 'Quantitative Aspects of the Economic Growth of Nations, VI Long Term Trends in Capital Formation Proportions', *Economic Development and Cultural Change*, 9, 1961
Larin, Yu. *Voprosy krest'yanskogo khozyaistva*, Moscow, 1923
Lavrent'ev, V. 'V.I. Lenin ob upravlenii i khozyaistvennom raschete v sovkhozakh', *Ekonomika sels'kogo khozyaistva*, 1, 1970
Lemeshev, M. 'Normativy kapital'nykh vlozhenii v sel'skom khozyaistve', *Voprosy ekonomiki*, 3, 1970
Lenin, V.I. *Collected Works*, vol. xlv, Moscow, 1970
Lewin, M. *Russian Peasants and Soviet Power*, Allen and Unwin, London, 1968
—— 'The Disappearance of Planning in the Plan', *Slavic Review*, 32, 1973
—— *Political Undercurrents in Soviet Economic Debates. From Bukharin to Modern Reformers*, Princeton University Press, Princeton, 1974
Lokshin, E. Yu. *Ocherk istorii promyshlennosti SSSR (1917-1940)*, Moscow, 1956
—— *Promyshlennost' SSSR, 1940-1963, ocherk istorii*, Moscow, 1964
Lorimer, F. *The Population of the Soviet Union*, UN, Geneva, 1946
McAuley, A. 'The Distribution of Earnings and Incomes in the Soviet Union', *Soviet Studies*, 29, 1977

—— *Economic Welfare in the Soviet Union. Poverty, Living Standards and Inequality*, Allen and Unwin, London, 1979

McCanley, M. *Khrushchev and the Development of Soviet Agriculture: The Virgin Land Programme 1953-64*, Macmillan, London, 1976

McKay, J.P. 'Foreign Enterprise in Russian and Soviet Industry', *Business History Review*, 48, 1974

Maddison, A. *Economic Growth in Japan and the USSR*, Allen and Unwin, London, 1969

Male, D. *Russian Peasant Organisation before Collectivisation*, Cambridge University Press, Cambridge, 1971

Malafeev, A.N. *Istoriya tsenoobrazovaniya v SSSR*, Moscow, 1964

Maksimov, M. 'Dvizhenie naseleniya SSSR 1959-1970', *Istoriya SSSR*, 5, 1971

Matthews, M. *Privilege in the Soviet Union*, Allen and Unwin, London, 1978

Maynard, Sir John, *Russia in Flux. Before the October Revolution*, Collier, New York, 1962

Miller, R.F. 'Soviet Agricultural Policy in the Twenties: The Failure of Cooperation', *Soviet Studies*, 27, 1975

Millar, J.R. 'Soviet Rapid Development and the Agricultural Surplus Hypothesis', *Soviet Studies*, 22, 1970

—— (ed.) *The Soviet Rural Community*, Urbana, Illinois, 1971a

—— 'A Reply to Alec Nove', *Soviet Studies*, 23 1971b

—— 'Mass Collectivisation and the Contribution of Soviet Agriculture to the First Five Year Plan', *Slavic Review*, 23, 1974

Milward, A.S. *War Economy and Society 1939-45*, Allen Lane, Harmondsworth, 1977

Moller, H. (ed.) *Population Movements in Modern European History*, Macmillan, London, 1964

Morskoi flot, 1, 1970

Moshkov, Yu. A. *Zernovaya problema v gody sploshnoi kollektivizatsii sel'skogo khozyaistva SSSR (1929-32)*, Moscow, 1966

Narkiewicz, O. 'Stalin, War Communism and Collectivisation', *Soviet Studies*, 20, 1966

—— *The Making of the Soviet State Apparatus*, Manchester University Press, Manchester, 1970

Narodnoe khozyaistvo SSSR, Statisticheskii ezhegodnik, published annually, Moscow

Narodnoe khozyaistvo SSSR 1922-1972, yubilennyi statisticheskii ezhegodnik, Moscow, 1972

Narodnoe khozyaistvo SSSR za 60 let, yubilennyi stat. ezhegodnik,

Moscow, 1977

NATO, Directorate of Economics Affairs, Colloquia published in Brussels on various themes:
1975, *Economic Aspects of Life in the USSR*
1976, *East-West Technological Cooperation*
—— Economics Directorate, *Regional Development in the USSR* Oriental Research Partners, Mass., 1979

Newth, J.A. 'The Soviet Population; War time Losses and the Post War Recovery', *Soviet Studies*, 15, 1964

Nove, A. *An Economic History of the USSR*, Allen Lane, Harmondsworth, 1969
—— 'The Agricultural Surplus Hypothesis; a Comment' *Soviet Studies*, 22, 1971
—— 'A Reply to a Reply', *Soviet Studies*, 23, 1972

Novikov, M. 'Vazhoe zveno agrarnoi politiki partii', *Kommunist*, 15, 1977

Oganovskii, P.I. *Revolyutsiya naoborot*, Petrograd, 1917

Pershin, P.N. *Agrarnaya revolyutsiya v Rossii*, 2 vols, Moscow, 1966

Politicheskaya Ekonomiya – sotsializm, pervaya faza kommunisticheskogo snosoba proizvodstva, Moscow, 1971

Pravda, published daily, Moscow

Preobrazhensky, N. *The New Economics*, Trans. B. Pearce, Clarendon, Oxford, 1965

Promyshlennost' SSSR, Statisticheskii sbornik, Moscow, 1964

Rashin, A.G. *Formirovanie rabochego klassa Rossii*, Moscow, 1958

Razvitie ekonomiki SSSR v desyatoi pyatiletke, Moscow, 1977

Razvitie sotsialisticheskoi ekonomiki SSSR v poslevoennyi period, Moscow, 1965

Resheniya partii i pravitel'stva po khozyaistvennam voprosam 1917-1967 gg., 5 vols, Moscow, 1967-8

Schroeder, G. 'Industrial Wage Differentials in the USSR', *Soviet Studies*, 17, 1966
—— 'Soviet Economic Reform: A Study in Contradictions', *Soviet Studies*, 20, 1968
—— 'The Reform of the Supply System in Soviet Industry', *Soviet Studies*, 24, 1972

Sel'skoe khozyaistvo SSSR po dannym nalogovykh svodov, 3 vols, 1925-6, Moscow, 1927
1926-7, Moscow, 1928
1927-8, Moscow, 1929

Sel'skoe khozyaistvo SSSR, statisticheskii sbornik, Moscow, 1960

Sel'skoe khozyaistvo SSSR, statisticheskii sbornik, Moscow, 1971

Senyavskii, S.L. 'Rabochii klass i sotsial'nye sdvigi v sovetskom osbsh-chestve', *Istoricheskie zapiski*, 100, Moscow, 1977

Shaffer, H.G. *Soviet Agriculture: An Assessment of its Contributions to Economic Development*, Praeger, New York, 1977

Shigalin, G.I. *Narodnoe khozyaistvo SSSR v period velikoi otechest-vennoi voiny*, Moscow, 1960

Simakov, V. 'Rubezhi obshcheevropeiskogo sotrudnichestva', *Ekonomicheskaya gazeta*, 42, 1977

Smith, W. Bedell, *Moscow Mission 1946-1949*, Heinemann, London, 1950

SSSR v novoi pyatiletke, spravochnik, Moscow, 1966

Stalin, J. *Problems of Leninism*, Moscow, 1947

—— *Collected Works*, vol. 12, Moscow, 1955

Strauss, E. *Soviet Agriculture in Perspective*, Allen and Unwin, London, 1969

Sutton, A. *Western Technology and Soviet Economic Development*, vol. 1, 1917-30, Stanford University Press, Stanford, 1968
vol. 2, 1930-1945, Stanford University Press, Stanford, 1971
vol. 3, 1945-1966, Stanford University Press, Stanford, 1973

Swaniewicz, S. *Forced Labour and Economic Development*, Oxford University Press, London, 1965

Tupper, S. 'The Mobilisation of Soviet Industry for Defence Needs 1937-41', unpublished Conference Paper, Birmingham, 1981

Trud v SSSR, stat. sbornik, Moscow, 1968

Tsentral'nyi komitet Rossiiskoi kommunisticheskoi partii (b), (T.S.K.R.K.P. (b)), *Materialy po obsledovaniyu devevni*, Moscow, 1923

Ts.S.U. *Osnovye elementy sel'sko-khozyaistvennogo proizvodstva SSSR 1916, i 1923-27 gg.*, Moscow, 1930

United Nations, *Economic Survey of Europe for 1960*, Geneva, 1961

—— *Yearbook of International Trades Statistics*, New York, 1976

—— *Economic Survey of Europe for 1978*, New York, 1979

Vestnik statistiki, 1978

Vneshnyaya torgovlya, published monthly, Moscow

Vneshnyaya torgovlya, stat. obzor, published annually, Moscow

Vneshnyaya torgovlya SSSR za 1918-1940 gg. stat. obzor, Moscow, 1960

Vneshnyaya torgovlya 1918-1966, stat. sbornik, Moscow, 1967

Volin, L. *A Century of Russian Agriculture*, Harvard University Press, Cambridge, Mass., 1970

Volkov, L. (ed.) *Razvitie sel'skogo khozyaistva v poslevoennye gody*, Moscow, 1972

Voprosy istorii KPSS, 5, 1975

Wadekin, E. *The Private Sector in Soviet Agriculture*, California University Press, Berkeley, 1973

Wheatcroft, S.G. 'Grain Production Statistics in the USSR in the 1920s and 1930s', *CREES Discussion Papers*, SIPS 13, Birmingham, 1977

—— 'On Assessing the Size of Forced Concentration Camp Labour in the Soviet Union, 1929-56', *Soviet Studies*, 33, 1981

Wiles, P. *Distribution of Income East and West*, North-Holland, Amsterdam, 1974

Wilkins, M. and Hill, F.E. *American Business Abroad*, Wayne State University Press, Detroit, 1964

Zaleski, E. *Planning for Economic Growth in the Soviet Union, 1918-32*, North Carolina University Press, Chapel Hill, 1971

—— *Stalinist Planning and Economic Growth 1933-1952*, North Carolina University Press, Chapel Hill, 1980

Zelenin, I.E. 'Kolkhozy i sel'skoe khozyaistvo SSSR v 1933-35 gg.', *Istoriya SSSR*, 5, 1964

Zoerb, C.R. 'From the Promise of Bread and Land to the Reality of the State Farm, *Studies on the Soviet Union*, VI, Munich, 1967

SELECT BIBLIOGRAPHY

Works on various aspects of Soviet economic history are legion. The following is but a brief guide to further reading on particular themes.

Basic statistical sources
Narodnoe khozyaistvo SSSR, published annually, Moscow
R.A. Clarke, *Soviet Economic Facts 1917-1970*, Macmillan, London, 1972, is a very useful, concise edition

General texts
A. Nove, *An Economic History of the USSR*, Penguin, Harmondsworth, 1975
M. Dobb, *Soviet Economic Development since 1917*, Routledge, London, 1966
R. Hutchings, *Soviet Economic Development*, Blackwells, Oxford, 1971

Economic history of the late nineteenth century
O. Crisp, *Studies in the Russian Economy before 1914*, Macmillan, London, 1976
M. Falkus, *Industrialisation of Russia, 1700-1914*, Macmillan, London, 1972
A. Gerschenkron, *Economic Backwardness in Historical Perspective*, Harvard University Press, Cambridge, Mass., 1962
M. Florinsky, *The End of Russian Empire*, Collier Books, New York, 1961
P.I. Khromov, *Ekonomicheskoe razvitie Rossii xix-xx vv.*, Moscow, 1950

NEP
E.H. Carr, *A History of Soviet Russia*, Penguin Books, Harmondsworth, in 14 vols
—— *The Russian Revolution from Lenin to Stalin*, Macmillan, London, 1979, is a summary volume of the massive and authoritative work on the 1920s
A.Erlich, *The Soviet Industrialization Debate 1924-28*, Harvard University Press, Cambridge, Mass., 1967

R. Day, *Leon Trotsky and the Politics of Economic Isolation*, Cambridge University Press, Cambridge, 1973

N. Preobrazhensky, *The New Economics*, Clarendon, Oxford, 1965

M. Dobb, *Russian Economic Development since the Revolution*, Routledge, London, 1928

O. Narkiewicz, *The Making of the Soviet State Apparatus*, Manchester, 1970

The Planned Economy from the 1930s

A. Baykov, *The Foundation of the Soviet Economic System*, Cambridge University Press, Cambridge, 1948

E. Zaleski, *Planning for Economic Growth in the USSR*, North Carolina University Press, Chapel Hill, 1971

E. Zaleski, *Stalinist Planning and Economic Growth 1932-1952*, North Carolina University Press, Chapel Hill, 1980

H. Schwartz, *The Soviet Economy since Stalin*, Gollancz, London, 1965

N. Spulber, *Foundations of a Soviet Strategy for Economic Growth*, Bloomington, Indiana, 1964

N. Jasny, *Soviet Industrialization 1928-52*, University of Chicago Press, Chicago, 1961

A. Nove, *Stalinism and After*, Allen and Unwin, London, 1975

Contemporary economic system

A. Nove, *The Soviet Economic System*, Allen and Unwin, London, 1977

D. Dyker, *The Soviet Economy*, Crosby Lockwood, London, 1976

M. Kaser, *Soviet Economics*, Weidenfeld, London, 1970

A. Nove and D. Nuti (eds.), *Socialist Economics*, Penguin, Harmondsworth, 1972

J. Wilczynski, *The Economics of Socialism*, Allen and Unwin, London, 1970

Agriculture

E. Strauss, *Soviet Agriculture in Perspective*, Allen and Unwin, London, 1969

L. Volin, *A Century of Russian Agriculture*, Harvard University Press, Cambridge, Mass., 1970

A.V. Chayanov, *The Theory of Peasant Economy*, Irwin, Illinois, 1966

D. Male, *Russian Peasant Organisation before Collectivisation*, Cambridge University Press, Cambridge, 1971

M. Lewin, *Russian Peasants and Soviet Power*, Allen and Unwin, London, 1968

R.W. Davies, *The Socialist Offensive, the Collectivisation of Soviet Agriculture 1929-30*, Macmillan, London, 1980

—— *The Soviet Collective Farm, 1929-30*, Macmillan, London, 1980

N. Jasny, *The Socialised Agriculture of the USSR*, Stanford University Press, Stanford, 1949

M. McCauley, *Khrushchev and the Development of Soviet Agriculture*, Macmillan, London, 1976

Finance

R.W. Davies, *The Development of the Soviet Budgetary System*, Cambridge University Press, Cambridge, 1958

Foreign trade

A. Boltho, *Foreign Trade Criteria in Socialist Economies*, Cambridge University Press, Cambridge, 1971

F.D. Holzman, *Foreign Trade under Central Planning*, Harvard University Press, Cambridge, Mass., 1974

G.A. Smith, *Soviet Foreign Trade: Organization, Operations and Policy 1918-71*, Praeger, New York, 1973

Incomes and consumption

P. Hanson, *The Consumer in the Soviet Economy*, Macmillan, London, 1969

A. McAuley, *Economic Welfare in the Soviet Union*, Allen and Unwin, London, 1979

M. Matthews, *Privilege in the Soviet Union*, Allen and Unwin, London, 1978

Labour

I. Deutscher, *Soviet Trade Unions*, Oxford University Press, London, 1950

G.V. Osipov (ed.), *Industry and Labour in the USSR*, Tavistock, London, 1966

E.C. Brown, *Soviet Trade Unions and Labour Relations*, Harvard University Press, Cambridge, Mass., 1966

M. Dewar, *Labour Policy in the USSR 1917-28*, Octagon, New York, 1979

D. Lane and F. O'Dell, *The Soviet Industrial Worker*, Robertson, Oxford, 1978

General political

M. McAuley, *Politics and the Soviet Union*, Penguin, Harmondsworth, 1977

R. Medvedev, *Let History Judge*, Macmillan, London, 1972

R. and Z. Medvedev, *Khrushchev, the Years in Power*, Oxford University Press, London, 1977

J. Nettl, *The Soviet Achievement*, Weidenfeld, London, 1967

D. Treadgold, *Twentieth-Century Russia*, Chicago University Press, Chicago, 1976

L. Schapiro, *The Communist Party of the Soviet Union*, Methuen, London, 1963

D. Lane, *Politics and Society in the USSR*, Robertson, London, 1978

INDEX

225